This book introduces a new method for determining the authorship of renaissance plays. Based on the rapid rate of change in English grammar in the late sixteenth and early seventeenth centuries, socio-historical linguistic evidence allows us to distinguish the hands of renaissance playwrights within play texts. The present study focuses on Shakespeare: his collaborations with Fletcher and Middleton, and the apocryphal plays. Among the plays examined are *Henry VIII*, *The Two Noble Kinsmen*, *Macbeth*, *Pericles*, and *Sir Thomas More*. The findings of the book allow us to be more confident about the divisions of the collaborative plays, and confirm the status of *Edward III* as a strong candidate for inclusion in the canon.

Using graphs to present statistical data in a readily comprehensible form, the book also contains a wealth of information about the history of the English language during a period of far-reaching change.

The authorship of Shakespeare's plays

# The authorship of Shakespeare's plays
# A socio-linguistic study

Jonathan Hope

*School of English, University of Leeds*

Published by the Press Syndicate of the University of Cambridge
The Pitt Building, Trumpington Street, Cambridge CB2 1RP
40 West 20th Street, New York, NY 10011–4211, USA
10 Stamford Road, Oakleigh, Melbourne 3166, Australia



First published 1994

Printed in Great Britain at the University Press, Cambridge

*A catalogue record for this book is available from the British Library*

*Library of Congress cataloguing in publication data*

Hope, Jonathan, 1962–
The authorship of Shakespeare's plays: a socio-linguistic study / Jonathan Hope.
p. cm.
Includes bibliographical references and index.
ISBN 0 521 41737 6 (hardback)
1. Shakespeare, William, 1564–1616 – Authorship. 2. English drama – Early modern and Elizabethan, 1500–1600 – History and criticism. 3. English drama – 17th century – History and criticism. 4. English language – Early modern, 1500–1700 – Grammar 5. Authorship – Collaboration – History. 6. Drama – Authorship – History. I. Title.
PR2937.H65 1994
822.3′3 – dc20 93–29834 CIP

IBN 0 521 41737 6 hardback

VN

. . . first I stood on that earthen floor
for a hundred years, while the language changed around me.

(Peter Didsbury, 'The Barn', in *The Classical Farm*,
Bloodaxe Books, Newcastle upon Tyne, 1987)

# Contents

# Tables

# Graphs

# Preface

In this book, I introduce a new method for determining the authorship of renaissance plays. This method relies on what I term socio-historical linguistic evidence. Simply put, the use of socio-historical linguistic evidence involves the determination and comparison of linguistic usages of renaissance dramatic authors: at this time the English language is changing so rapidly that it is possible to distinguish between the grammatical usages of certain writers, even though they are writing in the same place (London), and at the same time (*c*. 1590-1625).

The methodology I use to determine and compare linguistic usages is based on theories of language variation and change developed in the fields of socio-linguistics and socio-historical linguistics by William Labov and Suzanne Romaine (see Labov 1972, Romaine 1982). As I argue in the Introduction, the use of socio-historical linguistic evidence offers a more reliable means of resolving authorship debates surrounding Elizabethan and Jacobean plays than has previously been available.

This book is divided into three parts. The first part concerns the methodology of socio-historical linguistic evidence, and the grammatical features investigated in this particular study. It should be of particular interest to historical linguists and authorship scholars who want to understand the precise basis of the method. One of the strengths of socio-historical linguistic evidence as opposed to other current approaches to authorship, is that its basis should be readily appreciable by anyone familiar with the language or literature of the period: no statistical background is required.

The second part of the book consists of a series of studies of individual plays and groups of plays: first the Shakespeare–Fletcher collaborations; then the Shakespeare–Middleton collaborations; then the 1664 folio plays; then a more diverse group of apocryphal plays which have received varying degrees of support for inclusion in the Shakespeare canon. Although some refinements to the methodology set out in part I are presented in the first section of chapter 5, individual studies in part II should be clear to anyone who has read the Introduction and chapters 2 and 3.

Part III distils my findings on the authorship of individual plays, and is included so that those who want easy access to my conclusions can get at them quickly without having to follow the statistics and graphs of parts I and II. This section is designed for literary scholars who want to know the likely authorship of any play they happen to be working on, but do not have the time or inclination to get involved in the authorship studies themselves. They should be warned, however, that some ascriptions can be made more confidently than others: the background to the ascriptions made in this section can be found in part II.

In a work of this type, some statistics are inevitable, but this is a book written for literary and linguistic scholars, and I have tried to avoid opaque sets of figures and equations. Wherever possible, statistical information is presented graphically in the main text, or in simple percentages – those interested will find raw figures in the Statistical Appendix.

# Acknowledgements

The methodology applied in this book developed from work which owes much to the influences of three people: Sylvia Adamson, Anne Barton, and Rivkah Zim. Of the three, my greatest debt is to Sylvia, who was patient and generous with a very stubborn, and completely ignorant, PhD student. I hope she will take pleasure in, and credit for, whatever is worthwhile in this book.

Many others have helped me during the writing, revising, and reworking: John Kerrigan, Willy Maley, Sophie Tomlinson, Gordon McMullan, my thesis examiners Richard Proudfoot and Susan Wright, Charles Barber, Matti Rissanen, Merja Kytö, and all at Helsinki. The method has been presented, usually with audience participation and on the spot testing, at Helsinki University, Newcastle University (Continuing Education Department), Leeds University, and King's College, London – I am grateful to all my audiences. Richard Holdsworth and Katie Wales ('thou' and 'you'), and Vivian Salmon (auxiliary 'do') answered questions so long ago they have probably forgotten. I have enjoyed a lively correspondence with Thomas Merriam.

From 1989 to 1991 the Department of Speech at Newcastle University provided me with the most supportive and stimulating academic environment possible, and Professors James and Lesley Milroy kindly read and commented on unreasonable amounts of draft thesis in a very short time. It is also a pleasure to be able to thank Lisa McEntee and Katie Reid of the Department of Speech for advice on sections of the thesis. Towards the end, Laura Wright read large sections of this book in manuscript, saving me from many, but not I fear all, indiscretions. Dream FM, Genesis FM, and RCR Radio kept me entertained through long Leeds nights.

Portions of the research presented here have been funded by the British Academy, St John's College, Cambridge, my parents, and an Earl Grey Memorial Fellowship from the University of Newcastle upon Tyne. Further research was carried out at the University of Leeds.

This book is for Dorothy and Basil Hope, with love and thanks, and especially Sylvia Adamson, who patiently guided me into the world of linguistics, and looked after my welfare when the 'real' world impinged.

# Abbreviations

The following abbreviations are used throughout the text; others are explained when they occur. In some cases plays have the same, or similar, abbreviation – in context, it is always clear which one is meant. In the list, plays marked (1) form the early Shakespeare sample (abbreviation Sh1); plays marked (2) the late Shakespeare sample (Sh2); while plays marked (3) represent a reduced Fletcher sample used in chapter 3.

| *abbreviation* | *play* |
|---|---|
| Shak | Shakespeare |
| *AW* | *All's Well That Ends Well* |
| *AC* | *Antony and Cleopatra* (2) |
| *CE* | *The Comedy of Errors* (1) |
| *CO* | *Coriolanus* (2) |
| *CY* | *Cymbeline* (2) |
| *KL* | *King Lear* |
| *LL* | *Love's Labours Lost* (1) |
| *MM* | *Measure for Measure* |
| *MSN* | *A Midsummer Night's Dream* (1) |
| *MV* | *The Merchant of Venice* (1) |
| *O* | *Othello* |
| *R2* | *Richard II* (1) |
| *T* | *The Tempest* (2) |
| *TC* | *Troilus and Cressida* |
| *TG* | *The Two Gentlemen of Verona* (1) |
| *WT* | *The Winter's Tale* (2) |
| Flet | Fletcher |
| *B* | *Bonduca* (3) |
| *HL* | *The Humorous Lieutenant* |
| *IP* | *The Island Princess* |
| *LS* | *The Loyal Subject* |
| *ML* | *The Mad Lover* (3) |
| *MT* | *Monsieur Thomas* (3) |
| *P* | *The Pilgrim* |
| *V* | *Valentinian* (3) |

| | |
|---|---|
| *WG* | *The Wild Goose Chase* |
| *WP* | *The Woman's Prize* (3) |
| | |
| Marl | Marlowe |
| *E2* | *Edward II* |
| *T1* | *Tamburlaine part 1* |
| *T2* | *Tamburlaine part 2* |
| | |
| Dekk | Dekker |
| *IF* | *If This be Not a Good Play . . .* |
| *ML* | *Match Me in London* |
| *SH* | *The Shoemaker's Holiday* |
| *WB* | *The Whore of Babylon* |
| | |
| Midd | Middleton |
| *MW* | *A Mad World, My Masters* |
| *MT* | *Michaelmas Term* |
| *PH* | *The Phoenix* |
| *TC* | *A Trick to Catch the Old One* |
| *FG* | *Your Five Gallants* |
| | |
| Mass | Massinger |
| *BM* | *The Bondsman* |
| *DM* | *The Duke of Milan* |
| *MH* | *The Maid of Honour* |
| *RG* | *The Renegado* |
| *UC* | *The Unnatural Combat* |

# PART I

# METHODOLOGY

# Chapter 1
# Introduction

## Authorship studies in the early Modern period

There is a great number of Elizabethan and Jacobean plays which are either anonymous, wrongly ascribed, or thought to be the work of more than one writer. This situation is a result of the particular context in which early Modern plays were written, acted, and published – and an understanding of this context explains many of the most common authorship problems which arise (Bentley 1971, and Wells *et al.* 1987:1–68 provide excellent accounts of these issues in more detail than can be given here). Such an understanding can also help in explaining the shortcomings and limitations of much previous authorship work.

The single most important factor in this context is that early Modern plays were only very rarely regarded as 'literature' in a sense recognisable today. They are better regarded as raw material fuelling the profitable entertainment industry of early Modern London, much as film scripts are the raw material of today's film industry. Like film scripts, they were bought from writers by acting companies and, just as today, once a script was sold, the writer lost control over it.

The demand of the theatres for new material, especially in the later sixteenth and early seventeenth centuries, was insatiable, and, again as often in the film industry, this favoured collaboration as a means of producing material of the required standard in as short a time as possible. Writers might specialise in certain types of writing – opening scenes, closing scenes, comic scenes, love scenes; and unsatisfactory scripts might be touted round various authors who would add to and cut the script in the hope of producing something playable.

Furthermore, the fact that the ability and right to produce a play lay in the ownership of a licensed copy was a disincentive to publication. Acting companies had an interest in protecting their investment in a popular play by not publishing it. Plays might thus be in repertory, but unpublished, for a considerable time, during which time they would naturally be adapted for each new production, possibly with topical additions by different dramatists.

When plays *were* released for publication (significantly often in times of plague, when the theatres were closed, and companies had to find alternative income), the process of transmission of texts produced effects which are highly relevant to authorship studies (again, Wells *et al.* 1987:9–52, provide a detailed account). Most important is the recognition that certain aspects of the author's original manuscript – spelling, punctuation, even some word forms – would not necessarily have been transmitted faithfully by those who prepared subsequent versions of the text: scribes preparing fair copies to sell to acting companies; bookkeepers producing prompt texts; compositors setting type from handwritten pages, these may all have introduced changes to the original. The printing process is particularly relevant here, not only because many authors seem to have punctuated manuscripts very lightly, if at all, in the expectation that pointing would be supplied in the printing house if the text were ever printed, but because the practicalities of fitting text onto lines and pages often introduced expansions and contractions (see Wells *et al.* 1987:42, 44–5, for illustrations). In many cases, the effects of these factors are unpredictable: we know, for example, that some scribes regularly preserve original spelling, others do so intermittently, while others rarely do so.

This context has numerous consequences for authorship studies. The most theoretically challenging is that our very desire to fix the authorship of early Modern play-texts is something of an anachronism, stemming largely from what Stillinger calls the 'romantic myth of the author as solitary genius' (1991:203). Dramatic texts are inherently collaborative, and there comes a point at which we have to admit that we can never know who wrote which word. Even so, early Modern dramatic collaboration was a physical process, which left physical evidence in the texts it produced. Various processes have intervened to corrupt that evidence, but often it is still detectable and interpretable – if not to the extent we might wish.

In a more concrete way, this context of production means that we have to be alive to the nature of the evidence an early Modern play-text presents us with. We need to know which features of a text are stable, and which are not. We need to know that spelling, punctuation, lineation, contractions, sentence length, oaths, stage directions are all subject to being changed by hands which are not those of the 'author' of the play. If we are to use these features as evidence for the authorship of a text (and they all have been), we need to know the likelihood of their being changed, and the consequences if they were. We also need to know that any play in the repertory of a London company for any length of time might have been cut, revised, or had material added for a particular performance, a tour, or to bring it up to date. This work would probably have been done by the company's contracted playwright, whoever the original author of the play had been.

The consequence of this is that any expectation of textual integrity, or purity, in early Modern play-texts is misplaced. Modern authorship studies, like modern editing, is not about returning us to some 'original' text, neatly doled out to collaborators, or ascribed to a single author. What it tries to do – what I have tried to do in this book – is look at the evidence present in the texts we have, understand how that evidence got there, and reveal what that evidence tells us about the history of how the text came to be like it is.

## Early Modern English and socio-historical linguistic evidence

I approach the question of the authorship of early Modern English play-texts via the historical linguistic context in which they were written. Early Modern English is conventionally dated from 1500–1700, and while linguistic change is a continuous process rather than a collection of discrete events, these dates are generally accepted as being meaningful by historical linguists, encompassing as they do a period in which written texts in England can be seen to show progressively less variation in a number of linguistic features as a written Standard language emerges (as we await Lass (ed.) forthcoming, the best book on early Modern English remains Barber 1976).

The key to socio-historical linguistic evidence is the fact that linguistic change is a process: when a change is in progress, the alternative forms will co-exist in the language. Changes in progress in early Modern English offered alternatives to writers and speakers where Present-day Standard English offers none – for example, a choice between 'you' and 'ye' in the second person pronoun, and '-th' and '-s' as an ending for the third person singular present tense of verbs (e.g. 'hath' versus 'has').

Alternatives such as these have been used as evidence in authorship studies (notably in the work of Hoy on the Fletcher canon) – unfortunately, these features are textually unstable: scribes and compositors could, and did, alter them when transmitting texts. This means that any attempt to use such evidence as an indicator of authorship is likely to be beset by questions of possible interference: results which do not conform to the subjective prejudices of the researcher can be explained away, and the tendency will always be to dismiss or discount inconvenient evidence (see chapter 5, and my discussion of Hoy's work on *Henry VIII*).

However, there are linguistic changes in progress in the early Modern period whose alternates (or more accurately variants) are not regarded as interchangeable by scribes and compositors, and which are therefore textually stable. Furthermore, by drawing on modern advances in linguistics, it is possible to elucidate, and in some cases predict, differences in the usages of variants by writers.

Socio-linguistics, as developed by Labov (1972), offers techniques for analysing and explaining language variation and change, in relation to factors such as age, sex, and class of language users. These techniques depend on the abstract notion of the linguistic variable; that is, an element of language which has two or more possible realisations (variants), which vary within the usage of a group of speakers of a language. In classical socio-linguistics, linguistic variables are phonological (for example pronunciation or non-pronunciation of /r/ in words such as 'fourth' and 'floor'), and their use can be related to social factors such as age, class, and sex. Socio-historical linguistics (Romaine 1982) has attempted, with success, to apply a methodology developed for the study of contemporary speech, to historically distant writing, specifically treating relative marker choice as a linguistic variable.

Crucial for the value of socio-linguistics to authorship studies is the fact that quantitative socio-linguistic methods are explicitly designed to deal with variation in linguistic forms which is not categorical (either form A or form B appears in a text), but is a matter of more or less (forms A and B both occur in texts, but in differing proportions, depending on factors such as the age or class of the producer of the text, and the situation in which it was produced). Quantitative socio-linguistics can therefore enable the researcher to make statistical comparisons between texts on the basis of the usages of linguistic variants within them, as Romaine notes.

> Anyone can observe that two samples of speech or writing are different. Sociolinguistic analysis can show that these differences are objectively measurable, and that there are patterns in the choices which a speaker/writer does make, on the one hand, and can make, on the other.
>
> (Romaine 1982:13)

Socio-historical linguistic evidence attempts to use the predictable patterning of incoming and recessive variants during language change in order to detect the hand of a chosen author. The key to this is the 'S' curve model of linguistic change (Aitchison 1991:83–5).

To illustrate this, let us assume that a change is taking place within a linguistic feature of a language. This change involves an older variant (A) and a newer variant (B), which is replacing the older one. In the course of this change, B forms will not appear randomly in the language, nor will A forms disappear overnight. Socio-linguistic models of change would lead us to expect that the shift from A to B within the language will be patterned in time, within the speech community, and within the usage of individual members of the speech community.

If we were to draw a graph of this change, we would expect it to have a distinctive 'S' curve – B forms would appear first in certain restricted

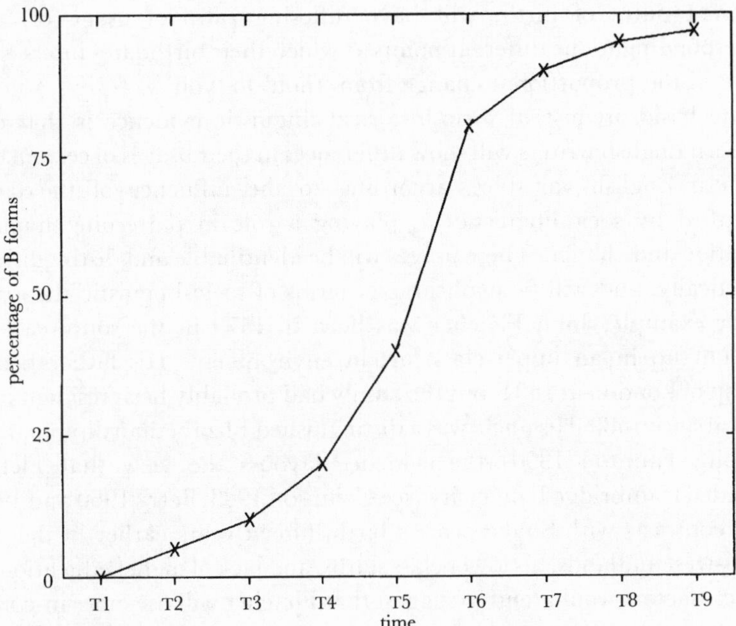


Graph 1.1 'S' curve of linguistic change (after Aitchison 1991:84)

contexts (restricted grammatically, geographically, and by individual) and would remain in a small proportion relative to A forms for some time. Then, as the change took off, B forms would increase exponentially, 'invading' contexts in which A had previously been the only variant found. Finally a third stage is reached, with B numerically dominant, but A retained in a few specific contexts (see graph 1.1, where T1 . . . T9 represent successive sampling points).

An example of such a change in Standard English would be the replacement of 'thou' by 'you' as the second person singular pronoun form. For this change, the 'S' curve begins with a few instances of singular 'you' in letters in the thirteenth century, has its exponential phase in the sixteenth and seventeenth centuries, and settles down from the eighteenth century to the present, with 'thou' retained only in highly specialised poetic and liturgical contexts.

The important point here is that during the exponential phase, an early Modern English speaker's frequency of use of 'thou' will be determined by a number of factors. We know that in-coming prestige variants like 'you' are used more frequently by younger, more educated, more urban members of the speech community. Because linguistic usages tend to be fixed early in life, two writers writing in the same year (even in the same text) who have different dates of birth, will have differing rates of usage of 'thou' corresponding to the different points at which their birthdates intersect the curve in the proportional change from 'thou' to 'you'.

The basic premise of socio-historical linguistic evidence is that early Modern English writers will show differences in their usages of certain early Modern English variables, according to the influence of the factors identified by socio-linguistics as playing a role in patterning linguistic variation and change. These usages will be identifiable and distinguishable statistically, and will be explicable in terms of socio-linguistic theory.

For example, John Fletcher was born in 1579 in the south-east and brought up in an upper-class, urban environment. His father became bishop of London in 1594, but the family had probably been resident in the capital since 1589. His uncle was a distinguished Elizabethan diplomat, and (despite Taunton 1990) the evidence favours the view that Fletcher attended Cambridge University (see Collinson 1983, Berry 1960 and 1964). This contrasts with Shakespeare's birth, fifteen years earlier in the rural south-west midlands, his lower class status, and lack of higher education. All of these factors would tend to suggest that Fletcher will use more in-coming prestige variants than Shakespeare.

In this ability to explicate, and even predict the differences it studies between authors, socio-historical linguistic evidence differs crucially from the most successful current approach to authorship studies: stylometry.

Stylometric tests typically involve the computational analysis of texts on the basis of factors such as average length of word, and the frequency of the appearance of certain words at the start of sentences. A wide range of other tests has been developed following the initial work in this area by A.Q. Morton (see Morton 1978; Kenny 1982 presents a more critical view of the claims of Morton and his followers). Leading workers in the field, whose studies are referenced in the Bibliography, include M. W. Smith, Morton, Stratil and Oakley, and Merriam. The work of Jackson, Lake, and Holdsworth at times draws on stylometric tools, as does that of the Shakespeare Clinic (see references to articles by Elliot and Valenza).

Stylometric tests can appear impressive, especially to those not familiar with the statistical tests used. Wells *et al.* however (1987:80), note difficulties which arise when Morton's techniques are applied to early Modern texts (not the least of which is how to define the sentence in texts punctuated in the printing house), as well as potential statistical problems (these are taken up in greater detail in various articles by M. W. Smith). Non-statisticians are also likely to suspect a fundamental methodological flaw in the basis of stylometric tests, which Furbank and Owens term the 'spectre of the meaningless' (1988:181). This is an unease with stylometric evidence based on its focus on apparently arbitrary factors, and the inability of its practitioners to explain either what exactly they observe and measure, or why authors should be different on these grounds. As A. Q. Morton puts it,

> the question which now arises naturally is, if it is not the grammatical, linguistic or philological role of words which is being investigated, what is it that is being studied? To this reasonable request the only reasonable reply is that we do not know.
>
> (Morton 1976:15)

This lack of understanding within stylometry of the nature of the object being measured must raise potential doubts about the methods used to measure it: how can the stylometricians be sure that their tests are appropriate?

In fact, I suspect that this difficulty is one of public relations rather than a fundamental methodological flaw. Literary scholars and non-statisticians are unwilling to accept the conclusions of work which they cannot understand, and which appears to be arbitrarily based. None the less, it is a major strength of socio-historical linguistic evidence that the differences it detects between the linguistic usages of authors are explicable, and that it does not rely on complex statistical tests for validation.

## Applying socio-historical linguistic evidence

The application of socio-historical linguistic evidence is essentially a two-stage process. In the first stage, the usages of the candidates for the authorship of a play, or number of scenes, are established from a comparison sample of their unaided work. In the second stage, results from the disputed texts are compared to those findings to indicate the possibility or otherwise of authorship by the suggested candidate. It will immediately be apparent that the application of the technique depends on the existence of a suitable comparison group of non-controversial texts.

The comparison samples analysed in chapters 2, 3, and 4 were selected on the basis of one over-riding factor: plays chosen had to be the unaided work of the named dramatist. This is easier for some writers than for others, and, as has been indicated, the very notion of an 'unaided' text at this time may be inappropriate.

When this study was begun, with the specific intention of separating Shakespeare and Fletcher's hands in *Henry VIII* and *The Two Noble Kinsmen*, an arbitrary decision was taken to include ten plays from each author in the samples. As work progressed, it became clear that this size of sample was not only time consuming to count by hand; it was unnecessary. As results in chapters 2 and 3 show, five plays give a more than adequate sample.

After initial work on auxiliary 'do' in Shakespeare and Fletcher therefore, comparison samples were reduced to five plays, and a second group of Shakespeare plays was selected from the early part of his career to allow assessment of the extent to which linguistic usages might change over an author's career. The selection of playwrights other than Shakespeare and Fletcher was done on the basis of those who had been suggested as possible authors of plays in the apocrypha. Suspicions of collaboration meant that in the cases of Marlowe and Dekker it was not possible to select five plays for the sample. (A list of the plays selected for each author can be found under Abbreviations at the front of the book.)

# Chapter 2

# The auxiliary 'do'

## Background

In Present-day Standard English, the auxiliary verb 'do' is used mainly in the formation of questions ('*Did* you go home?') and negatives ('I *didn't* go home'). Such usages are usually referred to as being 'regulated' (Barber 1976:263–7), which means that use of 'do' is obligatory in certain sentence types (negative declaratives, positive and negative questions) and absent from others (positive declaratives). The use of auxiliary 'do' in positive declaratives today automatically carries emphasis ('I *DID* go home').

In early Modern English however, the use of the auxiliary was optional in all of these cases – for example questions could be formed by inversion *or* by the use of auxiliary 'do': 'Went you home?' versus 'Did you go home?'. Positive declarative sentences in early Modern English could use the auxiliary without automatic implication of emphasis. Effectively early Modern speakers had a choice of two constructions whenever they formed any one of the four sentence types mentioned above. Constructions conforming to present-day usage are termed 'regulated', while those which would be unacceptable in Present-day Standard English are termed 'unregulated'. Table 2.1 illustrates the two systems (see also table 2.2 for actual examples of the sentence types from early Modern texts). Inevitably it has been necessary to simplify this account of one of the most researched and most contentious areas of historical English syntax. Fuller accounts of the modern and historical systems can be found in Tieken 1987, 31–4; Quirk *et al.* 1985 sections 2.49–51, 3.36–7, 12.21–6; Stein 1990.

The regulated system of auxiliary 'do' usage constitutes a rising variant over the period 1400–1700, conforming to the 'S' curve of linguistic change predicted in the Introduction. In 1400, auxiliary 'do' is hardly used, in the period 1500–1600 it is available in all sentence types, by 1700 it has been regulated in virtually all contexts: again, as stated in the Introduction, it can be assumed that younger, higher class, more educated, more urban individuals will be at the forefront of the change. For example, the assumption is that if regulation is the rising variant (as it will eventually be established as the standard), then Fletcher will show a more highly regulated usage than

Table 2.1 Regulated and unregulated use of the auxiliary 'do'

| *1 Regulated sentences (now standard)* | |
|---|---|
| (a) positive declarative: | I went home |
| (b) negative declarative: | I did not go home |
| (c) positive question: | Did you go home? |
| (d) negative question: | Did you not go home? / Didn't you go home? |
| *2 Unregulated sentences (now non-standard)* | |
| (a) positive declarative: | I did go home |
| (b) negative declarative: | I went not home |
| (c) positive question: | Went you home? |
| (d) negative question: | Went you not home? |

Shakespeare. This is based on his relative youth (date of birth 1579 as opposed to Shakespeare's 1564), his higher class (his father became bishop of London, while Shakespeare's was a yeoman-citizen), his greater degree of education (to university level, as opposed to Shakespeare who probably went no further than grammar school) and his more urban, south-eastern upbringing compared to Shakespeare's in the rural south-west midlands.

## History and development of the auxiliary 'do'

There is an extensive, and growing, literature on auxiliary 'do'. Hausmann (1974:158) goes so far as to say that 'There is probably no problem in the history of English syntax more carefully explored and reported on than the origin of modern English periphrastic "do"', and yet he goes on to quote Visser (1963–73:1488): 'there is hardly a point of syntax on which there is a greater cleavage of views'. This study does not attempt to offer a solution to the problems of the origin of auxiliary 'do', but it does constitute a contribution to a growing theme in recent work on the topic: focused approaches to the *use* of the auxiliary in specific contexts (see Stein 1990, Rissanen 1991, Nevalainen 1991).

Briefly summarised, theories as to the origin of auxiliary 'do' divide into semantic and syntactic. Semantic theories posit the reanalysis of one of the earlier forms of 'do', either the Old English causative 'do' (Engblom 1938, Ellegard 1953), or the main verb (Visser). Syntactic theories suggest either the creation of a new formal modal category, with 'do' filling the same structural slot as the new modals (Lightfoot 1979:116), or a logical, and expected, reordering of the rules which already existed governing the use of the Old English substitute verb usage (directly parallel to the modern English usage (Hausmann 1974:164–7)). Denison (1985) offers a synthesis of these analyses which posits a 'do' + infinitive construction arising in the thirteenth century, the status of which is derived from its context (thus sidestepping the vexed question of chronology, and the competing candidates for the semantic origin of auxiliary 'do'). This construction then enters the modal verb subsystem ('which it resembles formally' Denison 1985:54). Effectively Denison has it all ways – his 'do' first appears in the causative system, where its status is subject to semantic analysis on the basis of context, and then is syntactically reanalysed into the modal system, after which a further period of regularisation produces the modern system of NICE properties (negation, inversion, code, emphasis).

A more recent contribution to studies of the auxiliary 'do', Kroch 1989, attempts to link syntactic change, linguistic variation, and psycho-linguistics to explain the gradual nature of the regulation of 'do' use. Kroch's finding that his 'mediated influence model' applies to changes in the use of auxiliary 'do', supports the grouping of different sentence types into 'regulated' and 'unregulated' classes, since it implies that 'the increase in frequency of the use of *do* up to 1560 in all environments reflects an increase in the application of a single grammatical rule that introduces *do*' (1989:160; Kroch's findings are, however, contested by Ogura 1993).

Of prime importance to this study are accounts of the development, rather than the origin, of the auxiliary, since they often include factors which may interfere with the socio-linguistic patterning of the variable. Ard (1982) concentrates on the reasons for the changes in the relative frequencies of auxiliary use: the increase in its use in questions and negatives, and the decrease in positive declaratives. His attempt to relate the increase in auxiliary use in negatives and questions to the emphatic use of 'do' by analogy with other languages is less convincing than his suggestion of a multi-influence on the auxiliary – a series of different factors all tending to increase tendencies which eventually become obligatory. In a similar argument, Rissanen suggests that

> no single use, such as the causative one, lies behind the rise and development of do-periphrasis. The roots of the periphrasis can probably be found in the wide semantic scope of 'do' – a verb of 'basic action' as many scholars . . . have noted. Causativeness was just one of the many shades of meaning of this verb; it may well have supported its periphrastic use but it can hardly be specified as its sole origin. It seems that the popularity of do-periphrasis in spoken language has always been largely due to the influence of what could be called the three Es: emotion, emphasis, and euphony.
>
> (1985:177)

Further factors which favoured the use of the auxiliary include the principle of structural compensation, which identifies a tendency for the predicate of a clause to be longer than the subject (Quirk *et al.* 1972:968). Rissanen suggests that 'the need to increase the weight of the predicate became acute in late Middle English and early Modern English when the reduction of verbal endings – notably the loss of the unstressed vowel – produced a large number of monosyllabic verb forms' (1985:164). Increasing the weight of the verb phrase in this way can effect the emphasis of the expression – both in emotive, contrastive emphasis ('You did not go home' leading to contrastive emphasis 'I *DID* go home' versus unemphatic 'I went home'), and in what Rissanen calls 'textual emphasis', where the auxiliary forms function as textual markers (on the possible functions of auxiliary 'do' as a textual or topic marker see Stein 1985, 1990). Auxiliary 'do' can carry tense and person in cases when the main verb is delayed until the end of the sentence, and it seems to function as a rhetorical balance to phrases formed with modal or tense auxiliaries: 'they would never Eate till they did wash' (Rissanen 1985:165).

The auxiliary can also function as a verb phrase marker, marking predicates which are separated from the subject, and acting as a tense marker for potentially ambiguous verbs which have identical present and past tense forms (e.g. cut, cast, eat, put – giving 'I cut' as present but 'I did cut' as past). It can also carry tense in order to avoid potentially awkward consonant clusters (e.g. 'did jump' for 'jumpedest'). Specialised functions in poetry include the effect of the auxiliary on word order and its taking of the infinitive stem, which affect euphony and rhyme schemes, as well as the addition or deletion of extra syllables to the line (on phonotactic factors affecting the use of do periphrasis, see Stein 1987:420).

Characterising early Modern English usage, Barber states that there is a stylistic dimension to regulated or unregulated usage – 'the regulated use of "do" is more typical of a colloquial style, while the unregulated use is more literary' (1976:265). Support for this may come from John Fletcher's *The Faithful Shepherdess*, a consciously literary, and deliberately archaic piece, which makes extensive use of unregulated 'do' forms in positive declarative sentences.

Rissanen (1985) however, claims that unemphatic, unregulated 'do' in positive declaratives can be found in records of speech in early American English, which would challenge Barber's identification of regulated usage as speech-based. While the work on the present-day occurrence of this unemphatic auxiliary 'do' in non-standard Present-day English speech which Tieken notes might tend to support a survival in speech rather than writing (compare the case of 'tun' in German – Hausmann 1974), Rissanen's examples of the use of apparently unemphatic 'do' in church meetings and courts may be explained by the formality of the events recorded, and the desire to give a non-contrastive emphasis to assertions in such contexts. I think a similar explanation can be given for the findings of Rissanen 1991, which I consider at greater length in a forthcoming paper, 'The status of auxiliary *do*'.

This debate is important to the use of auxiliary 'do' as socio-historical linguistic evidence, since it concerns the status of the variable. The question of whether unregulated 'do' in positive declaratives has written or spoken connotations will relate to whether it carries overt or covert prestige, and hence its likely patterning in the speech community.

The above factors have been offered as explanations for the increase in auxiliary 'do' usage in the early Modern period. Given that the regulated system has become the standard form, the changes bringing this about can be expected to pattern socio-linguistically, with the regulated system behaving as a rising variant. However, there is a danger that formal or stylistic factors (such as the specialised use of the auxiliary in poetry) will intervene to skew any figures which are attempting to show socio-linguistic patterning, since they might function to alter an author's expected usage.

The usefulness of auxiliary 'do' regulation as an authorship tool will depend on the extent to which non-socio-linguistic factors interfere with the socio-linguistic patterning of the variants – and this is best assessed by collecting and analysing data from early Modern plays to determine whether or not a clear quantitative difference can be shown to exist between the usages of different writers.

## Counting methodology

As was stated in chapter 1, the application of socio-historical linguistic evidence is essentially a two-stage process. This chapter gives an account of the first stage of the process for using the auxiliary 'do' as an authorship tool: establishing the usages of a range of early modern dramatists.

In the course of this study, regulation rates were calculated for forty-three plays of known authorship, which formed the comparison samples, held to be representative of the usages of six early Modern dramatists. Collection of the raw data was done by hand, most often from modern facsimiles of the earliest available authoritative texts, and in some cases from microfilm copies, or from modern diplomatic editions (for example the Bowers edition of Fletcher's plays).

It may appear surprising that counting was done by hand rather than by computer, but in fact this emerged as the most reliable and efficient approach for a number of reasons. In the first place, when this project began, the availability of electronic editions of early Modern dramatic texts was much more haphazard than it has become (thanks largely to the Oxford Text Archive). In the second, computer counting would have had to have been performed on a grammatically tagged text in order to allow the computer to pick up regulated positive declaratives (in the event, the single most common sentence type in all plays) – since by definition these are distinguished by absence of the auxiliary with the tensed verb. A simple concordance program could not have picked these up. The production of tagged texts of early Modern drama, although a highly desirable research resource, is not yet possible on a large scale, since current tagging programs can only work with modernised editions, and are set up to deal with modern English grammar.

Human counting inevitably means a degree of error through inadvertence, or misclassification. Early in the project, certain counts were repeated on separate occasions to test for error. The results of this were encouraging, in that totals varied only by one or two out of several hundred instances – far below the level at which error would have affected the results. I performed all the counts myself, which guaranteed that decisions about classification were consistent (and presumably that any errors were consistent across comparison samples). Generally I collected raw data from each play in an author's comparison sample before any of those figures were converted into percentages – this avoided the possibility of my own expectations biasing the count while it was being made.

The actual physical process of counting involved making pencil marks on a tally sheet while reading the play. In most cases, figures were collected on a scene by scene basis. Certain sentence types were excluded from consideration before the count began: amongst these were imperatives and tag questions, because they are often ambiguous with substitute verb usage, and (following Rissanen 1985:179, note 12) constructions with the verbs 'be', 'have', and 'do', because they cannot vary with the simple verb form.

Because emphatic usages are often a question of interpretation, all instances of 'do' in positive declaratives were counted as unregulated. The number of emphatic usages thus misclassified (since they are strictly speaking regulated) was insignificant, and since all authors were treated in the same way, this did not affect the figures.

The above exclusions gave a basic set of eight sentence types (four regulated and four unregulated). These were coded in the following fashion: the coding first signals presence or absence of the auxiliary ('a' = contains auxiliary 'do' / 'x' = lacks auxiliary 'do'), then signals whether the sentence is positive or negative ('+' = sentence is positive / '−' = sentence is negative), and then identifies sentence type ('d' = sentence is declarative / 'i' = sentence is interrogative. Thus the coding 'x+d' indicates a positive declarative sentence ('+d') without the auxiliary ('x'). Examples of the sentence types, and the codings can be found in table 2.2.

The relative percentages of regulated sentences in any play can be calculated from the raw figures by the formula

$$\frac{R}{N} \times 100$$

where R is the number of regulated forms in a play, and N is the total number of regulated and unregulated forms. The resulting percentage allows comparison of regulation rates between samples of differing line length or N value.

## Comparison group results

Graph 2.1 shows the percentage regulation rate for each play in the comparison samples. The raw figures, and the average rates for each author (shown on graph 2.2), will be found in the Statistical Appendix. In graph 2.1, the number of plays in a sample with any one percentage regulation rate is plotted against the vertical axis, the regulation rates are plotted against the horizontal axis. Thus the first bar on the graph represents the three plays in the Shakespeare samples with regulation rates of 79 per cent.

The most striking fact evident from this graph is that at no point does Shakespeare's usage overlap with that of any other author: no other author shows a regulation rate below 85 per cent, and Shakespeare never exceeds 84 per cent. Every other author's usage overlaps at some point with at least one other author, and usually more than one. This is an indication that, in the case of Shakespeare at least, auxiliary 'do' can function as a very powerful authorship tool. Many stylometric studies (for example Horton's of Shakespeare and Fletcher) suffer because although they can describe consistent ranges of usages for linguistic features for authors, these ranges are not always distinct from each other, and so are not always reliable enough for use as tests of authorship.

It should also be pointed out from this graph that authors do show characteristic, and consistent, rates of regulation: plays in the samples group together. This graph indicates that given sufficiently large samples (N = 900 and over) certain authors could be ruled out of candidacy for plays showing certain rates of regulation: Fletcher for plays much below 90 per cent; Shakespeare for plays much above 85 per cent. This type of test will always be better at giving negative answers than positive ascriptions for the reasons discussed in the Introduction, but it is striking that of these six

Table 2.2 Alternative sentence structures in early Modern English

Unless otherwise stated, all examples are from *Henry VIII*

| *Sentence type* | *Status* | *Code* | *Example* | |
|---|---|---|---|---|
| Positive declarative | unregulated | a+d | 'I do know / Kinsmen of mine . . . ' | (1.01. 80–1) |
| | regulated | x+d | 'I know, his Sword / Hath a sharpe edge . . . ' | (1.01.109–10) |
| Negative declarative | unregulated | x−d | 'Alas, I know not' | (5.03. 15) |
| | regulated | a–d | 'I doe not know / What kinde of my obedience, I should tender' | (2.03. 65–6) |
| Positive questions | unregulated | x+i | 'Know you of this Taxation?' | (1.02. 40) |
| | regulated | a+i | 'But will the dainty Dominie, the Schoolemaster keep touch doe you thinke . . . ?' | (*The Two Noble Kinsmen* 2.03. 39–40) |
| Negative questions: | unregulated | x−i | 'Know you not / How your state stands i'th' world, with the whole world?' | (5.01. 126–7) |
| | regulated | a−i | 'Doe not I know you for a Favourer / Of this new Sect?' | (5.02. 115–16) |

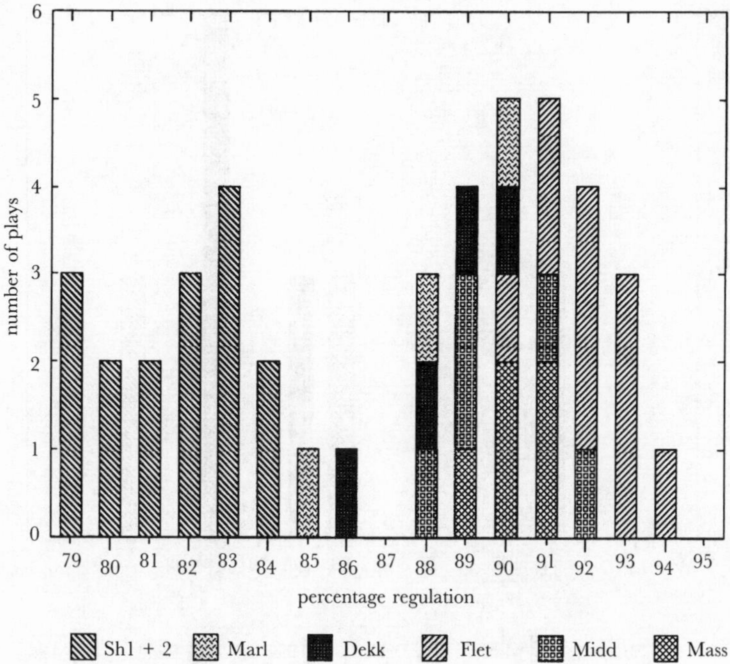


Graph 2.1 Auxiliary 'do' regulation: comparison samples (all plays)

playwrights, only Shakespeare has a regulation rate which is ever below 85 per cent for long periods. Of course, it is likely that if counts were performed on the whole extant corpus of early Modern drama, then playwrights closer in usage to Shakespeare would be found – but at the moment they remain elusive.

A basic presumption of the use of socio-historical linguistic evidence is that variants will pattern in the early Modern speech community according to socio-linguistic factors. Prior to the collection of the data, it was assumed that date of birth would function as a factor to determine the regulation rate in dramatists. Graph 2.2 shows the average regulation rates for each of the six sampled dramatists. Their names appear in the legend of the graph in order of birth (Shakespeare 1564, Marlowe 1564, Dekker 1572, Fletcher 1579, Middleton 1580, Massinger 1583). If the date of birth theory were correct, I would expect the samples to appear in the same order along the percentage regulation axis (the horizontal one).

That the trend of the graph is towards this pattern is clear, but there are two important exceptions to the progression of the graph. The first comes with the two earliest playwrights, Shakespeare and Marlowe, who are far apart in terms of their average regulation rates, despite sharing their year of

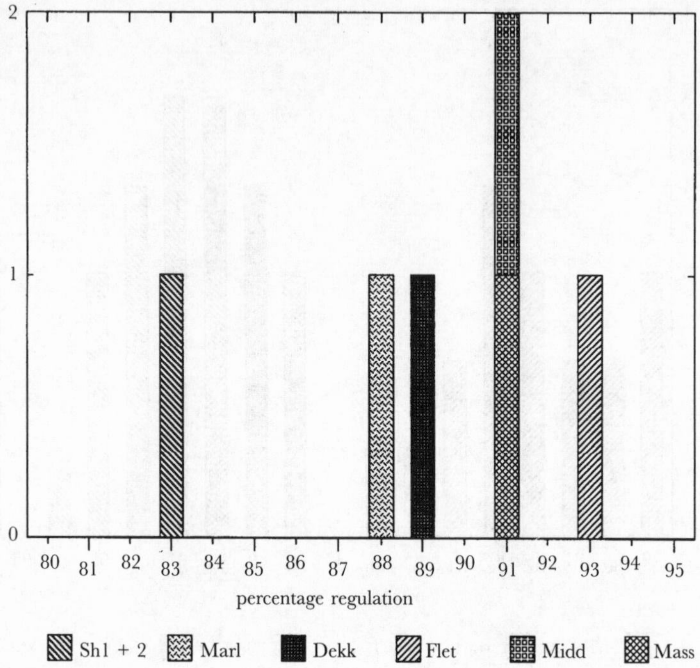


Graph 2.2 Auxiliary 'do' regulation: comparison samples (averages)

birth. Of course, a certain amount of individual variation around a central trend is to be expected, so it is perhaps not wise to make too much of this. It is also difficult to decide whether this result is because Shakespeare is 'old fashioned' in his usage of auxiliary 'do', or because Marlowe is ahead of the trend. Given the isolation of Shakespeare shown on graph 2.1, it might be inferred that Shakespeare is the anomaly here.

Looking at Fletcher's position though, also ahead of the later-born Middleton and Massinger, I am tempted to suggest that factors other than date of birth are also involved in the patterning of this variable: the possibility is that Shakespeare's south-western upbringing, as much as, or more importantly than, his date of birth, makes him a highly unregulated writer; while Fletcher's more urban birth and childhood push him to the fore of this innovation.

Pat Poussa's 1990 paper on the origin of auxiliary 'do' notes that usage is higher in western areas (possibly, she suggests, because it is a result of pidginisation of English in areas of contact with Celtic), and auxiliary 'do' remains in some western dialects today where it is used as a marker of habitual action. As yet, we do not know enough about early Modern English to say that unregulated usage of auxiliary 'do' is a western dialect

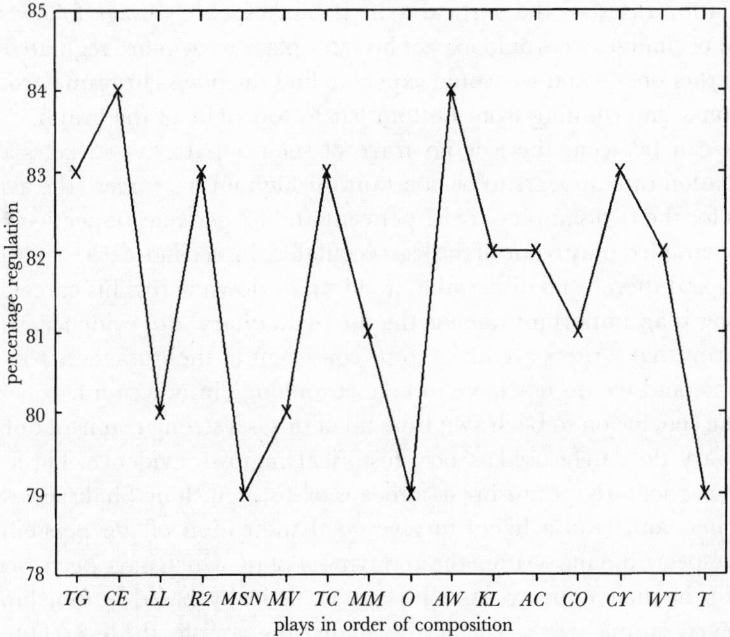


Graph 2.3 Regulation rates of Shakespeare's plays

feature, but it is possible that in graph 2.2, and Shakespeare's 'do' usage generally, we are seeing linguistic evidence of Shakespeare's birthplace.

It can also be pointed out here that despite the picture painted in literary studies of Shakespeare as a dramatic and linguistic innovator, this is one linguistic feature which could well have struck his contemporaries as old-fashioned. It is also possible that this could explain the tendency of the restoration theatre to prefer Fletcher to Shakespeare as more up to date dramatically and linguistically.

Graph 2.3 addresses a problem which has been encountered by other workers seeking to use linguistic features as evidence for authorship (for example feminine endings in verse lines): how can we know whether or not an author's usage of a feature is constant over his career, or whether he changes? We know that the percentage of feminine endings in Shakespeare's writing goes up substantially over his career – and yet in the case of a socio-linguistic variable, we would normally expect preferences formed in childhood to persist throughout later life.

This problem was addressed by the collection of samples from the early and late periods of Shakespeare's career – sixteen plays in all. These sixteen plays are listed along the horizontal axis of graph 2.3, with their respective regulation rates on the vertical axis. If Shakespeare's usage followed the trend of change, we would expect his later plays to be more regulated than his earlier ones – and we would expect to find the plays clustering around a diagonal line running from bottom left to top right of the graph.

As can be seen, there is no trace of such a pattern – Shakespeare's regulation rate appears to be constant throughout his career (the average rates for the two samples are 81 per cent and 82 per cent respectively); his latest sampled play is one of the least regulated; his second-earliest one of the most, and there is no discernible trend up or down across his career. This finding is an important one for the use of auxiliary 'do' evidence, since it confirms that writers are likely to be consistent in their usages across their careers, and we do not have to take chronology into account.

The conclusion to be drawn from all of this is a strong confirmation that auxiliary 'do' can be used as socio-historical linguistic evidence. The feature looks particularly promising as a means of distinguishing Shakespeare and Fletcher, and is also likely to give good indication of the possibility of Shakespeare having written the anonymous plays which have been ascribed to him in their entirety. As with any statistically based authorship tool however, sample size is crucial: the smaller the sample, the less reliable the test. We have to accept that even the best tests can tell us nothing significant about short passages or (and this is particularly relevant in the early Modern period) short poems.

Auxiliary 'do' regulation is therefore potentially a very powerful socio-historical linguistic authorship tool: on large samples it can be diagnostic of authorship between Shakespeare and Fletcher on the basis of quantitative analysis. However, one of the aims of this study is to produce a division of single plays: it is therefore necessary to work on single scenes rather than whole plays, giving very much smaller sample sizes. The question which now arises is, what is the minimum significant sample? How many sentence tokens (N) are needed to form an opinion on the likely authorship of a scene or passage?

## Establishing the minimum significant sample size

Milroy 1987:135–6, considers the work which has been done on sample sizes. In statistics, N = 30 is usually taken to be the dividing line between large and small samples – low samples are more and more subject to random fluctuations (and in studies such as this, where the results are expressed as percentages, conclusions based on small samples can be highly misleading, since one or two instances of a usage either way can bring about large swings in the percentages). One linguistic study Milroy discusses suggests that N = 35 gives 100 per cent conformity with the expected norm, but other work disputes that classical statistical procedures are appropriate for socio-linguistic analysis, where the variability of the factors studied may be extremely complex. For example, tossing a coin gives two variables for each 'token', or toss, and it would be surprising if a sample of twenty tokens were not close to the expected norm of 50 per cent heads. The 'variable' under consideration here, although it can be expressed as a binary opposition (regulated versus unregulated), is in fact made up of a series of related variables, one of which, the 'do' periphrasis in positive declaratives versus simple tensed verb, occurs far more frequently than any of the others. It was difficult to predict what effect this complexity would have on the number of tokens needed to produce a significant sample, and a further count was therefore made on a scene by scene basis of the two plays from the Shakespeare and Fletcher comparison groups which were closest in percentage regulation. The intention was to see at what level of sampling the regulated percentage continued to discriminate between Shakespeare and Fletcher.

The plays closest together from the two comparison groups are *The Wild Goose Chase* (90 per cent regulated usage) and *All's Well that Ends Well* (84 per cent regulated usage). Graph 2.4 shows the regulation rate for

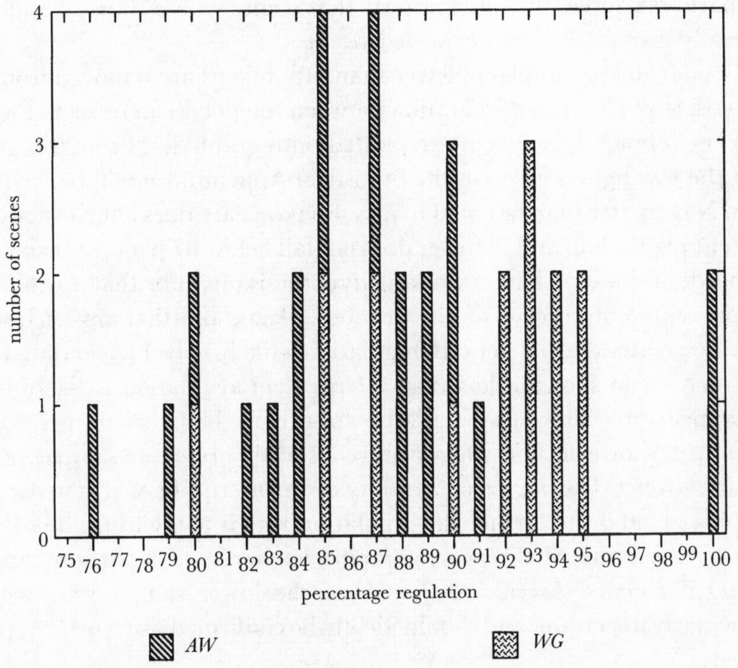


Graph 2.4 Scene by scene regulation in *All's Well* and *The Wild Goose Chase*

individual scenes in the two plays (for technical reasons I have included only those scenes where the regulation rate is 75 per cent or above). The raw figures for each scene will be found in the Statistical Appendix (see pp. 158–9).

Given that these two plays have been deliberately chosen as they show the least overall difference between Shakespeare and Fletcher's usages in the comparison samples, at what level is it still possible to discriminate between the two writers? The plays themselves are six percentage points apart, but, as might be expected with percentages based on smaller sample sizes, there is considerable overlap in the percentages for individual scenes, with two of Shakespeare's even showing 100 per cent regulated usage: at this level of sample size, the test is obviously no longer categoric for Shakespearean or Fletcherian authorship.

However, looking at the eleven highly regulated Shakespearean scenes (i.e. 87 per cent or over), it can be seen that only two (2.01, 4.03) have more than fifty tokens (seventy-two and eighty-nine respectively). Furthermore, the five most regulated Shakespeare scenes all have fewer than fifty tokens. Looking at the five Fletcher scenes showing regulation below 87 per cent, only two have more than fifty tokens (85 per cent regulated 4.01 has just sixty tokens and may be a borderline case), although the 167 tokens of the 87 per cent regulated 3.01 mean that this must be regarded as a good sample. Matching these results against the separation of usage found in the comparison samples, it would appear that scenes where $N = 50$ and over generally give close to the expected result.

If scenes giving samples of fewer than fifty tokens are removed from the analysis, a much clearer separation between the plays can be seen. Figures for scenes of over fifty tokens are plotted onto graph 2.5. From this graph (and the raw figures given in the Statistical Appendix) it will be seen that when N is greater than or equal to fifty, Shakespeare does not rise above 89 per cent regulation, and Fletcher does not fall below 87 per cent (except for the borderline 4.01). Thus a working hypothesis might be that a significant sample represents a scene of fifty or more tokens, and that any such scene showing greater than 89 per cent regulation is likely to be Fletcherian, while any such scene showing less than 87 per cent regulation is likely to be Shakespearean. This may initially appear to be a small percentage difference – however, the difference is constantly present in samples of fifty or more tokens. The degree of certainty of any ascription will increase with sample size, and the further the regulation rate is away from the overlap area between the Shakespearean and Fletcherian comparison samples (86–90 per cent). Ascriptions based on the lower sample sizes will be particularly uncertain, and should ideally be confirmed using other types of evidence.

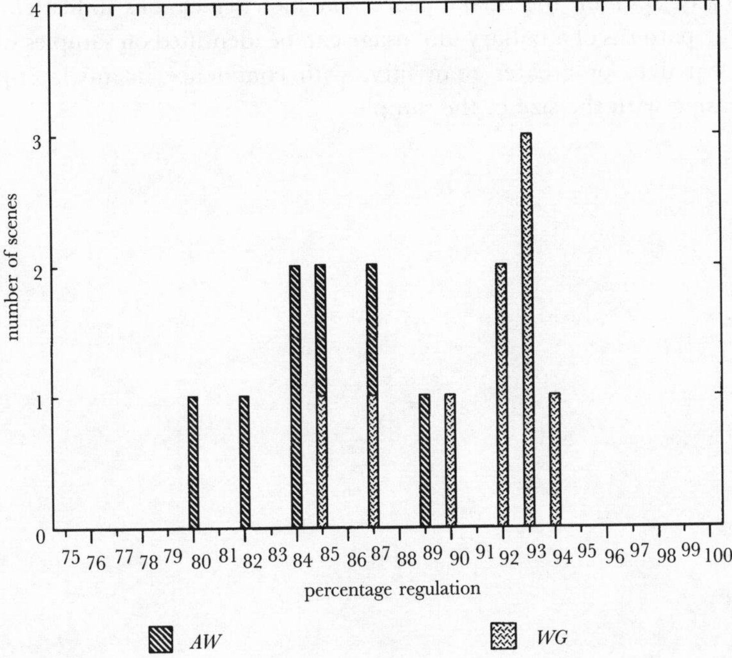


Graph 2.5 Scene by scene regulation in *All's Well* and *The Wild Goose Chase* (N=50+)

## Summary

This chapter has demonstrated that early Modern dramatists have consistent, and in some cases distinct, regulation rates of auxiliary 'do'. Ranges of usage for Shakespeare, Marlowe, Dekker, Fletcher, Middleton, and Massinger have been established. Some evidence for the expected correlation between early birthdate and low regulation of auxiliary 'do' has been found, but it also seems likely that place of birth (in terms of region, and also whether urban or rural) plays a role in patterning regulation in the speech community.

This chapter has also shown that auxiliary 'do' rates do not change over the lifetime of writers (at least in the case of Shakespeare). This is an important factor in the use of any linguistic feature as an authorship tool. Although formal and stylistic features which might affect the use of auxiliary 'do' were identified prior to the collection of data, the consistency of usage found within the comparison samples suggests that such factors do not operate to obscure the socio-linguistic patterning of the variants.

Finally, tests on the Shakespeare and Fletcher canons indicated that distinct patterns of auxiliary 'do' usage can be identified on samples where N is equal to or greater than fifty, with confidence in any ascription increasing with the size of the sample.

# Chapter 3

# Relative markers

## Background

As is the case with auxiliary 'do' usage, early Modern English shows the emergence of a system of relativisation which will eventually be standardised in Present-day English, but which exists alongside, and in competition with, other forms and conventions. Relativisation is rather more complex than auxiliary 'do' however, in that it is not possible to produce a binary 'regulated' / 'non-regulated' analysis of relativisation strategies corresponding to the dichotomy of auxiliary 'do' usage.

In the Present-day Standard English utterance

(The man [. . . I know])

The relative clause ([. . .]) can be introduced by any one of three relative pronouns:

The man that I know
The man who I know
The man (0) I know

(in the final example the pronoun is termed zero, represented by (0)). The relative pronoun 'which' would not be possible in this position in Present-day Standard English:

*The man which I know

because the antecedent ('The man') is human, and Present-day Standard English distinguishes between 'who' and 'which' on the basis of their antecedents.

In early Modern English, however, this distinction was not obligatory, as can be seen from the following examples from Shakespeare:

Where is that Slaue
*Which* told me they had beate you to your Trenches?

– 'which' with a personal antecedent (*Coriolanus* 1.06. 39–40);

the Elements
Of *whom* your swords are temper'd[. . .]

– 'who(m)' with a non-personal antecedent (*The Tempest* 3.03. 62).

Other differences between early Modern English and Present-day Standard English relativisation strategies include the use of 'that' in non-restrictive relative clauses (a restrictive relative clause delimits the range of reference of the antecedent):

I cheefely,
*That* set thee on to this desert, am bound
To loade thy merit[. . .]

– 'that' in a non-restrictive clause (*Cymbeline* 1.06. 72–4), and the use of zero relatives in the object position:

I haue a minde presages me such thrift,
That I should questionlesse be fortunate[. . .]

– zero in subject position (e.g. 'I have a minde (0) presages . . . ' – *The Merchant of Venice* 1.01. 175–6).

While these differences cannot be reduced to two competing systems as with auxiliary 'do', they do represent changes in progress in the language, and can be expected to pattern systematically within the speech community. Tables 3.1 and 3.2 summarise what was theoretically possible in the early Modern period, and what is taken to be Present-day Standard usage, respectively. It should be noted that the use of '+' is not intended to imply that all usages are numerically as likely as each other.

Changes in progress in the relative system in the early Modern period therefore include a tendency to distinguish 'who' and 'which' on the basis of their antecedent, a tendency to avoid using 'that' in non-restrictive clauses, and a tendency to avoid using zero in the subject position. For the reasons stated in the Introduction, younger, more urban, upper class authors are to be expected to show all of these tendencies more strongly. Furthermore, 'who' as a relative is itself a fairly recent innovation at this time, which might therefore be expected to be found more frequently in the work of younger playwrights (see Romaine 1982:53–80, and Rydén 1983 for more detailed accounts of the changes in the relative system at this time).

To take Shakespeare and Fletcher as examples, on the evidence of the more innovatory patterning of auxiliary 'do' in the work of Fletcher when compared to Shakespeare, it might be expected that Fletcher will show a corresponding increased tendency to distinguish between 'who' and 'which' on the basis of the antecedent ('who' being restricted to personal antecedents, 'which' to non-personals), to avoid zero relatives in the subject position, and

Table 3.1 Relative markers in early Modern English

Following Barber 1976:213–22; + = possible, – = not possible.

| | | *restrictive* | | *non-restrictive* | |
|---|---|---|---|---|---|
| | | *sub* | *obj* | *sub* | *obj* |
| who(m) | personal | + | + | + | + |
| | non-personal | + | + | + | + |
| which | personal | + | + | + | + |
| | non-personal | + | + | + | + |
| that | personal | + | + | + | + |
| | non-personal | + | + | + | + |
| zero | personal | + | + | – | – |
| | non-personal | + | + | – | – |

Table 3.2 Relative markers in Present-day Standard English

Following Quirk *et al.* 1985:366, 1248–9.

| | | *restrictive* | | *non-restrictive* | |
|---|---|---|---|---|---|
| | | *sub* | *obj* | *sub* | *obj* |
| who(m) | personal | + | + | + | + |
| | non-personal | – | – | – | – |
| which | personal | – | – | – | – |
| | non-personal | + | + | + | + |
| that | personal | + | + | – | – |
| | non-personal | + | + | – | – |
| zero | personal | – | + | – | – |
| | non-personal | – | + | – | – |

to confine his usage of 'that' largely to restrictive clauses. If however, as scholars suggest, 'that' and deletion are dominant, or increasing, in drama, we might expect Fletcher to show an increased usage of them in comparison to Shakespeare in accordance with the tendency shown in the analysis of auxiliary 'do' usage for him to use rising forms more than Shakespeare. However, if 'who' is also in some contexts a rising form, there might be a case for expecting Fletcher to employ that form more frequently than Shakespeare (especially as 'who' is the most recent form to enter the relative system).

It should be apparent that predicting differences between the relativisation strategies of authors is much more difficult than for auxiliary 'do'. This is because we understand less about the behaviour of the individual relative markers, since they function individually rather than as part of a single system, and because stylistic factors play a much greater role in patterning relative markers than in the patterning of auxiliary 'do' usage.

Romaine (1982) goes so far as to say that the variation she studies is due more to style than chronology – she feels that the relative system is diachronically stable, while showing synchronic variation due to register. Barber cites the city comedies of Middleton as plays which show an increased use of 'that' due to a supposed representation of the colloquial forms of contemporary speech (1976:218).

In the case of auxiliary 'do', although stylistic and prosodic factors which might potentially have blurred the socio-linguistic stratification of the variable were identified in advance of the collection of the data, they were not found to play a major role in patterning the use of auxiliary 'do'. In the case of relative marker choice however, most scholars argue that the choice of relative marker is sensitive not only to grammatical factors (such as the animateness of the antecedent, and whether the relative clause itself is restrictive or not), but also to register. Thus in her texts, Romaine detects a correlation between formality and 'qh' (i.e. 'who'/'which') relatives, and informality and 'that'/zero relatives. Barber too stresses the need to take text type into account – claiming that 'who' and 'which' increase in formal prose in early Modern English at the expense of 'that', but that 'that' continues to be dominant in drama (1976:221).

This link between text-type and relative pronoun choice is very important if relative pronoun choice is to be used as socio-historical linguistic evidence, since it is always necessary to understand any non-biographical factors which may affect the patterning of the variants when attempting to use a variable as socio-historical linguistic evidence. If drama can be considered as a homogeneous text-type with regard to relativisation it would be very convenient for the present study.

However, there is not much evidence which would allow this to be assumed in advance of the collection of data from the comparison samples: there is in fact disagreement about the stylistic register of the relatives in some contexts. Barber's suggestion that early Modern deletion is 'as likely to occur in formal as in colloquial style' (1976:221) directly contradicts the basis of Romaine's study, which hypothesises a relationship between colloquial style and deletion in Middle Scots ('The predominant opinion about the origin of 0 relatives is . . . that it is an indication of the colloquial language of the period' 1982:74).

Two factors therefore suggest that relativisation strategies are not quite as suitable for use as sociohistorical linguistic evidence as the auxiliary 'do'. The first is that there is no way to represent relative choice as a 'regulated'/'unregulated' dichotomy as with the auxiliary 'do'. This immediately makes the figures of usage more opaque, and dilutes them into more than two categories. Given that relativisation is less frequent than auxiliary 'do' use (or non-use), the need to divide the totals into separate values for each marker produces small samples, and therefore less reliable results.

The second is the stylistic factor, which blurs sociolinguistic stratification of the use of the variables (for example, it is easy to imagine that a writer predisposed by biography to use 'that' and zero forms might in fact produce a piece using entirely 'who' and 'which' forms in an attempt to write in a formal mode).

These are problems, but they are not fatal to the use of relativisation as socio-historical linguistic evidence – indeed, a certain stylistic level, and therefore a preference for one of the markers over the others, may be an identifiable trait of use as an indicator of possible authorship (for example, in his Arden edition, Hoeniger attempts to use zero forms as an indicator of the presence of Wilkins in *Pericles* – 1963:lxi, and note to 1.01.15).

Although the system of relatives, as a system which is undergoing standardisation, appears at first sight to offer a similar situation to that observed in the case of auxiliary 'do' use, stylistic factors threaten the socio-linguistic stratification of the variable. At the same time though, the fact that the different relative markers may pattern in accord with different stylistic levels, opens up the possibility that this factor may be of use as an authorship tool, once playwrights' characteristic usages have been established by results from the comparison samples.

## Counting and methodology

For the purposes of this study, the paradigm set of relative clause markers was taken to be 'who(m)', 'which', 'that', and 'zero' (or, 'deletion'). Missing from this set, amongst others, are 'the which', and 'whose', instances of which were not included in the final figures because of uncertainty about the relationship of 'the which' to 'which' and zero, and about the effect of case on the relationship of 'whose' to zero (the totals for each are too low to have affected the final results in any case). Also excluded are sentential relative markers (Quirk *et al.* 1985:1244), relatives with an initial preposition (Quirk *et al.* 1985:1252–3) and markers such as 'as', current in non-standard English today ('The man as I know').

The clauses were classified according to three intersecting criteria: whether they were restrictive or non-restrictive; whether the antecedent was personal or non-personal; whether the relative functioned as subject or object of its clause. These three factors, when matched to the four markers distinguished in this study, give thirty-two possible kinds of relativisation (that is, for any one of the relative markers, there are eight possible clause types: restrictive-personal-subject; restrictive-personal-object; restrictive-non-personal-subject; restrictive-non-personal-object, etc.). Many studies, in fact, refine the classification of clauses further, dividing non-restrictive clauses into 'progressive' and 'non-progressive' (Rydén 1966:xlviii–li) or 'continuative' (Romaine 1982:83–4), or increasing the complexity of the syntactic analysis of the position or function of the relative marker (Romaine 1982:92–8). In this case, it was felt that the thirty-two types provided by the basic analysis of relatives were ample to allow significant differences to emerge, and, as Romaine makes clear:

> Nothing in fact is gained by increasing the number of cells [types of clause] since the number of tokens representing each category becomes smaller each time a further subcategorization is made, until finally the numbers become too small to draw meaningful conclusions.
>
> (1982:88)

If there are too many clause types in an analysis, the initial sample will become too dilute to yield significant results; the only way around this is either to increase the sample size, or reduce the number of clause types. For the purposes of this study, as will be seen, even thirty-two cells proved to be too many to support authorship analysis.

One aspect of the classification system which has a potential for error is the restrictive/non-restrictive distinction (examples of ambiguous clauses are given in the *Pericles* section in chapter 6). In Present-day Standard English speech, these are distinguished by intonation, and in writing by punctuation (non-restrictive clauses are separated from the head by a comma), but in the case of early Modern English texts, intonation is absent, and punctuation is unreliable. There is therefore potential for ambiguity, and for subjective choice to play a role in the final figures of a count (indeed, as Romaine (1982:82) notes, Jacobsen has suggested that the distinction should be thought of as a continuum rather than as an opposition, and Fox and Thompson (1990), in a study of the grammar of relative clauses using tape recorded conversational data, abandon the distinction altogether). In the event, distinctions made here between authors do not generally rely on differences in the formations of these types of clauses.

The possibility of printing house standardisation of relative markers is something which must also be considered here. Relative markers can theoretically be interchanged much more easily than regulated and unregulated auxiliary 'do' usages, since their replacement or removal does not entail any syntactic reordering, or inflection of the verb.

Checks on the Shakespeare canon show that in all but one of the plays which exist in both folio and quarto, there is no evidence that the editors or compositors of the first folio modernised the relative markers. Evidence for alteration of relative markers between quarto and folio texts exists only in the case of *Richard III*, a particularly problematic text. In the case of Fletcher, none of the sample plays was printed in his lifetime, four appearing in the 1647 first folio, and *Monsieur Thomas* in a 1639 quarto. The delay in printing (he died in 1625, so the plays were thirty to forty years old when they came into the printing house) raises questions about the possibility of modernisation, but the only evidence available of the effects of transmission (manuscripts of *The Woman's Prize* and *Bonduca* which are presumed to pre-date the folio) shows that relative markers were retained. It will be seen below that only in the case of Dekker is there reason to suspect that relatives have been tampered with at some stage. None the less, it will be necessary to bear in mind that relative markers are textually less stable than auxiliary 'do' evidence.

The question of sample size must also be addressed here, since I have reduced the Fletcher and the second Shakespeare sample to five plays, in line with the sizes of other samples. Romaine makes clear (1982:106) that from what we know about sampling procedures it is not necessary to include all the instances of a variable in a statistical corpus – either in a period, as in Romaine's case, or in (say) Shakespeare and Fletcher, even if this were possible with computer analysis. What may be lost in this particular study by such a limitation of the corpus are 'freak' usages which fall far outside the normal range of a particular author due to special generic or stylistic circumstances.

The effects of this limitation of the corpus are not significant – as was said above, linguists and statisticians generally find that an N value greater than or equal to 35 gives 100 per cent conformity with expectations. Obviously the sensitivity of variables to sample size is not constant, especially with complex variables which need larger samples for patterns to emerge, but the sample here compares well with that of Romaine, which is 6,300 relative

Table 3.3 Relatives in Shakespeare sample 2

| | | *restrictive* | | *non-restrictive* | | | |
|---|---|---|---|---|---|---|---|
| | | *sub* | *obj* | *sub* | *obj* | *totals* | *%* |
| who(m) | personal | 29 | 24 | 53 | 45 | 151 | |
| | | | | | | 171 | 12 |
| | non-personal | 2 | 1 | 10 | 7 | 20 | |
| which | personal | 21 | 8 | 6 | 3 | 38 | |
| | | | | | | 458 | 33 |
| | non-personal | 96 | 117 | 124 | 83 | 420 | |
| that | personal | 277 | 24 | 40 | 2 | 343 | |
| | | | | | | 606 | 44 |
| | non-personal | 165 | 67 | 30 | 1 | 263 | |
| zero | personal | 13 | 21 | 0 | 0 | 34 | |
| | | | | | | 158 | 11 |
| | non-personal | 13 | 111 | 0 | 0 | 124 | |
| | | | | | | N=1393 | |

tokens from seven texts on a stylistic continuum from legal prose to verse (i.e. 900 from each text); the samples used here contain 6,204 tokens from six authors, with all texts belonging to the same genre. Nor have these tokens been subdivided into clause type categories to the same extent as those of Romaine, thus reducing dilution of the sample.

## The results: the comparison samples

### *Using relativisation evidence as an authorship tool: case study on Shakespeare and Fletcher*

Because of the complexity of relativisation as a variable, I decided to carry out a pilot study on the Fletcher and second Shakespeare comparison samples, in order to establish which features of the relativisation system seemed likely to be significant in authorship studies.

Tables 3.3 and 3.4 give the raw figures from the plays in the two chosen comparison samples, showing the numbers of relatives in each of the thirty-two cells of the analysis. In the initial analysis of the figures, it was found that the subject/object status of the relative marker was not useful in making a distinction between Shakespeare and Fletcher, and this factor was subsequently disregarded.

Table 3.4 Relatives in the Fletcher sample

| | | *restrictive* | | *non-restrictive* | | | | |
|---|---|---|---|---|---|---|---|---|
| | | *sub* | *obj* | *sub* | *obj* | *totals* | | *%* |
| who(m) | personal | 0 | 3 | 8 | 4 | 15 | 16 | 2 |
| | non-personal | 0 | 1 | 0 | 0 | 1 | | |
| which | personal | 0 | 1 | 3 | 1 | 5 | 117 | 13 |
| | non-personal | 18 | 12 | 42 | 40 | 112 | | |
| that | personal | 253 | 12 | 21 | 2 | 288 | 486 | 55 |
| | non-personal | 139 | 39 | 18 | 2 | 198 | | |
| zero | personal | 20 | 34 | 0 | 0 | 54 | 271 | 31 |
| | non-personal | 38 | 177 | 0 | 2 | 217 | | |
| | | | | | | N=890 | | |

Tables 3.5 and 3.6 show the effects of the animateness of the antecedent and the status of the relative clause (whether it is restrictive or non-restrictive) respectively. The percentages given here have been calculated using the individual totals of each relative marker in order to emphasise the effects of a shift between the factors (thus the figures show that 88 per cent of Shakespearean 'who' relatives occur with personal antecedents, as against 12 per cent with non-personals). In tables giving percentage values, totals may add up to 99 or 101 rather than 100 due to rounding up or down.

From the figures in tables 3.5 and 3.6, it will be seen that certain predictions about Fletcherian usage are confirmed. His use of 'who' and 'which' in respect of the animateness of their antecedents is more 'modern' than Shakespeare's, since Fletcher has 'who' with a personal antecedent 94 per cent of the time against Shakespeare's 88 per cent, and 'which' with a non-personal antecedent 96 per cent of the time as against Shakespeare's 92 per cent (these differences though are not great). Fletcher also observes the tendency for 'that' to occur increasingly in restrictive clauses (up from 88 per cent in Shakespeare to 91 per cent in Fletcher), and 'which' in non-restrictive (this last being particularly marked: up from 47 per cent in Shakespeare to 74 per cent in Fletcher, so that where a Shakespearean 'which' is slightly more likely to occur in a restrictive clause, a Fletcherian

Table 3.5 Effect of animateness of antecedent

| | *who* | *which* | *that* | *zero* |
|---|---|---|---|---|
| *Shakespeare 2* | | | | |
| Personal | 88 | 8 | 57 | 22 |
| Non-personal | 12 | 92 | 43 | 79 |
| *Fletcher* | | | | |
| Personal | 94 | 4 | 59 | 20 |
| Non-personal | 6 | 96 | 41 | 80 |

Table 3.6 Effect of restriction

| | *who* | *which* | *that* | *zero* |
|---|---|---|---|---|
| *Shakespeare 2* | | | | |
| Restrictive | 33 | 53 | 88 | 100 |
| Non-restrictive | 67 | 47 | 12 | 0 |
| *Fletcher* | | | | |
| Restrictive | 25 | 27 | 91 | 99 |
| Non-restrictive | 75 | 74 | 9 | 1 |

one is highly likely to be in a non-restrictive one). These differences conform to Fletcher's general tendency to show a more 'modern' language use than Shakespeare, using more examples of rising variants, and (because rising variants at this time represent developing norms) showing less variation in his language and more standardisation.

However, although this study has confirmed expectations of socio-linguistic differences in Shakespearean and Fletcherian usages of the relative markers, the differences discovered are not great enough to allow their use as an authorship tool. Only in the case of the use of 'which' in relation to the restrictive or non-restrictive nature of the clause is the observed difference likely to yield significant results, and the frequency of 'which' forms in the plays of Shakespeare and Fletcher is not great enough to make this useful as a statistical tool for ascribing doubtful scenes. Further, more statistically complex, analysis of these figures might produce more differences between the writers, but unfortunately the infrequent occurrence of relative markers means that differences in the usage of individually conditioned markers (e.g. 'who' in non-restrictive clauses) are unlikely to appear in the short

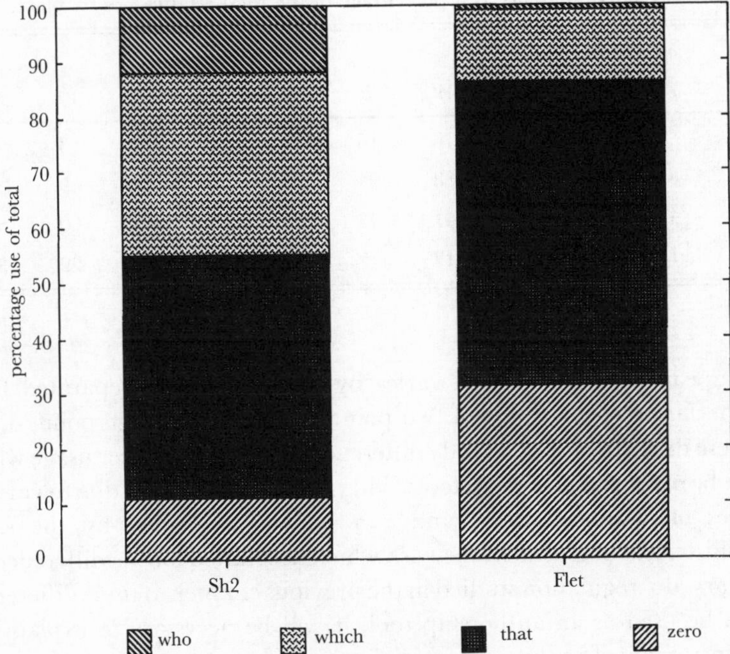


Graph 3.1 Average relative marker use in the Shakespeare 2 and Fletcher samples

passages studied in authorship tests – sometimes they may not even appear over whole plays.

If grammatical conditioning of individual markers does not look promising as evidence for authorship, one feature of relative marker choice does offer the possibility of being used as authorship evidence. When the focus of the study is shifted to the percentages for overall use of the relative markers, significant differences do occur, although they do not appear to be due to socio-linguistic factors.

Graph 3.1 shows the average usage of each relative marker by Shakespeare and Fletcher in the comparison samples. From the graph it can be seen that, compared to Shakespeare, Fletcher avoids 'who' and 'which' forms in favour of 'that' and particularly zero forms (socio-historical linguistic expectations had been that Fletcher might use more 'who' forms than Shakespeare). Of the four markers (see table 3.7), differences between three are such that the ranges of each author's usage do not overlap. Of these three, the rate of zero forms is the most differentiated, since the gap in percentage points between Shakespearean and Fletcherian usage (twelve points from 15 per cent to 27 per cent) is greater than the internal range of variation between the plays of either author (eight percentage points in each case). The next best differentiation comes with 'who' usage where

Table 3.7 Relative markers as a percentage of the total relative use by play

| | *Shakespeare* | | | | | *Fletcher* | | | | |
|---|---|---|---|---|---|---|---|---|---|---|
| | *AC* | *CO* | *CY* | *WT* | *T* | *MT* | *WP* | *B* | *V* | *ML* |
| who | 9 | 14 | 13 | 10 | 16 | 1 | 1 | 2 | 3 | 1 |
| which | 37 | 30 | 28 | 38 | 34 | 23 | 16 | 12 | 9 | 8 |
| that | 42 | 47 | 44 | 41 | 43 | 45 | 53 | 58 | 60 | 55 |
| zero | 12 | 9 | 15 | 12 | 7 | 31 | 31 | 27 | 29 | 35 |

Shakespearean usage (which varies by seven points) is separated from Fletcherian usage (a range of two points) by six percentage points.

These then, appear to be wide differences in relative marker usage which might be of use as authorship tools. They are not differences due to varying degrees of standardisation, and can not be explained by the same socio-historical linguistic framework which accounted for the differences in auxiliary 'do' regulation studied in the previous chapter. If these differences are to be used as an authorship tool, it will be necessary to explain the differing usages of Shakespeare and Fletcher in order to avoid the 'spectre of the meaningless' which has been felt to haunt the evidence of the stylometricians.

The pattern of the differences is that Fletcher avoids 'who' and 'which' forms in favour of 'that', and particularly zero forms, thus moving strongly in the direction of those forms Romaine identifies as least formal. Although 'who' is a rising form (and one which will establish itself as a standard), Fletcher avoids it, probably because of its formal connotations. The explanation for this, and the high percentage of zero forms in Fletcher, might be a desire on his part to reproduce the forms of speech. It is probably worth stressing here, in view of Barber's implication that 'that' is associated with the presumably colloquial speech of Jacobean city and restoration comedy, that the Fletcher sample includes tragedy and tragicomedy. This suggests that 'that' and deletion could be features of all speech, from whatever class, while 'who' may be strongly marked as a formal, written form.

Support for this view of 'who' as written-based (and therefore my explanation of why Fletcher might avoid it) comes from accounts of the rise of the form. In the historical contexts in which it first appears, 'who' refers exclusively to God (Rydén 1983:129). Rydén suggests that the need arose in the 1400s for a strongly personal relative marker to replace 'that' and 'which' in this type of sentence, and that 'who' was the obvious choice, since 'whom' and 'whose' had already been borrowed and had become established within the relative system.

Rydén seems to see the spread of 'who' in the sixteenth century as literature based:

> the first writers to avail themselves of this relative regularly were Lord Berners (the 1520s) and Thomas Elyot. By 1600 *who* had clearly got the upperhand of personal *which*. But not until the beginning of the 18th century – some 300 years after its first appearance in our extant records – did it reign supreme vis-a-vis *which*,
>
> (1983:132–3)

and Barber adds that the 'spread of *who* and *which*, and the recession of *that*, are especially characteristic of a formal style of writing' (1976:218). This is in spite of theories that 'who', because it is first found in letters, has its origin in spoken English (Romaine 1982:62). Much more likely in view of Fletcher's failure to pick up on 'who', is the theory which sees its appearance in letters as influenced by Latin letter-writing manuals (Rydén 1983:131, and note 13).

Rydén goes on to note the origin of 'who' use in association with strongly personal antecedents, and he categorises its spread with the formula '(heavily [+Human] > vaguely [+Human])' (1983:133). He says that 'who' is first employed with 'words' which

> occupy the highest position on the scale of personhood (the Deity, personal proper names, etc.) and then spread to entities lower down the scale, down to collectives and other words of a less outspoken personal character.
>
> (1983:130)

Looking at Shakespearean and Fletcherian 'who' use in the comparison sample, it is possible to see just these distinctions being made. Shakespearean use is the more general (on Rydén's terms more modern), 'who' being applied as expected to personal proper names,

> Sycorax, who with Age and Enuy[. . .]
>
> (*The Tempest* 1.02. 230–2)

as well as un-named personals,

> A Roman,
> Who had not now beene drooping[. . .]
>
> (*Cymbeline* 5.03. 89–90)

but also with collectives,

> The mariners . . . / Who . . . / I haue left asleep[. . .]
>
> (The Tempest 1.02. 230–2)

and less personal terms,

> This is some Monster of the Isle, with foure legs; who hath got . . . an Ague[. . .]
> (*The Tempest* 2.02. 66–7)

> A braue vessell
> (Who had no doubt some noble creature in her)[. . .]
> (*The Tempest* 1.02. 6–7)

In the Fletcher sample, usage is much more restricted, as well as being much less frequent: 'who(m)' tends to occur only with proper names or titles ('Diocles / (Whom long experience had begot a leader)', *The Mad Lover* 1.01. 15–6), or with un–named, but obviously personal, antecedents ('she that I love, / Whom my desires shall magnifie', *The Mad Lover* 1.02. 82–3). These distinctions will be drawn upon subsequently as indicators of likely authorship.

### Comparison sample results

Each section below gives the results for the comparison samples: tables give the raw figures for the whole samples, graphs show the range of variation within plays in the individual samples.

#### *The Shakespeare comparison samples*

Table 3.8 shows the raw figures and overall proportions of relative marker choice in the early Shakespeare sample. Noteworthy features of this sample include the high rate of 'which' usage and low rate of zero forms. It can also be seen from the 'who(m) non-personal' and 'which personal' rows in table 3.8 that Shakespeare tends not to observe the 'who' / 'which' distinction.

Graph 3.2 shows that the internal variation of the sample is not great for most plays – but there is one strikingly anomalous result: 'which' usage in *The Comedy of Errors* is much lower than in any other play of this date. This result calls for explanation, but it is not easy to know what to say about it. Compared to the other samples, deviations from idiolectal ranges like this are rare.

Looking forward to his later sample (graph 3.3), we can see that Shakespeare's relativisation pattern seems to become more consistent later in his career, so there may be a case for seeing this as an example of a young playwright experimenting with the texture of his language. However, I find this an unsatisfactory explanation of the result – in no other early play do we find such experimentation. Nor do I think that this result can be explained by any special circumstance in the genre or plot of *The Comedy of Errors*. Nor can some sharp overall decline in relativisation in this play be blamed – for one thing, this is a percentage drop for another, *A Midsummer Night's Dream*, which has thirty-five fewer relative markers overall than *The Comedy of Errors*, has twenty more 'which' forms.

Table 3.8 Relative markers in Shakespeare sample 1

| | | *restrictive* | | *non-restrictive* | | | |
|---|---|---|---|---|---|---|---|
| | | *sub* | *obj* | *sub* | *obj* | *totals* | *%* |
| who(m) | personal | 9 | 8 | 18 | 12 | 47 | |
| | | | | | | 55 | 7 |
| | non-personal | 2 | 0 | 6 | 0 | 8 | |
| which | personal | 10 | 0 | 5 | 2 | 17 | |
| | | | | | | 171 | 21 |
| | non-personal | 32 | 42 | 42 | 38 | 154 | |
| that | personal | 212 | 17 | 26 | 4 | 259 | |
| | | | | | | 477 | 58 |
| | non-personal | 101 | 106 | 11 | 0 | 218 | |
| zero | personal | 13 | 9 | 0 | 0 | 22 | |
| | | | | | | 119 | 15 |
| | non-personal | 7 | 90 | 0 | 0 | 97 | |
| | | | | | | N=822 | |

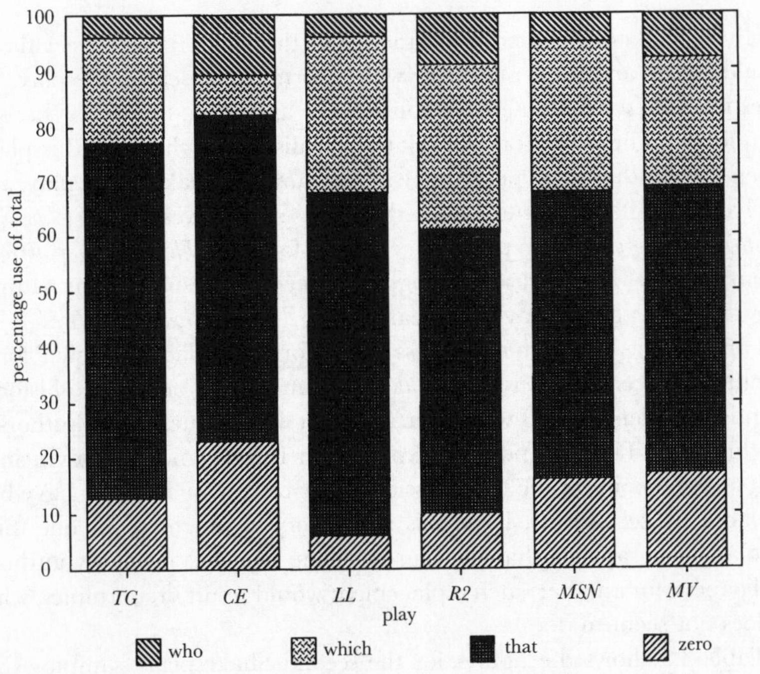


Graph 3.2 Relative marker use in the Shakespeare 1 sample by play

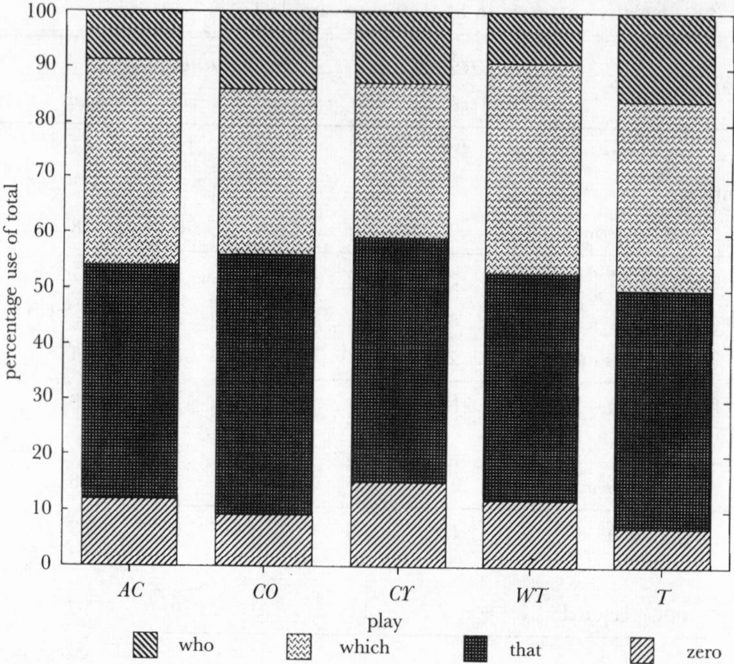


Graph 3.3 Relative marker use in the Shakespeare 2 sample by play

Given Shakespeare's normal practice at this stage in his career then, I would expect about twenty more 'which' forms to appear in the play. The question as to where these have gone can be answered: they have 'become' zero forms. The percentage of relatives realised as 'which' in this play is seven – by far the lowest percentage in any sampled Shakespeare play, a full twelve percentage points lower than the next lowest play (*The Two Gentlemen of Verona*). The percentage of zero forms in *The Comedy of Errors* is twenty-three – in this case, the highest percentage result for any sampled play, and six points above the nearest play (*The Merchant of Venice*).

I am unable to explain this excess of zero forms and lack of 'which' forms. In other respects the play is fully Shakespearean in terms of the socio-historical linguistic evidence, and I would certainly not wish to question its authorship on this basis. The only possible explanation I find remotely convincing is that at some point in the transmission of the text, 'which' forms have been replaced by zero forms. Even this is not very satisfactory: for one thing, scholarship is satisfied that the source for the folio was probably authorial foul papers; for another, such replacement would result in short lines, which it does not seem to do.

Table 3.9 shows the figures for the second Shakespeare sample – here 'which' usage is even higher than in the early sample, and zero usage is

Table 3.9 Relative markers in Shakespeare sample 2

| | | *restrictive* | | *non-restrictive* | | | |
|---|---|---|---|---|---|---|---|
| | | *sub* | *obj* | *sub* | *obj* | *totals* | *%* |
| who(m) | personal | 29 | 24 | 53 | 45 | 151 | |
| | | | | | | 171 | 12 |
| | non-personal | 2 | 1 | 10 | 7 | 20 | |
| which | personal | 21 | 8 | 6 | 3 | 38 | |
| | | | | | | 458 | 33 |
| | non-personal | 96 | 117 | 124 | 83 | 420 | |
| that | personal | 277 | 24 | 40 | 2 | 343 | |
| | | | | | | 606 | 44 |
| | non-personal | 165 | 67 | 30 | 1 | 263 | |
| zero | personal | 13 | 21 | 0 | 0 | 34 | |
| | | | | | | 158 | 11 |
| | non-personal | 13 | 111 | 0 | 0 | 124 | |
| | | | | | | N=1393 | |

lower. Contrasting the two samples, it can be seen that in neither does Shakespeare fully observe the 'who' / 'which' distinction – about 10 per cent of the forms of each marker are non-standard in today's terms.

As was suggested above, it can be seen from graph 3.3 that there is much less internal variation in the second sample, possibly implying that Shakespeare had attained a more stable style towards the end of his career.

Graph 3.4 shows the averages for the two samples plotted against each other – and it clearly shows a shift from 'that' and zero to 'who' and 'which' (that is, the more formal end of the scale) over the course of Shakespeare's career. This graph gives the first firm evidence that relative markers do not behave in the same way as auxiliary 'do', which was shown to be consistent over Shakespeare's career. It should be stressed that this shift is not necessarily the result of standardisation: although 'who' and 'which' are in theory rising forms, results from later samples will show that the status of 'who' at this time is highly complex. 'Which' does not become an explicitly preferred feature until the late seventeenth century. A more likely explanation is that the genre of the early and late plays results in this shift: the early plays being mainly comic, the late plays more tragic. I would expect such a shift in genre to be reflected in a shift up the formal scale of relatives (indeed, such stylistic shifts can be seen within Shakespeare's plays).

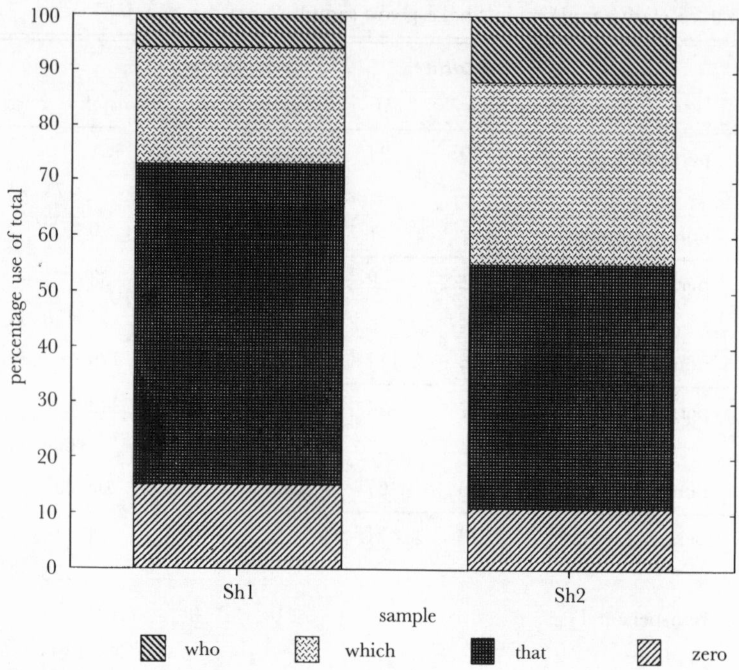


Graph 3.4 Average relative marker use in the two Shakespeare samples

In terms of their usefulness as socio-historical linguistic evidence, this is not good news about relatives. One of the main advantages of auxiliary 'do' is that it does not appear to change over the course of a dramatist's career; another is that it is not affected by generic or stylistic considerations. As soon as we have to include consideration of time and genre, the statistics regarding the use of socio-historical linguistic evidence become much less clear-cut. The danger is that statistics will be 'interpreted' in the direction consciously or unconsciously favoured by the researcher. This is not to rule out the use of relatives in this type of study – but their use will usually be ancillary to the use of auxiliary 'do'.

*The Marlowe comparison sample*

Table 3.10 and graph 3.5 show the results for the Marlowe comparison sample.

Although this sample is restricted to three plays (N = 577) because of sampling difficulties, an interesting pattern does emerge. Comparing this sample to the early Shakespeare sample (to which it is closest in time), we can see that although Marlowe is like Shakespeare in not restricting 'which' to non-personal antecedents (his percentage of personal 'which' – eleven per cent – is similar to Shakespeare's), he *does* restrict 'who' to personal ones.

Table 3.10 Relative markers in the Marlowe sample

| | | *restrictive* | | *non-restrictive* | | | | |
|---|---|---|---|---|---|---|---|---|
| | | *sub* | *obj* | *sub* | *obj* | *totals* | | *%* |
| who(m) | personal | 1 | 5 | 15 | 7 | 28 | 28 | 5 |
| | non-personal | 0 | 0 | 0 | 0 | 0 | | |
| which | personal | 4 | 2 | 2 | 1 | 9 | 81 | 14 |
| | non-personal | 15 | 14 | 31 | 12 | 72 | | |
| that | personal | 160 | 2 | 62 | 0 | 224 | 374 | 65 |
| | non-personal | 118 | 26 | 6 | 0 | 150 | | |
| zero | personal | 11 | 5 | 0 | 0 | 16 | 94 | 16 |
| | non-personal | 7 | 71 | 0 | 0 | 78 | | |
| | | | | | | N=577 | | |

As a variable therefore, restriction by antecedent behaves independently of relative marker: 'which' and 'who' are both undergoing a process of grammatical restriction, but the process of restriction does not necessarily move at the same rate for both forms.

Potentially this is a useful authorship distinction between Shakespeare and Marlowe: on this evidence, a piece of writing containing a non-personal 'who' is more likely to be by Shakespeare than Marlowe. Unfortunately, the relative infrequency of non-personal 'who' forms, even in Shakespeare's work, means that we would be very lucky to find such a form in a piece of disputed writing (there are only eight such forms out of a total relative count of 822 in the early Shakespeare sample, and twenty out of 1393 in the late sample – a numerical increase, but in fact a slight percentage decrease, again suggesting possible standardisation across Shakespeare's career).

A further point arises from graph 3.5. Intuitively, it would seem reasonable that of the three plays sampled, the two *Tamburlaine* plays would be more like each other than they would be like *Edward II*. Subjectively, these two plays share a set piece declamatory style characterised by long speeches and relatively little rapid interchange between characters, whereas *Edward II* would seem to feature rather more short speeches, argument, and

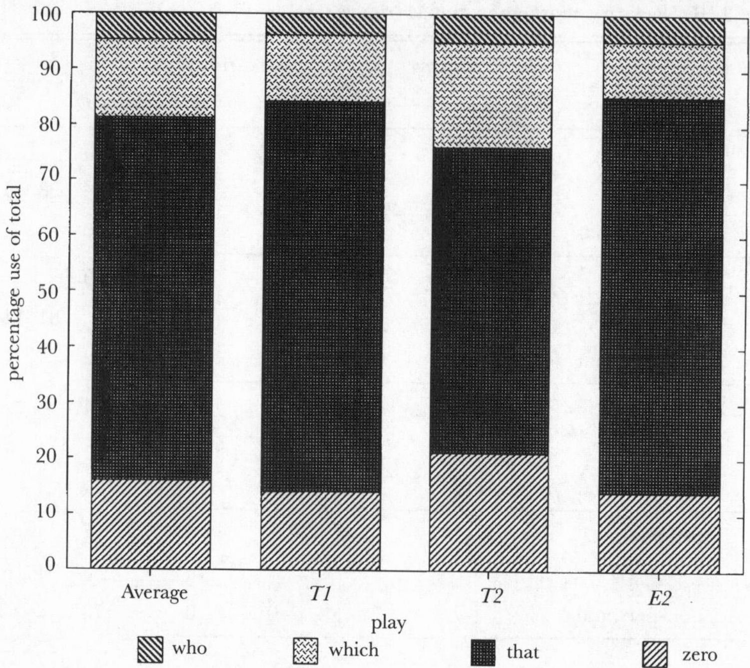


Graph 3.5 Relative marker use in the Marlowe sample (including average use)

interchange. These subjective characterisations may well hold good, but if so they are not evident in the relativisation strategies in the three plays: from the graph it can be seen that in terms of their relatives *Edward II* and *Tamburlaine part 2* are the most similar plays, while *Tamburlaine part 1* differs strikingly from the other two plays in terms of 'that' usage (lower) and 'which' and zero usage (higher). Not only is it puzzling that this play, rather than *Edward II*, should be aberrant, but it is difficult to explain the pattern of its aberrancy: if 'which' usage was lower, and 'that' and zero higher, then a shift down the formality scale would have occurred, but here the two increased markers have opposite stylistic implications.

Wright 1992 deals with similar internal variation in relative marker usage in the Addison canon, which can be related to explicit concerns about relative usage, but which also seems to respond to text type and audience. The only conclusion to be drawn from Wright's work, and these figures here, is that we do not yet know enough about intra-idiolectal variation to explain such shifts. Wright's work, and these figures, stress the dangers of using mean or average scores to characterise idiolectal usage – especially in the case of variables which are genre, or style, sensitive.

Table 3.11 Relative markers in the Dekker sample

| | | *restrictive* | | *non-restrictive* | | | | |
|---|---|---|---|---|---|---|---|---|
| | | *sub* | *obj* | *sub* | *obj* | *totals* | | *%* |
| who(m) | personal | 31 | 15 | 13 | 6 | 65 | 67 | 10 |
| | non-personal | 2 | 0 | 0 | 0 | 2 | | |
| which | personal | 2 | 0 | 2 | 0 | 4 | 139 | 20 |
| | non-personal | 59 | 54 | 17 | 5 | 135 | | |
| that | personal | 178 | 1 | 3 | 0 | 182 | 326 | 46 |
| | non-personal | 125 | 17 | 2 | 0 | 144 | | |
| zero | personal | 47 | 8 | 0 | 0 | 55 | 176 | 25 |
| | non-personal | 19 | 102 | 0 | 0 | 121 | | |
| | | | | | | N=708 | | |

*The Dekker comparison sample*

From the conflated figures in table 3.11, there would seem to be little to comment on in the Dekker sample: 'who' and 'whom' are both very close to being restricted by antecedent, and the relative percentage usages of each relative marker are roughly similar to those found in the Shakespeare and Marlowe samples.

When the individual scores for each play are plotted onto a graph however, a very different picture emerges, one which underlines the danger of using averages, means, or totals to sum up idiolects. Compared to the graphs so far seen, graph 3.6 shows a huge degree of intra-idiolectal variation: the plots for the plays differ widely for all markers except 'which'. In fact, the degree of variation here is such that it virtually exceeds the variation between the idiolects of the other writers sampled (see graph 3.10).

It should be stressed immediately that Dekker seems to be unique in the degree to which his idiolectal usage of relative markers varies: other dramatists may vary in one play in one marker (for example *The Comedy of Errors* in the early Shakespeare sample), none vary in every play, for virtually every marker. This result does not therefore necessarily undermine the use of relativisation as socio-historical linguistic evidence: rather it

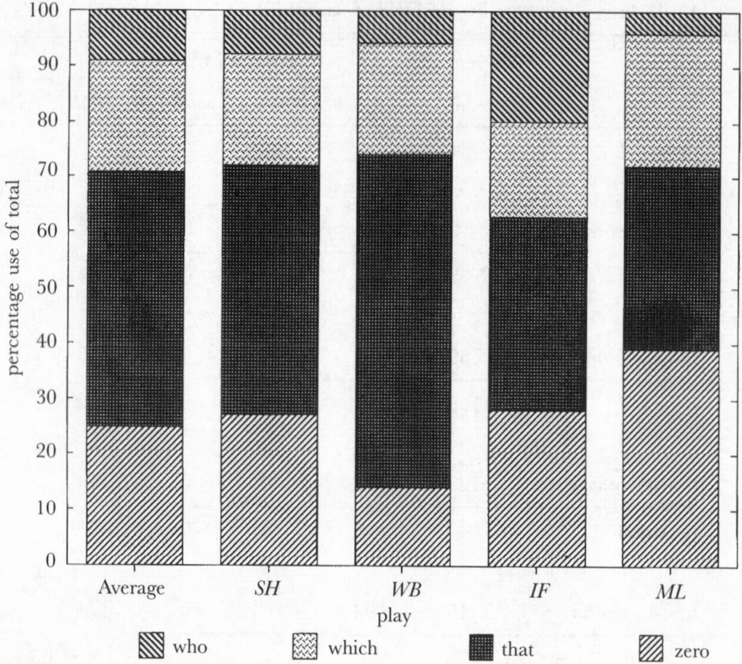


Graph 3.6 Relative marker use in the Dekker sample (including average use)

stresses that relativisation *may* be greatly affected by generic or stylistic factors. In Dekker we apparently see a writer who uses relativisation as a stylistic strategy more than other early Modern dramatists, and who is capable of shifting his usage and maintaining that shift over the course of a whole play.

Alternative explanations for this variation would be that it is evidence either for collaborative authorship, or for textual interference. Of the two, I would find the latter the most convincing. The reason for this is that in each play in which a relative marker appears at a much higher rate than in any other (for example 'who' in *If This Be Not A Good Play . . .*, zero in *Match Me in London*, and 'that' in *The Whore of Babylon*), the increased usage of that marker is spread evenly throughout the play. If the increase were due to collaboration, I would expect to find instances of the increased marker grouped in certain scenes – which does not occur. We know though that in theory relatives can be altered in the course of the transmission of a text much more easily than auxiliary 'do' forms (although in fact this does not seem to happen very often). Given that Dekker is the only popular playhouse writer sampled here, and that his play texts may therefore have a more confused history, and have been transmitted less carefully, it is possible that these sudden and extreme shifts in relative marker use are

Table 3.12 Relative markers in the Fletcher sample

| | | *restrictive* | | *non-restrictive* | | | |
|---|---|---|---|---|---|---|---|
| | | *sub* | *obj* | *sub* | *obj* | *totals* | *%* |
| who(m) | personal | 0 | 3 | 8 | 4 | 15 | |
| | | | | | | 16 | 2 |
| | non-personal | 0 | 1 | 0 | 0 | 1 | |
| which | personal | 0 | 1 | 3 | 1 | 5 | |
| | | | | | | 117 | 13 |
| | non-personal | 18 | 12 | 42 | 40 | 112 | |
| that | personal | 253 | 12 | 21 | 2 | 288 | |
| | | | | | | 486 | 55 |
| | non-personal | 139 | 39 | 18 | 2 | 198 | |
| zero | personal | 20 | 34 | 0 | 0 | 54 | |
| | | | | | | 271 | 31 |
| | non-personal | 38 | 177 | 0 | 2 | 217 | |
| | | | | | | N=890 | |

evidence for different copyists (be they scribes or compositors) imposing their own idiolectal usages on Dekker's texts. This would explain the suddenness of the shifts, the huge variations involved, and the fact that the increases seem to be consistent across each of the texts in which they occur. Again though, our lack of knowledge about intra-idiolectal variation prevents a full explanation at present.

### *The Fletcher comparison sample*

The most striking feature of Fletcher's relativisation choices, clear from graph 3.7, is his extreme avoidance of 'who' – a feature I have already considered. As will become clear (see graph 3.10), this avoidance of the most formally marked relative pronoun correlates with the highest use in the sampled writers of zero, the most informally marked pronoun. Fletcher's idiolect also shows observation of the 'who'/'which' distinction.

### *The Middleton comparison sample*

Middleton's proportions of usage of relative markers do not provide a basis for distinguishing him from other early Modern writers. 'Who' and 'which' are almost totally restricted by antecedent. The only slightly unusual features of Middleton's relativisation strategies are a preference for personal

Table 3.13 Relative markers in the Middleton sample

| | | restrictive | | non-restrictive | | | |
|---|---|---|---|---|---|---|---|
| | | *sub* | *obj* | *sub* | *obj* | *totals* | *%* |
| who(m) | personal | 9 | 18 | 13 | 15 | 55 | |
| | | | | | | 56 | 8 |
| | non-personal | 0 | 0 | 1 | 0 | 1 | |
| which | personal | 0 | 0 | 2 | 3 | 5 | |
| | | | | | | 89 | 13 |
| | non-personal | 16 | 24 | 30 | 14 | 84 | |
| that | personal | 228 | 7 | 22 | 0 | 257 | |
| | | | | | | 363 | 55 |
| | non-personal | 77 | 28 | 1 | 0 | 106 | |
| zero | personal | 57 | 21 | 0 | 0 | 78 | |
| | | | | | | 156 | 24 |
| | non-personal | 20 | 58 | 0 | 0 | 78 | |
| | | | | | | N=664 | |

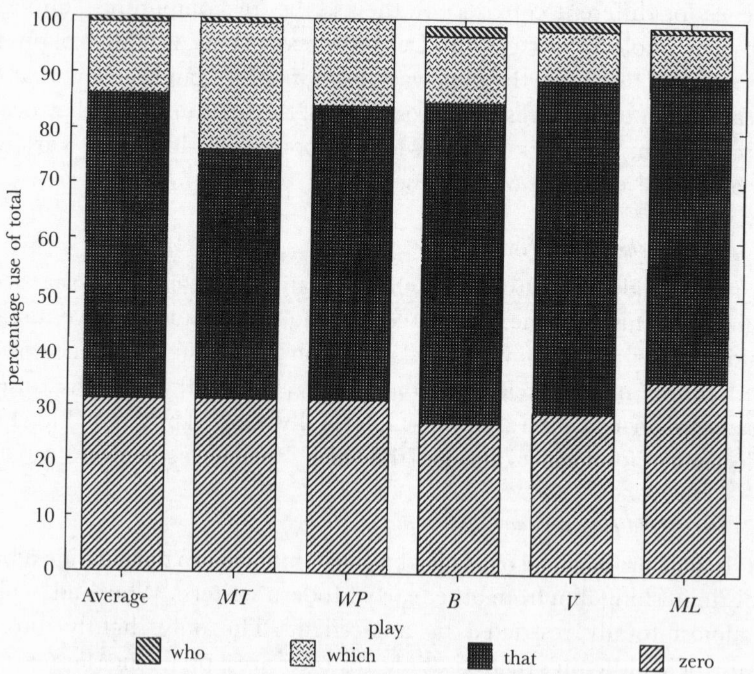


Graph 3.7 Relative marker use in the Fletcher sample (including average use)

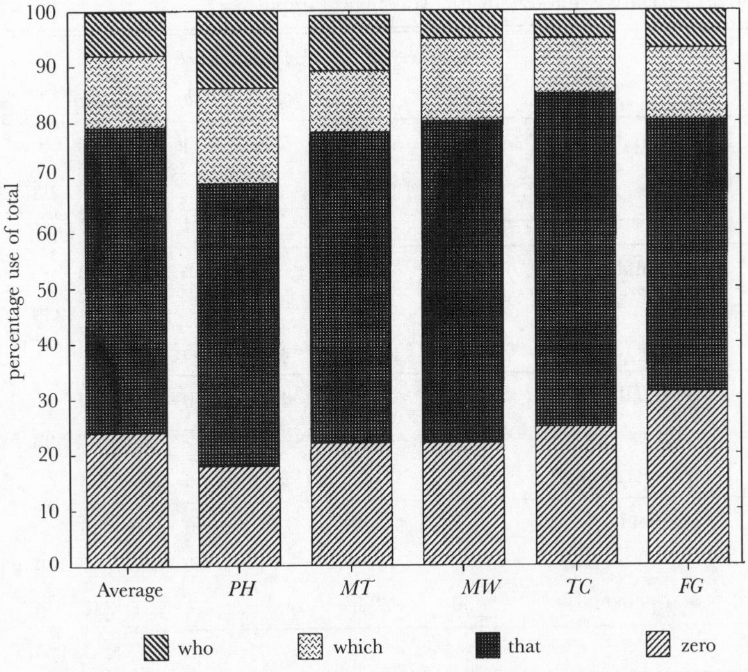


Graph 3.8 Relative marker use in the Middleton sample (including average use)

antecedents with 'that' (all other writers sampled favour non-personal antecedents with 'that'), and a lack of any strong preference in antecedent with zero (all other writers favour non-personal antecedents with zero – see Statistical Appendix). Unfortunately, none of these differences is likely to occur at frequencies useful as evidence for authorship.

*The Massinger comparison sample*

Like Middleton, Massinger presents a relativisation strategy which is not easily distinguishable from those of other writers – his usage is also highly consistent from one play to the next. Of all the playwrights sampled, Massinger is the closest to complete regulation of 'who' and 'which' according to antecedent.

## Summary

The main aim of this chapter has been to establish whether early Modern writers have distinct usages of relative markers. From graph 3.10 it can be seen that the writers sampled show wide differences in their proportional usages of the relative markers. Graph 3.10 consists of average usages, but the earlier graphs have shown that for all writers except Dekker, writers maintain a consistent usage of the relative markers.

Table 3.14 Relative markers in the Massinger sample

| | | restrictive | | non-restrictive | | | | |
|---|---|---|---|---|---|---|---|---|
| | | *sub* | *obj* | *sub* | *obj* | *totals* | | *%* |
| who(m) | personal | 6 | 7 | 19 | 11 | 43 | 44 | 4 |
| | non-personal | 0 | 0 | 0 | 1 | 1 | | |
| which | personal | 1 | 1 | 1 | 0 | 3 | 239 | 21 |
| | non-personal | 28 | 77 | 65 | 65 | 236 | | |
| that | personal | 204 | 6 | 80 | 0 | 290 | 598 | 52 |
| | non-personal | 199 | 80 | 26 | 3 | 308 | | |
| zero | personal | 5 | 26 | 2 | 0 | 33 | 269 | 23 |
| | non-personal | 30 | 202 | 3 | 1 | 236 | | |
| | | | | | | N = 1150 | | |

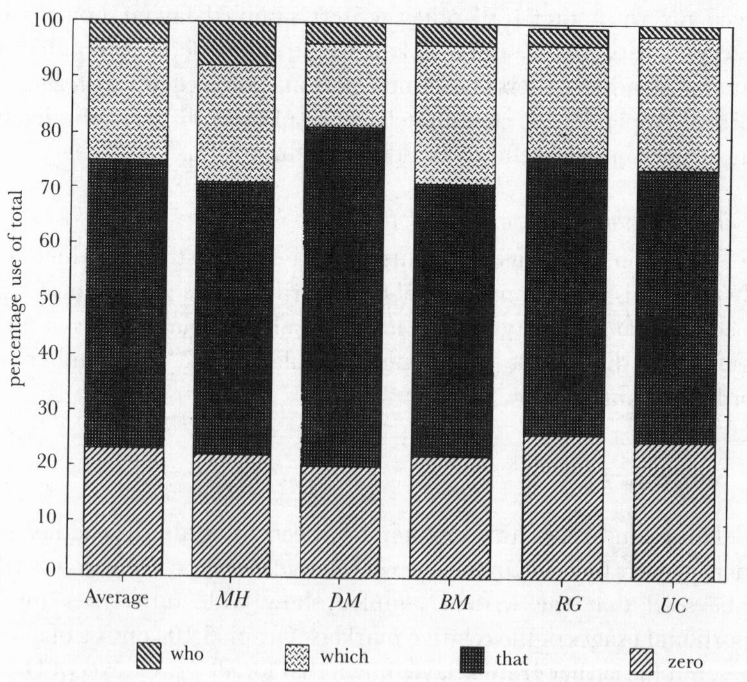


Graph 3.9 Relative marker use in the Massinger sample (including average use)

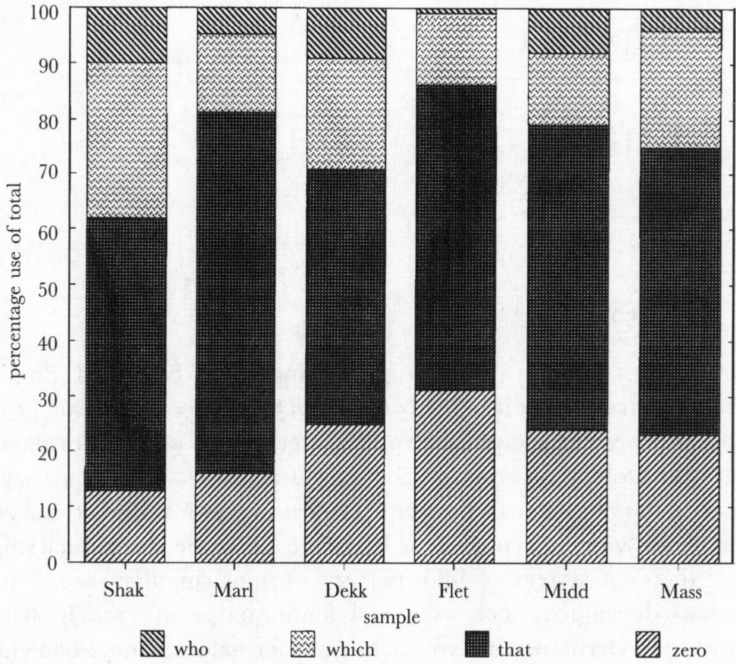


Graph 3.10 Average relative marker use in the comparison samples

Since the two Shakespeare samples are averaged together in graph 3.10, it does not show the fact that over the course of his career Shakespeare develops a style which is less like the style of other playwrights – graph 3.4 shows that Shakespeare samples 1 and 2 show a shift in the direction of formality, especially in the case of 'which'. As with auxiliary 'do', graph 3.10 indicates that of all playwrights sampled, Shakespeare and Fletcher have the least similar usages – Fletcher's usage being significantly less formal than Shakespeare's (Shakespeare 2 has the highest 'who' and 'which' proportions sampled, Fletcher shows the highest rate of zero relatives).

The usages of other writers tend to fall between those of Shakespeare and Fletcher, and for this reason relativisation evidence is less able to distinguish between these writers. The use of relative markers as socio-historical linguistic evidence is further complicated by the susceptibility of relatives to textual interference. These factors combine to make relative marker evidence less dependable than auxiliary 'do' evidence. None the less, this chapter has established ranges of usage for six early Modern authors which will be used as a supplement to auxiliary 'do' evidence in the authorship studies presented in chapters 5 and 6.

# Chapter 4

# 'Thou' and 'you'

## Background

Amongst present-day European languages, Standard English is slightly unusual in that it has only one form for the second person pronoun in both the singular and plural: 'you'. The current system comes about as a result of a historical process whereby the plural form ('ye' or 'you') began to be used in the singular as a marker of respect to persons of great rank. Once this singular 'you' had entered the language alongside the original singular form, 'thou', a system of informal and formal singular second person pronouns developed, such as is still found today in French, Russian, Spanish, and German, with 'you' acting as a formal pronoun. Following the status in French of 'tu' and 'vous', linguists term the informal form in any language 'T' and the formal 'V'.

In English however, this T/V distinction in pronoun forms was not maintained: as 'you' passed from being used only to persons of great rank, to being exchanged between members of the upper classes, to being given as a marker of respect to all in a position of authority (be it familial, economic, or political authority), it began to replace 'thou' as the most commonly used form of address. This process continued so that by 1700, 'thou' had virtually disappeared, leaving only the dialectal and liturgical exceptions which remain today (for the general history of the pronoun forms see Strang 1970; Barber 1976:203–13; Wales 1983; and Leith 1984 give accounts of usage specific to the early Modern period).

The status of singular 'you' as a rising form in the early Modern period, and the decline of 'thou', provides a third instance of a linguistic change which may be suitable for use as socio-historical linguistic evidence, since the graph of the replacement of 'thou' by 'you' follows the expected 'S' curve of linguistic change. This chapter considers the suitability of the 'thou'/'you' variable for use as an authorship tool in the light of Richard Holdsworth's 1982 attempt to use the variable to distinguish the hands of Shakespeare and Middleton in *Timon of Athens*.

## The use of 'thou'/'you' as an authorship tool

### *Holdsworth's use of T/V choice as an authorship tool*

Holdsworth (1982:168–74) attempts to follow-up a suggestion by Berry (1958:85) that T/V choice can be used 'to help determine certain questions of authorship'. Holdsworth suggests that by about 1600 'thou' would have been in decline in spoken English for some time, and that 'the drama, which would naturally tend to preserve the usage as a ready means of securing emotional effects and indicating social status, probably gives a false impression of its currency' (1982:168 – this suggestion is supported by empirical evidence given in Hope 1993). Furthermore Holdsworth states, in the context of his study of possible collaboration between Shakespeare and Middleton in *Timon of Athens*, that 'It would not be surprising to find that some dramatists in the early seventeenth century were more inclined to make use of *thou* than others, particularly, perhaps, one born in the early 1560s, as was Shakespeare, rather than one born in 1580, such as Middleton' (1982:168).

To test this hypothesis, Holdsworth collects totals for use of 'thou' and its contractions ('thou'rt', 'th'art', etc.) in Shakespeare and Middleton's work (twenty plays by Shakespeare, twelve by Middleton). He finds that Shakespeare uses 'thou' and its contractions on average 135 times in each play, while Middleton uses it only sixty-four times (1982:170). Applying this to his own division of *Timon of Athens*, Holdsworth finds that '*thou* is almost three times more common in *Timon* S [his proposed Shakespeare scenes] than in *Timon* M [his proposed Middleton scenes]' (1982:171).

This result appears impressive, but Holdsworth goes on to offer some criticisms of his own approach, and the use of T/V choice as authorship evidence, which demand that it be treated with caution. One initial problem with Holdsworth's study is his collection of data: his figures do not include forms such as 'thee' and 'thy', and offer no indication of the ratio of T forms to V. He assumes implicitly that 'thee' and 'thy' forms will be proportional to 'thou' forms, but this is not always the case. For example, his figures for 'thou' in *Macbeth* (1982: 169) give the impression that this play is particularly lacking in T forms when compared to Shakespeare's other tragedies (he finds only forty-three 'thou' forms in *Macbeth*, but never less than 100 in any other tragedy). Given the suggestion that work thought to be by Middleton appears in *Macbeth* as well as in *Timon of Athens*, this low total might appear significant.

However, not only does this total exclude 'thee' and 'thy' forms, it makes no allowance for length, which is an important factor in the case of *Macbeth*. When all T forms are included, and allowance is made for length, the play does not, in fact, look anomalous at all. This is shown by the figures in table 4.4 (see p. 62), which provides a comparison of the relative number of T forms in each play of the Shakespeare canon.

This problem can easily be overcome by including all forms of the pronouns. A more intractable problem with T/V evidence is what Holdsworth terms 'the large number of variables governing the use of *thou* in the drama of the period, involving emotional implication, social relationship, grammatical context, and simple inconsistency on the part of the author' (1982:171). To illustrate this, Holdsworth cites two meetings between Timon and Apemantus in *Timon of Athens*. In the first, Timon uses the T form ('Good morrow to thee' 1.01. 178), while in the second he uses V ('you are welcome' 1.02. 23). Holdsworth suspects that 'the main explanation of the change' is that

> Shakespeare wrote the first speech and Middleton the second, but it is quite possible to find each pronoun appropriate and deliberately chosen, *thou* signalling an attempt at relaxed intimacy, and *you* sounding a note of formal courtesy suited to the occasion of the feast in 1.2. One could, of course, come up with equally plausible explanations if the choice of pronouns were reversed.
> (Holdsworth 1982:172)

At this point, Holdsworth has pinpointed a basic issue in using socio-historical linguistic evidence: the interaction of biography and style. At what point do biographical factors stop patterning linguistic choice, and stylistic ones take over? In the variables discussed so far, auxiliary 'do' and relative marker choice, I have shown that stylistic factors were less prominent in structuring the patterning of auxiliary 'do' use than relative marker choice, and for this reason auxiliary 'do' use is a more reliable form of socio-historical linguistic evidence. This is because the effect of stylistic factors is to make the distribution of the variants of a variable in a text non-random in the sense that they will be concentrated in some portions of a text, and absent from others, according to stylistic demands.

On the basis of these problems, Holdsworth concludes his attempt to use T/V choice as authorship evidence by ruling it out from his own study. He suggests, however, 'that with more work it could be so counted' (i.e. as useable evidence). For this to be the case however, it will be necessary to understand the stylistic, or non-biographical, factors which can affect the patterning of the variants ('thou' and 'you'). Fortunately, there has been a great deal of work done on the semantics of early Modern English T/V choice, especially in Shakespeare. Many articles, most notably Barber 1981, have attempted to show the complex emotional and attitudinal changes which can be marked by the T/V pronouns, and also to trace the formal social relationships which can be encoded by T/V usage (on the literary use

Table 4.1 T/V choice and social relationship

*T forms* non-reciprocal (unequal power relationship) used by superior to inferior, e.g.:

husband to wife; parent to child

master or mistress to servant

monarch to subject

male to female

reciprocal (equal power relationship/solidarity) used to signal equality of social power (lower class) or shared concern/interest, e.g.:

between lower class members, between siblings, lovers, close friends

*V forms* non-reciprocal (unequal power relationship) used by inferior to superior, e.g.:

wife to husband; child to parent

servant to master or mistress

subject to monarch

female to male

reciprocal (equal power relationship, neutral or uncertain power relationship), e.g.:

between upper class members as a neutral form to strangers, and increasingly as the general second person singular pronoun

of T/V choice see also Byrne 1936, McIntosh 1963 a and b, Mulholland 1967, Jones 1981, Gurr 1982, Blake 1987, and Calvo 1992).

An attempt to extract a consensus of such factors affecting choice of pronoun shows the complexity of the system, which seems rather to be a series of intersecting and competing systems giving different implications to the forms. Brown and Gilman (1960) produced an analysis of T/V choice in a European context which fixed the source of the respectful singular use of the plural form in Latin plural address to the Emperor. This lead to an influential 'power and solidarity' model for T/V choice, which characterised usage in terms of social relationship: within unequal power relationships, the weaker individual gives V and receives T, while within relationships between social equals, the same pronoun is exchanged – stratified according to class so that lower class relationships are marked by mutual T, upper class by mutual V. This model provides an explanatory context for the early Modern English usages listed in table 4.1.

Working explicitly on the English context alone, Wales (1983) extends Brown and Gilman's model to take more account of the 'expressive' meanings which T/V can encode, and which can result in changes of forms between individuals, who are none the less in a stable social relationship, by emphasising the encoding of emotional proximity by T, and distance by V. Thus transient feelings of affection or anger can be encoded by use of T and V respectively.

Brown and Gilman's model can be still further extended by placing it within the context of the work of Brown and Levinson (1987) on universal politeness strategies. Strikingly, Brown and Levinson show that singularisation of plural pronouns, and the iconic representation of unequal power relationships by asymmetric (non-reciprocal) pronouns, are features of many unrelated languages (1987:45). This refutes the claim that T/V systems in European languages can be explained by a common Latin source. Brown and Levinson's models of intimate and non–intimate exchanges, and positive and negative politeness, provide a more complete context for our understanding of early Modern English T/V usage; but it is perhaps significant that an explicit attempt to read Shakespeare's plays through politeness theory by Brown and Gilman (1989) finds 'thou' and 'you' less easy to account for than other politeness markers.

The situation is then ripe for confusion, with at least three competing systems – a social system, an emotional/politeness-based system, and a system in which 'you' is the only available form – all open to use by speakers. Of these, it can be said that the socially based system would lead to 'thou' and 'you' choice being related to factors such as plot and character (since the social relationships between characters would dictate the patterning of the variants in any text). The emotional system would tie 'thou' and 'you' choice to factors of moment to moment event and response. Only the emergence of the 'you'-only system could be expected to show socio–historical linguistic patterning consistently – each of the other systems would be expected to disrupt it. As with relative markers, initial analysis suggests that the usefulness of 'thou'/'you' choice as socio-historical linguistic evidence may be limited. To test this, I carried out two pilot studies, one on the sampled plays of Shakespeare and Fletcher, and one on the whole canon of Shakespeare's plays, which was intended to investigate the relationship between genre and 'thou' and 'you' choice.

### *Count and analysis*

In contrast to Holdsworth 1982, figures for all forms of T and V were collected (that is, 'thou', 'thy', 'thine', 'thee', 'you', 'ye', 'your', etc.). Forms such as 'prithee', which by this time is functioning as a tag without reference to the pronoun system (as its frequent use in otherwise purely 'you' relationships shows), were not counted. Since it had been decided in advance of the count to compare the proportions of T and V forms used according to sex of speaker and addressee, pronouns used in personification

Table 4.2 Percentage of V forms in the comparison sample plays

| Shakespeare | | | | | |
|---|---|---|---|---|---|
| | *T* | *WT* | *CY* | *CO* | *AC* |
| total V | 226 | 610 | 541 | 451 | 425 |
| total T | 374 | 260 | 357 | 273 | 294 |
| N | 600 | 870 | 898 | 724 | 719 |
| %V | 38 | 70 | 60 | 62 | 59 |

| Fletcher | | | | | |
|---|---|---|---|---|---|
| | *MT* | *WP* | *B* | *V* | *ML* |
| total V | 772 | 726 | 355 | 604 | 580 |
| total T | 216 | 220 | 289 | 186 | 210 |
| N | 988 | 946 | 644 | 790 | 790 |
| %Y | 78 | 77 | 55 | 77 | 73 |

and apostrophe were not included in the figures, as these do not constitute dyadic relationships; self-address, aside, and address in absence were included where the addressed was a person.

As with relative markers, the count was restricted to five plays from each of the comparison groups. Since the plays each gave mean N values of between 600 and 1000, this gave a more than adequate total sample size (N = 3811 for Shakespeare, N = 4158 for Fletcher).

Table 4.2 shows the results of the count for the comparison sample plays, along with the percentage of second person singular pronouns realised by V in each play. To a certain extent, table 4.2 confirms the expectation that Fletcher would show a higher usage of V forms than Shakespeare, since his usage is usually above 70 per cent V forms, while the percentage of V forms in Shakespeare is always at or below this figure. However, it will be noticed that the pronoun usages of Fletcher and Shakespeare are much less consistent than their usages of auxiliary 'do' or relative markers, with an internal variation of thirty-two percentage points in the Shakespeare sample, and twenty-three in Fletcher. This compares with internal variations of only five and four percentage points respectively for auxiliary 'do' usage. Not only does this mean that the comparison samples overlap in their ranges (38–70 per cent for Shakespeare and 55–78 per cent for Fletcher), but it suggests that factors other than the social or biographical ones identified in chapter 2 are affecting the choices made by Shakespeare and Fletcher.

This suggestion stems from the fact that biographical factors can be assumed to be constant during an author's career, since they have to do with fixed items such as date and place of birth, class, and education. Patterning of linguistic variables due to biographical factors will therefore be expected to be consistent. When, as here, the expected patterning due to biographical factors is obscured, or only partially present, then it is reasonable to assume that some less fixed factors are operating to affect the patterning of the variable. In this case it can be noted that two plays in particular disrupt the appearance of consistent patterning in the comparison samples: *The Tempest* and *Bonduca*. If these are removed, then a much clearer separation is possible (the Shakespeare sample then ranges from 59–70 per cent, with an internal variation of eleven percentage points, while the Fletcher sample would then range from 73–78 per cent, with an internal variation of only five percentage points). It is therefore possible that while biographical factors control the patterning of T/V choice in most of the plays in the sample, other factors intervene in the cases of these two plays to affect T/V choice and obscure the effects of biographical factors.

A further set of figures was prepared which analysed the percentage of V forms used according to the sex of the speaker and addressee. The intention was to investigate the possibility that certain situations (e.g. female to male address) might favour the rising form, and it was suspected that any such tendency would be more marked in Fletcher, as his usage was expected to be more standardised. These figures are given in table 4.3

Table 4.3 shows that, while there is a general tendency towards the predicted weighting of V forms from women to men, and that this is more marked in Fletcher than in Shakespeare, again the results are not consistent enough for the statistics to be used as indicators of authorship. A number of factors combined to bring this about: a general lack of female characters meant that these relationships were characterised by much lower N than male speech, allowing one particularly 'thouful' speech to skew the figures; similarly, one 'thouful' relationship (such as Lucina's to the emperor in *Valentinian*) could dilute other pure 'you' ones; above all, and even though the general trend was for women to use more 'you' forms, and Fletcher's women especially, immediate contextual factors might intervene at any moment to produce a passage of sustained 'thou' use which would dilute the figures – for example an outburst of anger.

## *Qualitative analysis*

### *The role of T/V choice in authorship studies: qualitative assessment*

In the previous section, it was repeatedly noted that T/V evidence gave an inconsistent picture, with apparent biographical patterning of the variable often breaking down. It was suggested that in cases of break down, some further non-fixed factors were intervening to disrupt the consistent patterning

Table 4.3 Values for relationships by sex of speaker/addressed

Shakespeare

| | *T* | *WT* | *CY* | *CO* | *AC* |
|---|---|---|---|---|---|
| MM | | | | | |
| N | 477 | 476 | 453 | 533 | 390 |
| %V | 35 | 64 | 66 | 64 | 47 |
| MF | | | | | |
| N | 79 | 151 | 219 | 36 | 201 |
| %V | 29 | 66 | 59 | 83 | 75 |
| FM | | | | | |
| N | 44 | 211 | 210 | 124 | 90 |
| %V | 82 | 85 | 50 | 42 | 78 |
| FF | | | | | |
| N | 0 | 32 | 16 | 31 | 38 |
| %V | – | 78 | 63 | 94 | 53 |

Fletcher

| | *MT* | *WP* | *B* | *V* | *ML* |
|---|---|---|---|---|---|
| MM | | | | | |
| N | 417 | 325 | 523 | 468 | 416 |
| %V | 72 | 78 | 57 | 78 | 72 |
| MF | | | | | |
| N | 223 | 207 | 39 | 154 | 189 |
| %V | 75 | 67 | 59 | 75 | 73 |
| FM | | | | | |
| N | 260 | 267 | 50 | 107 | 109 |
| %V | 93 | 91 | 44 | 65 | 77 |
| FF | | | | | |
| N | 88 | 147 | 32 | 61 | 76 |
| %V | 73 | 63 | 38 | 85 | 76 |

MM = male to male, MF = male to female, etc.

expected with biographical factors. The particular variations of usage found in *The Tempest* and *Bonduca* (see table 4.2) can indeed be explained by such non-biographical factors: in the case of *The Tempest*, the high usage of T forms can be ascribed to factors such as Prospero's holding all of the other

Table 4.4 T index for plays in the Shakespeare canon by genre

Histories:

| *play* | *3H6* | *1H6* | *2H6* | *R2* | *1H4* | *R3* | *KJ* | *2H4* | *H5* |
|---|---|---|---|---|---|---|---|---|---|
| index | 18 | 16 | 16 | 15 | 15 | 14 | 14 | 10 | 8 |

Comedies:

| *play* | *TG* | *CE* | *12N* | *TS* | *MSN* | *AY* | *MA* | *LL* | *MW* |
|---|---|---|---|---|---|---|---|---|---|
| index | 15 | 14 | 13 | 11 | 11 | 11 | 8 | 8 | 6 |

Roman/Greek:

| *play* | *TA* | *TAN* | *AC* | *TC* | *JC* | *CO* |
|---|---|---|---|---|---|---|
| index | 19 | 14 | 12 | 10 | 8 | 7 |

Problem/Late:

| *play* | *T* | *P* | *WT* | *MV* | *AW* | *MM* | *CY* |
|---|---|---|---|---|---|---|---|
| index | 17 | 10 | 9 | 9 | 9 | 8 | 8 |

Tragedies:

| *play* | *RJ* | *KL* | *M* | *O* | *H* |
|---|---|---|---|---|---|
| index | 19 | 16 | 9 | 9 | 7 |

characters prisoner, and therefore being able to use the captor's T, and Ariel's use of the spirit's T (spirits tend to give and receive T forms); in *Bonduca*, the hysterical notion of honour which pervades the play (especially in the person of the Briton Catarach), the importance of the relationship between Catarach and the young boy Hengo, and the prolonged defiance of Bonduca and her daughters of the Romans, produce an abnormally large number of T forms.

It can also be shown quantitatively that there may be a degree of correlation between genre and relative percentages of T and V forms. Table 4.4 provides a comparison of the relative number of T forms in each play of the Shakespeare canon.

In this study, the total number of T forms (i.e. 'thou', 'thy', 'thine', 'thee' (sometimes appearing as 'the'), and forms beginning with 'thou', e.g. 'thou'lt', 'thou'dst', but not 'thyself', or any compounds ending in 'thou' such as 'prithee') was counted, and this was converted into an index comparable between plays of differing lengths by the following equation,

$$\frac{\text{total number of T forms}}{\text{number of lines in play}} \times 100$$

giving a basic 'index of thoufulness' for each play (the lower the number, the lower the use of T forms).

It will be remembered that Holdsworth's figures had suggested that *Macbeth* was unusual in terms of its T/V usage. In table 4.4, *Macbeth* does not look at all anomalous, either in terms of its genre, or the canon as a whole. Holdsworth's low total of 'thou' forms for this play is most likely to be due to its relative shortness.

This failure to include all T forms and account for length also leads Holdsworth to find similarities between *Henry VIII* and *The Two Noble Kinsmen*; data presented in chapter 5 challenges this conclusion. According to Holdsworth, *Henry VIII* and *The Two Noble Kinsmen* both have very low totals for 'thou': *Henry VIII* has 'by far the lowest total for thou in the whole canon'; and *The Two Noble Kinsmen* 'is also unusually low for Shakespeare'. He concludes from this that 'Such proximity [in terms of their rank order within the canon based on total 'thou' usage] between the two Fletcher collaborations seems unlikely to be coincidence' (1982:174). However, as results presented below will show, *Henry VIII* is so lacking in T forms that it is anomalous even in terms of Fletcher's normal usage – use of total 'thou' forms, and placing the plays in rank order as Holdsworth does, indicates a shared lack of T forms in these two collaborations which is highly misleading. There is no 'proximity' between these plays in terms of their T usage at all.

The results of this survey suggest that while it is possible to say that Histories usually have high proportions of T forms (they average fourteen), and Comedies lower (they average eleven), the ranges of variation within genres mean that no consistent relationship can be made between genre and the number of forms. It looks as though non-fixed factors are in operation here again: history as a genre tends to favour T forms, but certain History plays have very low counts, presumably because of specialised, individual circumstances (*Henry V*, for example, is one of the few Histories to show a relatively stable court – possibly resulting in a lack of the chivalric T usages common in the other plays). It is not difficult to guess that the high proportion of T forms in *Romeo and Juliet* is due to the use of the lovers' 'thou'; and that in *Timon of Athens* may be due to the excess of accusation in that play (in fact Holdsworth notes that 'over half' of the uses of 'thou' in the play occur in 4.03. 1–457, which contains Timon's most sustained 'invective'(1982:171)).

In a computer-based study of the relationship between pronoun usage and genre, Brainerd (1979) collected figures of pronoun usage in all of the plays of the Shakespeare canon as well as *Henry VIII* and *The Two Noble Kinsmen*. He found that pronoun usage was indeed sensitive to genre, but his figures are flawed in that he makes no comparison between T and V forms, and, most surprising of all, because he does not distinguish between singular and plural 'you' (presumably a consequence of relying on a concordance programme to count 'you' forms and hence having no way to distinguish singular and plural). His results confirm, however, that Holdsworth misrepresents the T/V evidence on the relationship between *Henry VIII* and *The Two Noble Kinsmen*, since Brainerd gives totals for all T forms, and word counts by which the length of plays can be taken into account. On the basis of these figures, *Henry VIII*, of average length, has by far the lowest number of T forms and the highest number of V forms (this is of course singular and plural forms) in the Shakespeare canon. *The Two Noble Kinsmen*, in contrast, does not look at all out of keeping with the rest of the canon. This confirms the suggestion that *Henry VIII* is highly unusual in its usage of T/V, even in comparison to *The Two Noble Kinsmen*. The significance of this result is discussed in chapter 5.

Any attempt to use T/V choice as purely quantitative evidence for authorship is bound to be clouded by the extent to which their occurrence is affected by style, genre, character, and transient emotion in literary texts. These factors (which I shall group under the heading 'stylistic' to distinguish them from biographical factors such as age, sex, birthplace, and class of author) have a more pervasive effect on the final statistics of usage of T/V forms than stylistic factors had on the other variables. This is because of the restriction of this variable to two realisations (T and V) where the others have more. The effect of this is to blur the influence of biographical factors. Within the relative marker system, for example, stylistic factors can gain expression within a biographical pattern because of the (at least) four variants involved. Hence Shakespeare can move into 'that' relativisation to indicate a different style of language, while Fletcher can move into deletion, or non-relativisation, to express the same shift in style. Thus the same stylistic information is given by a different linguistic choice, which may itself be affected by biographical factors, and the authorship can remain distinct; with T and V, stylistic choices obscure biographical differences. It would, for instance, be perfectly possible for Fletcher to write quite a long scene in which all of the pronoun forms were T, and Shakespeare to do the same using only V forms, if factors such as genre, character or emotion demanded it. The same could not be said of auxiliary 'do' positive declarative sentences or 'who' relatives in the case of Fletcher, or deleted relatives in the case of Shakespeare.

Any attempt to use T/V choice as evidence for authorship is therefore bound to be highly speculative, because it is impossible to allow for stylistic patterning of the variants. Unfortunately therefore, T/V choice has only a minor role to play in authorship studies.

# PART II

# APPLICATIONS

# Chapter 5

# Shakespeare as collaborator

## The Shakespeare–Fletcher collaborations

In this section I consider three plays which have been linked to the names of Shakespeare and Fletcher: *Henry VIII*, *The Two Noble Kinsmen*, and *The Double Falshood* ('Cardenio'). I begin each study with a consideration of the auxiliary 'do' evidence, because this is generally the most reliable indicator of likely authorship, especially between Shakespeare and Fletcher. The implications of this are then reviewed in the light of evidence from relative marker choice, and, in the case of *Henry VIII*, T/V choice. Because T/V choice has such serious limitations as socio-historical linguistic evidence, I have not used it in subsequent studies.

### *Henry VIII*

The authorship of *Henry VIII* was not called into question until the mid-nineteenth century, when two critics working independently (Hickson 1850, Spedding 1850) published articles which suggested that the play was in fact a collaboration between Shakespeare and John Fletcher, a younger playwright who eventually succeeded Shakespeare as contracted dramatist to the King's Men theatre company. A series of articles since then, culminating in the work of Cyrus Hoy (1962), has confirmed the presence of two hands in the play (see Farnham 1916, Partridge 1949, Oras 1953, Law 1959, Horton 1987). The major divisions of the play are summarised in table 5.1.

Doubts remain, however, about the precise shares of Shakespeare and Fletcher in the play: before Hoy, a consensus had developed, but his work reassigned to Shakespeare several scenes traditionally given to Fletcher. This reduction of Fletcher's share was welcomed by many literary critics, who had remained reluctant to accept *Henry VIII* as collaborative (see, for example the Arden edition of the play, edited by R. Foakes), but it has never been satisfactorily tested on the basis of any alternative evidence. For this reason, in his edition of the play, Fredson Bowers is cool about Hoy's claims, finding them at best 'not proven' and stating that it is 'unfortunate

Table 5.1 Divisions of *Henry VIII*

| Act | | *one* | | | | *two* | | | | *three* | | | *four* | | *five* | | | | |
|---|---|---|---|---|---|---|---|---|---|---|---|---|---|---|---|---|---|---|---|
| Scene | P | *1* | *2* | *3* | *4* | *1* | *2* | *3* | *4* | *1* | *2a* | *2b* | *1* | *2* | *1* | *2* | *3* | *4* | E |
| Hickson/Spedding 1850 | F | S | S | F | F | F | F | S | S | F | S | F | F | F | S | F | F | F | F |
| Fleay 1886 | F | M | S | F | F | F | F | S | S | F | M | F | F | F | M | F | F | F | F |
| Farnham 1916 | F | S | S | F | F | F | F | S | S | F | S | F | F | F | S | F | F | F | F |
| Hoy 1962 | – | S | S | F | F | S* | S* | S | S | F | S | S* | S* | S* | S | F | F | F | – |

S = Shakespeare; F = Fletcher

*Scenes mainly by Shakespeare with ‘mere Fletcherian interpolation’ (Hoy 1962:82) that no scholar to date . . . has made a closer study of the evidence' (Bowers (7) 1989:4–7).

Hoy terms his evidence 'linguistic'. His division of *Henry VIII* is based on the occurrence in the text of certain linguistic forms and contractions which can be identified with either Shakespeare or Fletcher. For example, Fletcher has a tendency to contract 'them' to ''em', and to use 'ye' for 'you' at a higher rate than Shakespeare. Shakespeare, on the other hand, is more likely to use the older, southern, '-th' endings in third person singular present verbs such as 'hath' and 'doth' (Hoy 1962:72–5).

Using this evidence, Hoy divides *Henry VIII* into three sections: scenes by Shakespeare (subsequently section A); scenes by Fletcher (section B); and scenes in which Hoy discovered Fletcherian features but was 'convinced that Fletcher has [here] done nothing more than touch up a Shakespearean passage, or insert a passage of his own in a Shakespearean context' (Hoy 1962:79) (section C). These section C scenes are those which had previously been assigned to Fletcher, and the effect of Hoy's tripartite division was to reduce substantially Fletcher's share in the play.

Although it will be seen from table 5.2 that the section C scenes contain Fletcherian features (i.e. 'ye' forms), Hoy focuses on what he sees as a suspicious tendency for these features to cluster: 'ye' in 2.01 at lines 1, 130, 131, and 132; 'ye' in 2.02 at lines 68, 69, and 137; 'ye' in 3.02b at lines 239, 240, 241, 242, 278, and 365; 'ye' in 4.01 at lines 114, 115, and 117; 'ye' in 4.02 at lines 22, 83, 84, and 86. These clumpings Hoy takes as evidence for Fletcherian interpolation into a Shakespearean original (Hoy 1962:80–1).

There are at least two reasons for treating this ascription of the section C scenes to Shakespeare with caution. On the one hand, a positive ascription (to Shakespeare) is being made on the basis of negative evidence: the lack of Fletcherian features, rather than presence of Shakespearean ones. On the other, as Hoy admits, scribes and compositors, inevitably involved in the transmission of these texts from author's manuscript to printed page, did not necessarily preserve the very features he studies. For example, the folio text of John Fletcher's *The Woman's Prize* contains only eighty-four 'ye' forms, against an average of 336 in his other unaided plays. Comparison with an independent manuscript of the play which has survived indicates that this lack of 'ye' forms is due to the tendency of Knight, the bookkeeper of the King's Men, to change 'ye' to 'you' when copying texts (Adams 1974, Bowers (4) 1979:13). It is also known that Compositor B, responsible for setting parts of *Henry VIII*, had a similar tendency (Walker 1953:29).

Other features Hoy uses as evidence, such as 'th' and 's' endings, are similarly unstable, as is shown by switches in usage between texts of *Measure for Measure*, *King Lear* and *Othello* (Walker 1953:62, Honigmann 1967:189, Stein 1987:417). Furthermore, practical requirements of lineation and

Table 5.2 Hoy's 1962 division of *Henry VIII*

| *Scene* | *Ascription* | | *Evidence* | | | | | |
|---|---|---|---|---|---|---|---|---|
| | | section | ye | you | hath | doth | 'em | them |
| 1.01 | S | A | 1 | 22 | 5 | 0 | 2 | 5 |
| 1.02 | S | A | 0 | 24 | 3 | 1 | 2 | 5 |
| 1.03 | F | B | 0 | 2 | 0 | 0 | 7 | 0 |
| 1.04 | F | B | 4 | 23 | 0 | 0 | 12 | 1 |
| 2.01 | S(F) | C | 4 | 20 | 0 | 0 | 4 | 0 |
| 2.02 | S(F) | C | 3 | 12 | 1 | 0 | 2 | 1 |
| 2.03 | S | A | 0 | 25 | 1 | 0 | 0 | 0 |
| 2.04 | S | A | 0 | 50 | 3 | 0 | 0 | 2 |
| 3.01 | F | B | 20 | 30 | 0 | 0 | 5 | 0 |
| 3.02a | S | A | 0 | 38 | 7 | 1 | 1 | 3 |
| 3.02b | S(F) | C | 6 | 37 | 1 | 0 | 2 | 1 |
| 4.01 | S(F) | C | 3 | 13 | 0 | 0 | 3 | 1 |
| 4.02 | S(F) | C | 5 | 20 | 0 | 0 | 3 | 2 |
| 5.01 | S | A | 0 | 41 | 3 | 0 | 0 | 4 |
| 5.02 | F | B | 12 | 42 | 0 | 0 | 6 | 0 |
| 5.03 | F | B | 7 | 13 | 0 | 0 | 13 | 0 |
| 5.04 | F | B | 6 | 3 | 0 | 0 | 1 | 0 |

spacing could often influence spelling and the contraction of words in the printing house (see Wells *et al.* 1987:42, 44–5). The following sections therefore re-examine *Henry VIII* in the hope of producing positive evidence either way for the ascriptions of these section C scenes.

### *Auxiliary 'do' evidence in* Henry VIII

The scene by scene regulation rates for *Henry VIII* will be found in the Statistical Appendix (p. 163). Graph 5.1 shows the regulation rates of the sections of *Henry VIII* in Hoy's tripartite division ('Shakespearean' A = 80 per cent, 'Fletcherian' B = 93 per cent, section C = 95 per cent) plotted against the comparison sample results for Shakespeare and Fletcher. It will be noted that sections A and B lie thirteen percentage points apart, each within the ranges of the proposed author as established by the comparison sample analysis. It is impossible to select two groups of scenes from any single play in the comparison samples which give percentage regulations this far apart. Despite the repeated literary claims that *Henry VIII* is wholly,

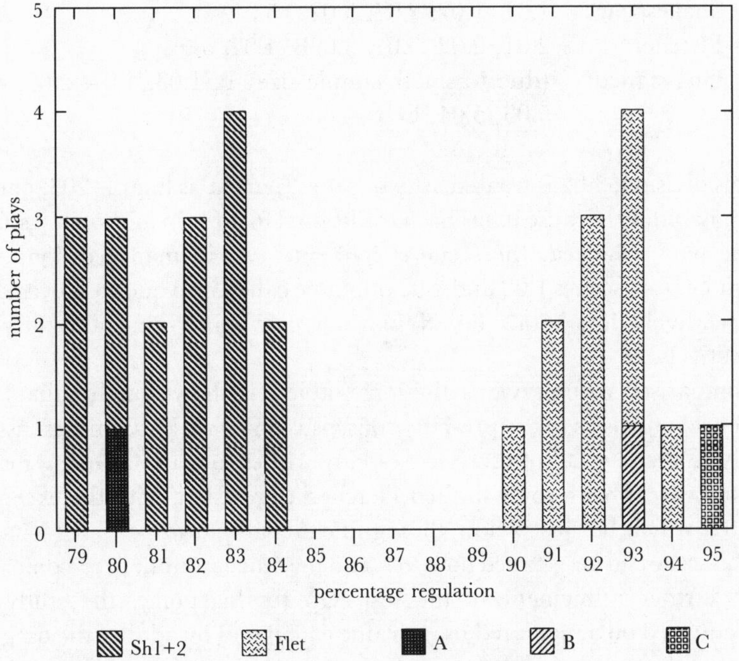


Graph 5.1 Auxiliary 'do' regulation in *Henry VIII* sections A, B, C

or mainly, by Shakespeare, the evidence for the presence of two hands in the play is overwhelming.

As for the section C scenes, in which Hoy is 'convinced' that Fletcher has 'done nothing more than touch up a Shakespearean passage, or insert a passage of his own in a Shakespearean context' (1962:79), it can be said that these results make Hoy's thesis appear very unlikely indeed. Were he correct, these scenes would be expected to show regulation rates in the range 85–90 per cent, since the original unregulated Shakespearean usages would tend to dilute the more highly regulated Fletcherian usage. The least likely outcome, given this hypothesis of revision or interpolation, would be for section C to show a degree of regulation slightly higher than the upper limit of the Fletcherian comparison sample, as is in fact the case (given that section C represents a smaller sample than those of the comparisons, this variation is to be expected).

Given that Hoy's division now looks unlikely as a whole, it is necessary to re-examine the ascriptions of individual scenes. On the basis of the scene by scene analysis of the comparison sample plays, the figures in table A5.1 give the following division of *Henry VIII* (see Statsistical Appendix):

| | |
|---|---|
| Shakespeare: | 1.01, 1.02, 2.04, 3.02a, 5.01 |
| Fletcher: | 2.01, 2.02, 3.01, 3.02b, 4.02, 5.02 |
| Unassigned: | (due to small sample size) P, 1.03, 1.04, 2.03, 4.01, 5.03, 5.04, E |

In this division, 3.02 is treated as two scenes (part 'a' is lines 1–203, part 'b' the remainder) because it has been traditional to do so in authorship studies of the play – indeed, the scene is split into two in many editions. The assignments of scenes 1.02 and 2.02 might be called into question because of the relatively low totals for N in each case (sixty-nine and fifty-one respectively).

Comparison with previous divisions (table 5.1) shows that auxiliary 'do' evidence returns us to the pre-Hoy consensus on *Henry VIII*: this test assigns firmly to Fletcher all of those scenes Hoy wishes to claim as being mainly Shakespearean with some limited Fletcherian revision, with the exception of 4.01, which lies just below the significant sample size.

This scene can be assigned however, and the other ascriptions re-confirmed, by a further refinement of the test. Up to this point, the study has concentrated on a regulated usage value calculated by adding the usages of several different types of sentence; by looking at the characteristic usages of Shakespeare and Fletcher in the most frequent sentence type, positive declaratives, it becomes possible to comment on the likely authorship of short scenes, and make confident statements about the likely authorship of scenes which, although they give significant token samples, fall into the overlap areas of the ranges of the two authors.

Table 5.3 shows the percentage of tokens formed with the auxiliary for each positive declarative sentence in the comparison samples. The table shows that Shakespeare's unregulated use of the auxiliary in this sentence type never falls below 8 per cent, while Fletcher's never rises above 4 per cent. This is an important difference, since the frequency of positive declarative sentences allows this distinction between Shakespeare and Fletcher to emerge over relatively short portions of text. Also, figures quoted by Barber (1976:263–7) show that unregulated positive declarative sentences are generally less than 10 per cent in the period, making Shakespeare's usage particularly marked.

As can be seen from table 5.3, Fletcher's highly regulated usage makes him very unlikely indeed to use auxiliary 'do' in positive declaratives, while Shakespeare is frequently doing so. In fact, in the comparison sample Fletcher never uses 'do' in this function more frequently than once every ninety lines, while Shakespeare never uses it less frequently than once every thirty-seven. Furthermore, when Fletcher does use this auxiliary 'do', it tends to be in syntactically and lexically restricted ways – with 'if' clauses

Table 5.3 Percentage of positive declarative sentences formed with auxiliary 'do'

| Shakespeare | | | | | | | | | | |
|---|---|---|---|---|---|---|---|---|---|---|
| play | *TC* | *MM* | *O* | *AW* | *KL* | *AC* | *CO* | *CY* | *WT* | *T* |
| % 'do' | 9 | 12 | 16 | 8 | 9 | 12 | 11 | 10 | 11 | 17 |

| Fletcher | | | | | | | | | | |
|---|---|---|---|---|---|---|---|---|---|---|
| play | *MT* | *WP* | *B* | *V* | *ML* | *LS* | *HL* | *IP* | *P* | *WG* |
| % 'do' | 4 | 4 | 2 | 2 | 3 | 2 | 1 | 1 | 1 | 1 |

(seven out of eleven usages in *The Pilgrim* are of this type) and with pleading verbs (especially 'beseech'). Indeed, Shakespeare's preference for auxiliary 'do' in positive declarative sentences has been noted before as a stylistic feature, and used to a limited extent as an authorship tool with special reference to *Henry VIII*, in tandem with the more familiar evidence of characteristic contractions, and variant forms (Partridge 1949).

In the case of *Henry VIII*, the pattern of individual auxiliary usage confirms the suggestion of the initial test that Hoy has gone awry in his conviction that the play is predominantly Shakespearean. As was suggested, Hoy draws this conclusion in spite of the fact that he finds no positive indicators for Shakespeare in the section C scenes. On his terms, the only positive indicators in these scenes are for Fletcher. He discounts these however, because they appear to cluster, and assumes that they represent Fletcherian interpolations into a Shakespearean original. Lacking positive evidence either way, Hoy ascribes the section C scenes to Shakespeare by default, even though there is good reason to suspect that his Fletcherian features (notably 'ye' forms) have been suppressed in the process of copying and printing the play.

The socio-historical linguistic evidence used in this procedure does not suffer at the hands of scribes and compositors in the way Hoy's does: to explain this, it is important to draw a distinction here between semantically equivalent variants (that is, 'ye' and 'you', or 'them' and ''em') and variant constructions, which may be functionally equivalent, but which carry implicational or semantic weight as well as exhibiting morphological change. Despite the ancient nominative/accusative implication of 'ye' and 'you' (see Barber 1976:204), Fletcher, in common with most writers close to him in date, seems to use them indiscriminately, while showing a personal preference for 'ye' (possibly for metrical reasons, as it seems to represent an unstressed form, and may be a laconic, upper-class usage). As has been seen, some compositors and scribes have a similarly haphazard approach,

Table 5.4 Unregulated positive declarative sentences as a percentage of all positive declarative sentences in *Henry VIII*

'Shakespearean' scenes (section A)

| | *1.01* | *1.02* | *2.03* | *2.04* | *3.02a* | *5.01* |
|---|---|---|---|---|---|---|
| %'do' | 10 | 7 | 12 | 20 | 19 | 8 |

'Fletcherian' scenes (section B)

| | *P* | *1.03* | *1.04* | *3.01* | *5.02* | *5.03* | *5.04* | *E* |
|---|---|---|---|---|---|---|---|---|
| %'do' | 0 | 0 | 0 | 2 | 2 | 3 | 0 | 0 |

Section C

| | *2.01* | *2.02* | *3.02b* | *4.01* | *4.02* |
|---|---|---|---|---|---|
| %'do' | 2 | 0 | 1 | 0 | 2 |

sometimes preserving forms, sometimes altering 'ye' to 'you', sometimes the reverse.

In contrast, there is no evidence of such interference with regulated and unregulated auxiliary forms. The use or not of the auxiliary involves a substantial difference in word order (and indeed, the effect of the auxiliary on word order is important in Engblom's discussion of its history and use) – especially in poetry. Evidence afforded by auxiliary use is therefore much more stable than that supplied by contractions and Hoy's linguistic forms.

Table 5.4 shows a scene by scene analysis of *Henry VIII* on the basis of the percentage of unregulated positive declarative usages in each scene. This analysis produces a bipartite division of the play into scenes showing total regulation of positive declaratives and those with a percentage of unregulated forms. Again, these sections conform to the traditional division of the play between Shakespeare and Fletcher, with those scenes showing the least percentage of unregulated usages matching the group of scenes traditionally assigned to Fletcher. Significantly, Hoy's section C scenes show very low percentages of unregulated forms.

If Hoy was correct in his theory that Fletcher's presence in these scenes is limited to revisions or interpolations inserted in Shakespearean originals, then this test would be expected to place these scenes in the Shakespearean portion of the play, since it would detect Shakespearean usage of unregulated positive declaratives. The absence of these forms in these scenes has two possible explanations. The first is that these scenes are originally and wholly Fletcherian, as earlier authorship work has suggested, and as Professor Bowers implies in his edition of the play. The second explanation is that Hoy was right in his hypothesis, and that Fletcher's revision of the scenes included the removal of Shakespearean unregulated forms, possibly because they struck Fletcher as archaic.

This second explanation is highly unlikely. Fletcher's own usage of unregulated positive declarative forms shows that they were not anathema to him: although this usage is infrequent, it is constant throughout the Fletcher comparison sample; and his shift in usage in *The Faithful Shepherdess* shows that he was happy to use the form on occasion as a stylistic device.

Most telling against this hypothesis however, is the impracticality of a revision which attempted to remove unregulated positive declarative forms from verse. The time and effort this would have involved would not have been justified given the limited gains in increased linguistic modernity. Such linguistic modernisation as was done in the early seventeenth century was done in the printing house on forms which did not have syntactic consequences (for example, the replacement of 'doth' and 'hath' with 'does' and 'has', and modernisation of spelling in the successive Shakespeare folios). Revisions by playwrights to Jacobean plays are dramatic, and are aimed at topicality, improving the dramatic force of a play, or reducing the number of characters for the sake of economy: for example, the addition of a topical scene concerning *Histriomastix* to Fletcher's *The Nightwalker* after his death; Shakespeare's revisions to *King Lear* (Kerrigan 1983); and the other revisions noted in Knutson 1985.

To illustrate the problems this mooted linguistic revision would have raised, it is enlightening to examine Shakespeare's scene 1.01 from *Henry VIII* from the point of view of a potential reviser. In the first long speech by Norfolk in this scene (lines 13–38), which describes the meeting of Henry VIII and the French king on the Field of the Cloth of Gold, there are three unregulated positive declarative usages:

> Their Dwarfish Pages were
> As Cherubins, all gilt: the Madams too,
> Not us'd to toyle, *did almost sweat to beare*
> The Pride upon them[ . . . ]
>
> The two Kings
> Equall in lustre, were now best, now worst
> *As presence did present them:* Him in eye
> Still him in praise[ . . . ]
>
> When these Sunnes
> (For so they phrase 'em) by their Heralds challeng'd
> The Noble Spirits to arms, *they did performe*[ . . . ]
>
> (*Henry VIII* 1.01. 22–35)

At the basic level of syllable counting, the removal of 'did' from each of these instances, and the inflection of the verb for past tense ('sweated', 'presented', 'performed') would preserve the required ten syllables. However, such modernisation would ruin the iambic stress of the lines:

> Not us'd to toyle, did almost sweat to beare

is natural;

> Not us'd to toyle, almost sweated to beare

is not. Similarly for

> As presence did present them: Him in eye

into

> As presence presented them: Him in eye;

and

> The Noble Spirits to arms, they did performe

into

> The Noble Spirits to arms, they performed.

Rewriting these lines without the auxiliaries but retaining natural stress patterns is time consuming, and tends to produce weaker, or hypermetrical, lines, for example:

> Not us'd to toil, seem'd like to sweat to bear . . .
> As presence there present'd 'em: him in eye . . .
> The noble spirits to arms, they all perform'd . . .

That a professional playwright should undertake such linguistic modernisation is not credible: the economics of the Jacobean stage are against it.

*Relative marker evidence*

Raw figures for relative marker usage in *Henry VIII* will be found in the Statistical Appendix. Graph 5.2 shows the values for section A plotted against the value for the second Shakespeare comparison sample, and that for the Fletcher comparison sample – from this it will be seen that the usage in section A conforms to Shakespearean rather than Fletcherian practice.

Graph 5.3 shows the values for section B plotted against the values for the second Shakespeare comparison sample and the Fletcher comparison sample. Again, this graph gives the expected result, with the section showing Fletcherian, rather than Shakespearean, usage.

Graph 5.4 shows the values for the disputed section C plotted against the

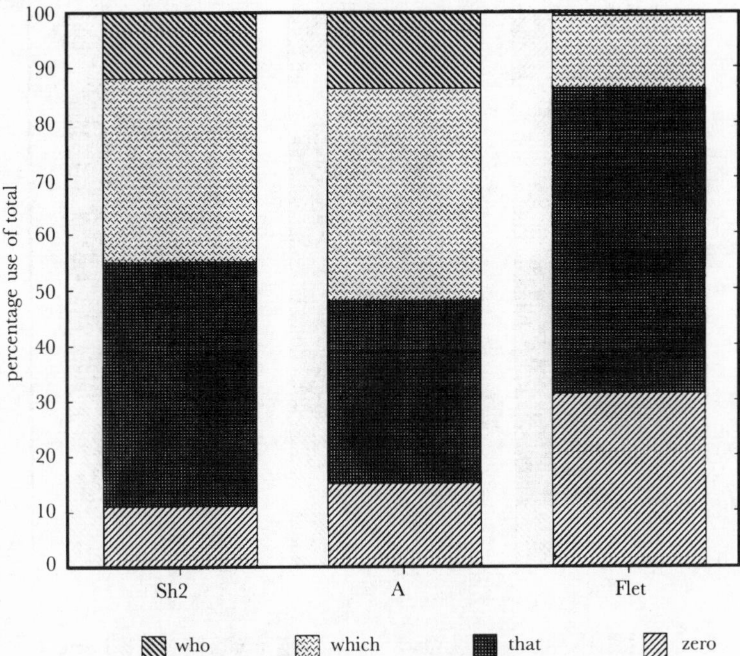


Graph 5.2 Relative marker use in *Henry VIII* section A

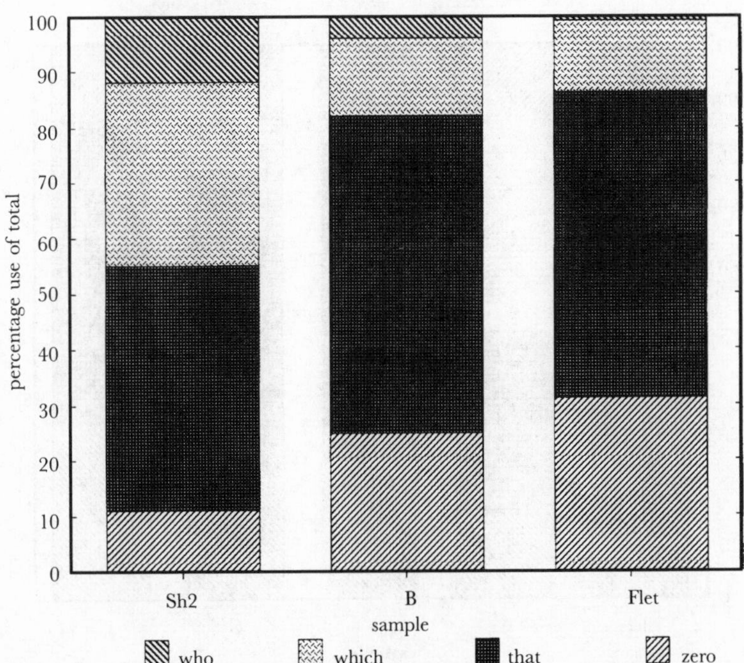


Graph 5.3 Relative marker use in *Henry VIII* section B

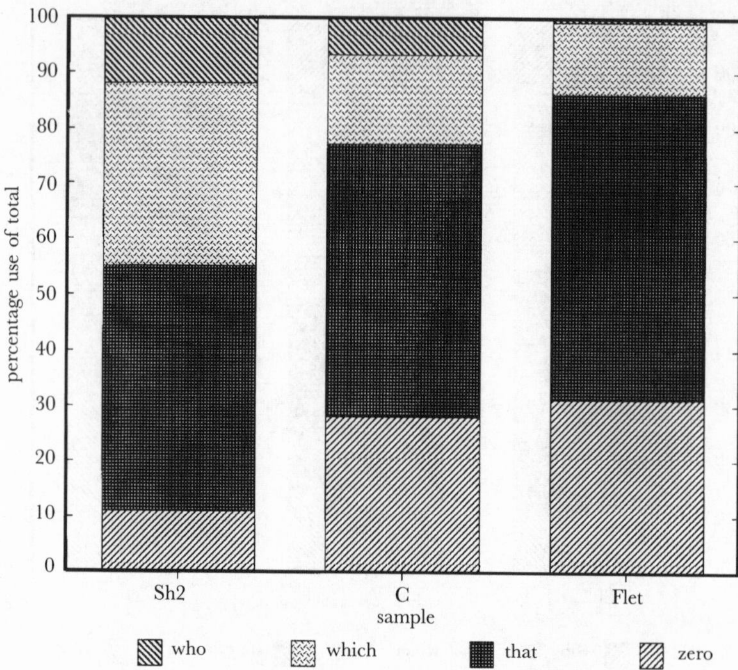


Graph 5.4 Relative marker use in *Henry VIII* section C

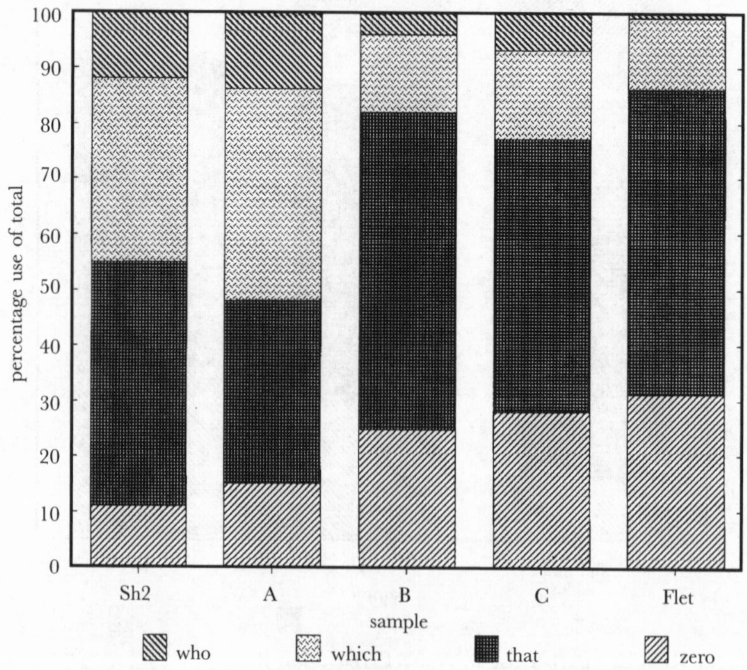


Graph 5.5 Relative marker use in *Henry VIII* sections A, B, C

values for the Shakespeare and Fletcher comparison samples. Here, section C is clearly closer to the Fletcherian comparison sample than to the Shakespearean one, confirming the indication of auxiliary 'do' evidence that section C is Fletcherian.

One interesting feature of the graph, however, is the fact that each relative in section C shows a movement in the direction of Shakespearean usage from Fletcherian – thus 'who' and 'which' usage are higher than in the Fletcher comparison sample, and zero and 'that' usage lower. This 'movement' is not great enough, however, to bring into doubt the Fletcherian authorship of this section. Graph 5.5, which plots values for the three sections of *Henry VIII*, shows that in this play Fletcher's usage throughout shifts towards Shakespearean (that is, sections B *and* C show very similar relatives, and *both* show a slight shift towards Shakespearean usage).

This phenomenon can probably best be explained by accommodation theory (see Street and Giles 1982, Beebe and Giles 1984), which suggests that in any interaction the usages of the participants are likely to shift towards each other, without necessarily meeting.

An alternative explanation is that this is precisely the kind of mixed evidence which would be expected if, as Hoy suggests, these scenes contain material by both authors. If this *is* evidence for mixed scenes, however, it is evidence for mainly Fletcherian scenes with minor Shakespearean survivals or interpolations: the opposite of what Hoy proposes. Although the results for these scenes do show movement towards Shakespearean relatives, it is very slight, and leaves the final figures for zero and 'which' still firmly within the Fletcherian ranges, and the figures for 'that' within the Fletcherian range, two points away from the upper limit of the Shakespearean range. Only the figure for 'who' is closer to the Shakespearean range than the Fletcherian, and this is the relative whose results are calculated on the lowest number of tokens (N = 8), and is therefore subject to most error.

To gauge the significance of this 'who' result, it will be necessary to move the focus of the analysis down to the level of individual usages. Looking at 'who' usage in *Henry VIII*, it is possible to make certain distinctions between Shakespearean and Fletcherian usage. Shakespearean usage is the more general, 'who' being applied to animals,

> Anger is like
> A full hot Horse, who being allow'd his way
> Selfe-mettle tyres him[ . . . ]
>
> (1.01. 132–4)

un-named personals,

This man so compleat,
Who was enrold 'mongst wonders[ . . . ]

(1.02. 118–19)

Sir, a Chartreux Fryer,
His Confessor, who fed him every minute
With words of Sovereignty[ . . . ]

(1.02. 148–50)

and collectives,

. . . they had gather'd a wise Councell to them
Of every Realme, that did debate this Businesse,
Who deem'd our Marriage lawful[ . . . ]

. . . the elect o'th' Land, who are assembled
To pleade your Cause[ . . . ]

(2.04. 49–51, 58–9)

as well as occurring with proper names,

. . . th'Bishop of Bayon, then French Embassador,
Who had beene hither sent[ . . . ]

(2.04. 170–1)

and particularly with reference to the king,

. . . they moved,
Have broken with the King, who hath so farre
Given eare to our Complaint[ . . . ]

(5.01. 46–7)

In the Fletcherian scenes (section B), there are only three usages of 'who', two of which conform to the more rigid system, occurring with a proper name, or title,

. . . his Grace of Canterbury,
Who holds his State at dore[ . . . ]

(5.02. 23–4)

and of the king (although out of context this looks like a less personal usage, in fact it comes from Cranmer's prophecy, and refers to James VI and I),

So shall she leave her Blessednesse to One,
(When Heaven shal call her from this cloud of darknes)
Who, from the sacred Ashes of her Honour
Shall Star-like rise[ . . . ]

(5.04. 43–6)

The third comes in the prose of 5.03, and is probably prompted by the need for variation, since both a relative and demonstrative 'that' have just been

Table 5.5 Pronoun choice in *Henry VIII*

| | *A* | *B* | *C* |
|---|---|---|---|
| total V | 330 | 150 | 138 |
| total T | 22 | 12 | 40 |
| N | 352 | 162 | 178 |
| %V | 94 | 93 | 78 |

used of the head (Fletcher is usually happy to mix relative and demonstrative 'that', but three usages in close proximity would probably be too many),

> There was a Habberdashers Wife of small wit, neere him, that rail'd upon me . . . I mist the Meteor once, and hit that Woman, who cryed out Clubbes[ . . . ]
> (5.03. 42–6)

The 'who(m)' usages of the section C scenes, of which there are more than would be expected if, as I claim, these scenes are Fletcher's (eight tokens in five scenes, whereas the comparison sample of five of Fletcher's plays yields only fifteen in total), conform to this more personal type as well. The two 'who' usages of 2.01 occur with proper names ('Sir Nicholas Vaux, / Who undertakes you to your end', 'Henry of Buckingham, / Who first rais'd head against Usurping Richard' 2.01. 96–7, 107–8), two further usages refer to the king ('Heare the Kings pleasure Cardinall, who commands you' 3.02b. 228, 'The Kings request, that I would visit you, / Who greeves much for your weaknesse' 4.02. 116–7); and a final usage,

> . . . our Issues,
> (Who if he live, will scarse be Gentlemen)[ . . . ]
> (3.02b. 291–2)

appeared in the first folio as 'whom', and was altered in the second.

My conclusion from this is that the increase in 'who' forms in the section C scenes is not necessarily positive evidence for Shakespeare's presence. These forms are acceptable Fletcherian usage, if not his normal frequency, and it is probable that he uses more of them here because of the formality of the situations, or because he is being influenced by Shakespeare's style. The overall pattern of relative formation in the section C scenes remains Fletcherian.

### *T/V evidence*

I have already indicated that T/V choice is not a good form of socio-historical linguistic evidence for authorship, however I am going to consider the pattern of pronoun form choice in *Henry VIII* because the figures for the play are so extraordinary. In *Henry VIII*, both Shakespeare and Fletcher seem to alter their normal pronoun usage to achieve a stylistic effect (table 5.5). This evidence suggests that the collaboration of Shakespeare and Fletcher in this play was interactive – that the two men wrote and planned together, rather than Fletcher finishing-off a play abandoned by Shakespeare.

In terms of its use of pronoun forms, *Henry VIII* is the most unusual play in the Shakespeare canon. This is because it uses so few 'thou' forms, and is so dominated by 'you' forms. This tendency shows up both in terms of a very low percentage of 'thou' and mixing relationships, and in the total number of 'thou' forms used in the play. It is not just that this is the play with the lowest number of 'thou' forms, but that the figure is so far below that found in any other play. On the 'thou' index, *Henry VIII* scores two, while the other plays range from six to nineteen, and can be graduated according to score so that no play is more than two points different from its neighbours. *Henry VIII*, at least four points different from any other play, stands out as a major change in the way pronoun forms are used in the canon (see table 4.4 on p. 62).

As Brainerd's figures show, statistical comparison with *The Two Noble Kinsmen* shows that the difference cannot be explained simply by Fletcher's presence. Furthermore, the total number of all pronoun forms in *Henry VIII* is what we would expect for a play of its length. The play is characterised by a marked reluctance to modulate (except for the latter half of one scene), despite the fact that elsewhere, Shakespeare's writing, in whatever genre, seems to have a constant level of modulation.

These figures have obvious implications for the question of authorship, but the high 'you' percentages are not evidence for sole Fletcherian authorship – they are too far outside his normal range – nor do I take them as evidence that someone other than Shakespeare or Fletcher wrote the play. The absence of 'thou' forms, and of modulation, has to be addressed, as does the fact that thirty-five of the eighty-four 'thou' forms in the play occur in one half of one scene (3.02. 203–459), the first half of which contains only one 'thou' form.

It seems to me that what they are evidence for, rather than authorship, is conscious and planned collaboration on the part of Shakespeare and Fletcher; the adoption of a specific linguistic tactic in support of an attempt to write what was perceived as a new form of historical drama. The alternative title, and the Prologue, both stress 'truth' as being a dramatic value of the piece. I think that there is a case for seeing *Henry VIII* as a new genre – a sort of documentary history, prepared to abandon dramatic form and structure in favour of the factual portrayal of historical events.

It is not unreasonable to suggest that a consciousness of authenticity might manifest itself in the language of the play, and specifically in the language of upper-class court interchange: perhaps the language of the play is deliberately modern, aping contemporary court usage, just as the events portrayed are self-consciously related to the contemporary events of the Jacobean court. I have suggested before that 'thou', even as early as Elizabethan times, may be more of a literary phenomenon than is thought. If that is correct, then we here see the casting off of a further literary convention to that of plot structure, the use of 'thou', in the interests of factual drama. In many ways, *Henry VIII* evinces a voyeuristic obsession with the detail of court display and intrigue: the tone of the play's presentation, from Prologue to the elaborate stage directions, is one of authoritative description. It is possible (as Holdsworth suspects) that by this time 'thou' had completely disappeared from court speech (preserved only in songs and literature) – perhaps *Henry VIII* records the modern system of pronouns in triumph in the Jacobean court.

I think that the pattern of 'thou' forms in 3.02b, coinciding with the un-named, rather impersonal 'who' at line 292 ('our issues / (Who if he live, will scarce be gentlemen)'), may suggest that the exchange between Surrey and Wolsey is based on a Shakespearean original (mainly I think lines 251–316). This is not to concede Hoy's point, which sees all of this part-scene as mainly Shakespearean with Fletcherian additions: the rest of the scene remains wholly Fletcherian, in my opinion, on the basis of the evidence of relative markers and auxiliary 'do' use (the consistent 'thou' forms from Wolsey to Cromwell at the end of the scene are typically Fletcherian and contrast well with the rapid modulation of the Wolsey/Surrey exchange).

*Summary*

Auxiliary 'do' and relativisation evidence combine to confirm strongly the likely Fletcherian authorship of section C of *Henry VIII*, and to confirm the previous ascriptions of sections A and B to Shakespeare and Fletcher respectively.

### *The Two Noble Kinsmen*

The origin of the linguistic case for the attribution of *The Two Noble Kinsmen* to Shakespeare and Fletcher, thus confirming the title page attribution of the 1634 first quarto, can be traced through the work of Weber (1812), Spalding (1833), and Hickson (1847). Major twentieth century work on the play includes that of Farnham (1916), Hart (1934), Mincoff (1952), Muir (1960), Merriam (1985:136–44), and Horton (1987). There is less controversy about the division of this play than *Henry VIII*, as can be seen from the main divisions, recorded in table 5.6: Spalding's 1833

Table 5.6 Divisions of *The Two Noble Kinsmen*

| Act | | *one* | | | | | *two* | | | | | | *three* | | | | | | *four* | | | *five* | | | | | |
|---|---|---|---|---|---|---|---|---|---|---|---|---|---|---|---|---|---|---|---|---|---|---|---|---|---|---|---|
| Scene | P | 1 | 2 | 3 | 4 | 5 | 1 | 2 | 3 | 4 | 5 | 6 | 1 | 2 | 3 | 4 | 5 | 6 | 1 | 2 | 3 | 1a | 1b | 2 | 3 | 4 | E |
| Spalding 1833 | – | S | S | S | S | S | F | F | F | F | F | F | S | F | F | F | F | F | F | F | S | S | S | F | S | S | – |
| Hickson 1847 | – | S | SF | S | S | S? | S | F | F | F | F | F | S | S | F | F | F | F | F | F | F | S | S | F | S | S | – |
| Fleay 1886 | – | S | S | S | S | S | S | S | F | F | F | F | S | F | F | F | F | F | F | F | S | F | S | F | S | S | – |
| Farnham 1916 | – | S | S | S | S | S | S | S | S | F | F | F | S | S | F | F | F | F | F | F | S | S | S | F | S | S | – |
| Hart 1934 | – | S | S | S | S | S | F | F | F | F | F | F | S | F | F | F | F | F | F | F | F | S | S | F | S | S | – |
| Hoy 1962 | – | S | S | S | S | S | S | F | F | F | F | F | S | S | F | F | F | F | F | F | F | F | S | F | S | S | – |
| Waith 1989 | F | S | S | S | S | S | S? | F | F | F | F | F | S | S | F | F | F | F | F | F | S? | SF | S | F | S | S | F |

S = Shakespeare; F = Fletcher

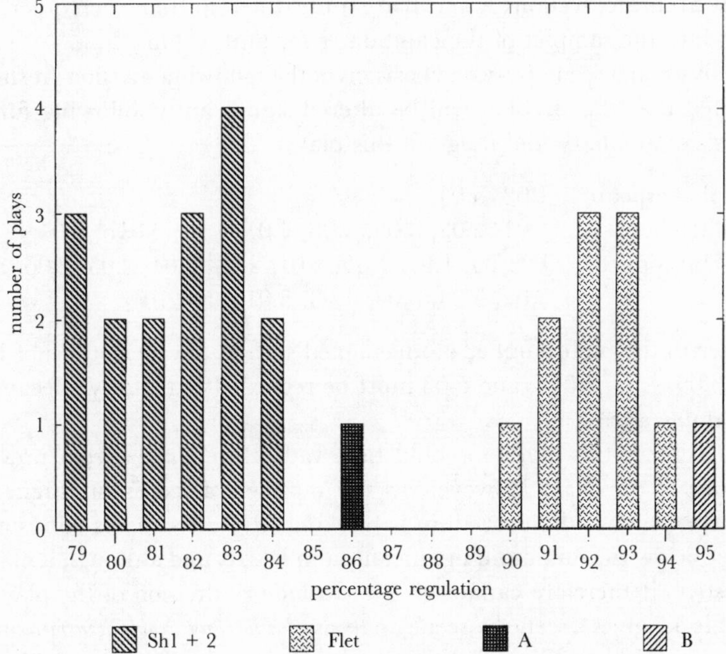


Graph 5.6 Auxiliary 'do' regulation in *The Two Noble Kinsmen* sections A, B

division was supported by Hickson, and subsequent studies using various types of evidence did no more than reassign one or two short scenes.

Although such a large measure of agreement amongst studies employing different types of evidence is impressive, there have been some dissenting voices. Massinger and Chapman have been offered as candidates for the 'Shakespearean' parts of *The Two Noble Kinsmen* (Boyle 1880–5:443–87; Sykes 1919:19–47) but neither suggestion has subsequently been supported. Bertram (1965) claims sole Shakespearean authorship for *The Two Noble Kinsmen*, but misrepresents or ignores the evidence for Fletcher in a study which has claimed no subsequent following.

*Auxiliary 'do' evidence*

The scene by scene regulation rates for *The Two Noble Kinsmen* will be found in the Statistical Appendix. Graph 5.6 shows the regulation rates of the sections of *The Two Noble Kinsmen* in the currently accepted division (Shakespearean A = 86 per cent, Fletcherian B = 95 per cent) plotted against the results for the second Shakespearean and the Fletcherian comparison samples.

Graph 5.6 shows that the traditional division of the play is probably largely accurate: sections A and B are quite different from each other, and lie close to the samples of the candidates for authorship.

Analysis on a scene-by-scene basis gives the following division (it should be noted that this division will be altered significantly following further analysis of auxiliary 'do' usage in this play):

| | |
|---|---|
| Shakespeare: | 1.02, 5.03 |
| Fletcher: | 1.01, 2.02, 3.05, 3.06, 4.01, 4.02, 5.01b, 5.04 |
| Unassigned: | P, 1.03, 1.04, 1.05, 2.01, 2.03, 2.04, 2.05, 2.06, 3.01, 3.02, 3.03, 3.04, 4.03, 5.01a, 5.02, E |

Further to the high number of unassigned scenes, the ascriptions of 1.01, 1.02, 3.05, 4.02, 5.01b, and 5.03 must be regarded as tentative because of low sample sizes.

If accepted, this division would be a radical departure from previous divisions of the play. However, as the number of scenes unassigned or borderline shows, the procedure is working here on samples consistently near or below the minimum significant sample size, and although it may be suggestive, it therefore cannot give a satisfactory division of the play.

Table 5.7 gives a scene by scene analysis of *The Two Noble Kinsmen* on the basis of regulation of positive declarative sentences. This test divides the play into two: one set of scenes in which unregulated positive declaratives occur, and another where regulation is total (i.e. unregulated forms are 0 per cent of the total). The degree to which these two sets of scenes conform to the traditional division of the play between Shakespeare and Fletcher is striking (the scenes are grouped according to this division in table 5.7). Only two traditionally Fletcherian scenes show anything other than total regulation in this sentence type. Only three traditionally Shakespearean scenes show less than 5 per cent usage of unregulated forms, all of them very short.

This analysis enables socio-historical linguistic evidence to be brought to bear on individual scenes which do not provide substantial samples. In this case, the test confirms the traditional division, with scenes such as 1.01, 1.02, 1.03, 5.01b, 5.03, and 5.04 all having high numbers of positive declaratives expressed with the auxiliary. Scenes 1.01 and 5.04, originally assigned to Fletcher on relatively low sample sizes, and with only 90 per cent regulation, now begin to look Shakespearean. Even short scenes containing a single unregulated positive declarative sentence usage can be tentatively assigned to Shakespeare using this analysis, since Fletcher's infrequent usage of the construction makes it unlikely that it would occur in a short scene, except in one of his formulaic phrases. Of course, such evidence could not be as firm as overall regulation rates based on good samples, but it can provide strong indications of likely authorship which may be accepted if

Table 5.7 Unregulated positive declarative sentences as a percentage of all positive declarative sentences in *The Two Noble Kinsmen*

'Shakespeare' scenes (section A)

| | *1.01* | *1.02* | *1.03* | *1.04* | *1.05* | *2.01* | *3.01* | *3.02* | *5.01b* | *5.03* | *5.04* |
|---|---|---|---|---|---|---|---|---|---|---|---|
| % 'do' | 5 | 13 | 9 | 8 | 0 | 6 | 3 | 0 | 12 | 19 | 7 |

'Fletcher' scenes (section B)

| | *P* | *2.02* | *2.03* | *2.04* | *2.05* | *2.06* | *3.03* | *3.04* | *3.05* | *3.06* | *4.01* | *4.02* |
|---|---|---|---|---|---|---|---|---|---|---|---|---|
| % 'do' | 0 | 0 | 0 | 0 | 0 | 0 | 0 | 0 | 2 | 0 | 0 | 0 |
| | *4.03* | *5.01a* | *5.02* | *E* | | | | | | | | |
| % 'do' | 4 | 0 | 0 | 0 | | | | | | | | |

accompanied by other types of evidence. On this basis, a tentative complete division of the play can be offered for confirmation by subsequent tests:

Shakespeare: 1.01, 1.02, 1.03, 1.04, 1.05, 2.01, 3.01, 3.02, 5.01b, 5.03, 5.04

Fletcher: P, 2.02, 2.03, 2.04, 2.05, 2.06, 3.03, 3.04, 3.05, 3.06, 4.01, 4.02, 4.03, 5.01a, 5.02, E

### *Relative marker evidence*

Figures for the proportions of relative markers in each of the two proposed sections of *The Two Noble Kinsmen* are given in the Statistical Appendix. Graph 5.7 shows the values for section A plotted against the values for the second Shakespeare comparison sample and the Fletcherian comparison sample.

From graph 5.7 it will be seen that, as expected, section A shows Shakespearean, rather than Fletcherian usage of relative markers, confirming the generally accepted ascription of these scenes to Shakespeare.

Graph 5.8 shows the relative marker values for section B plotted against the values for the second Shakespearean and the Fletcher comparison samples. This graph confirms the traditional ascription of these scenes to Fletcher, as is clearly shown by the similarity of the graph for section B to the graph for the Fletcher comparison sample.

Graph 5.9 shows the values for section A plotted against those for section B. This graph constitutes strong evidence for the presence of two hands in the play, given the marked differences in relativisation strategies in the two sections. This graph may also tell us something about the nature of the collaboration between Shakespeare and Fletcher, since evidence presented

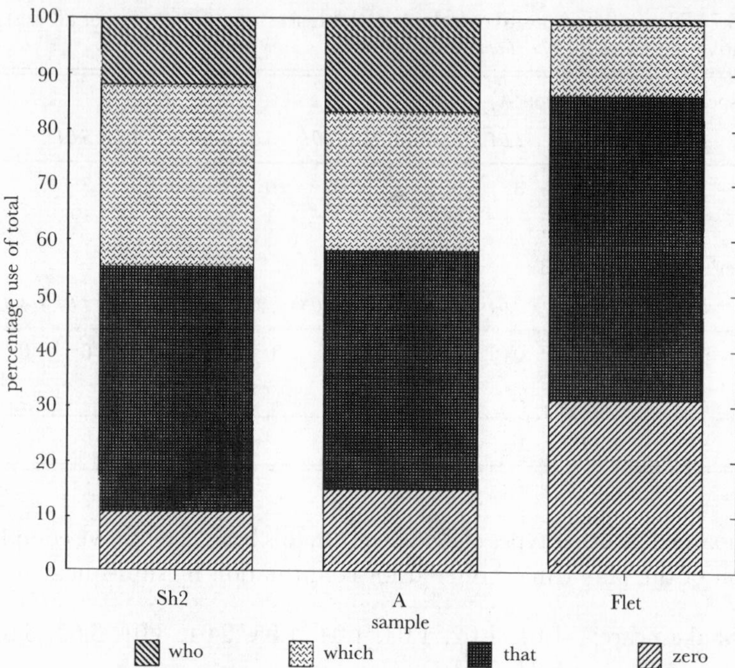


Graph 5.7 Relative marker use in *The Two Noble Kinsmen* section A

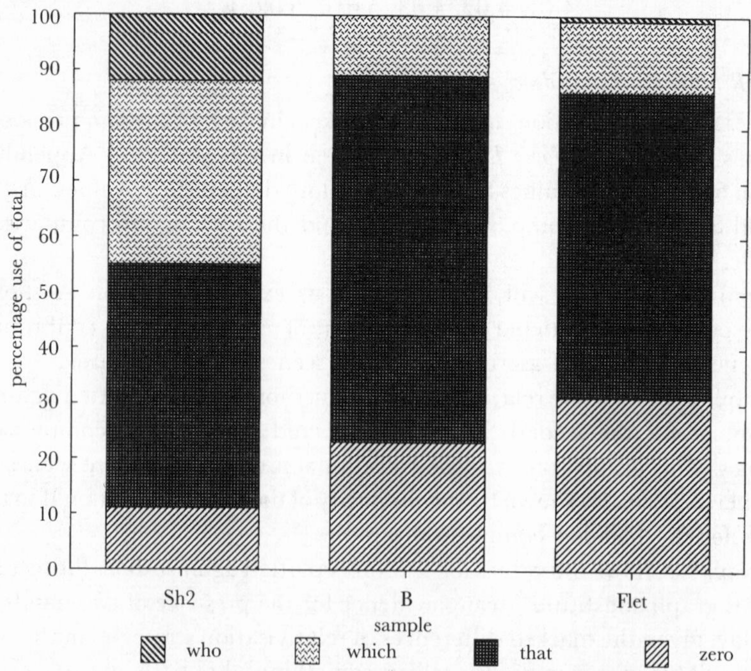


Graph 5.8 Relative marker use in *The Two Noble Kinsmen* section B

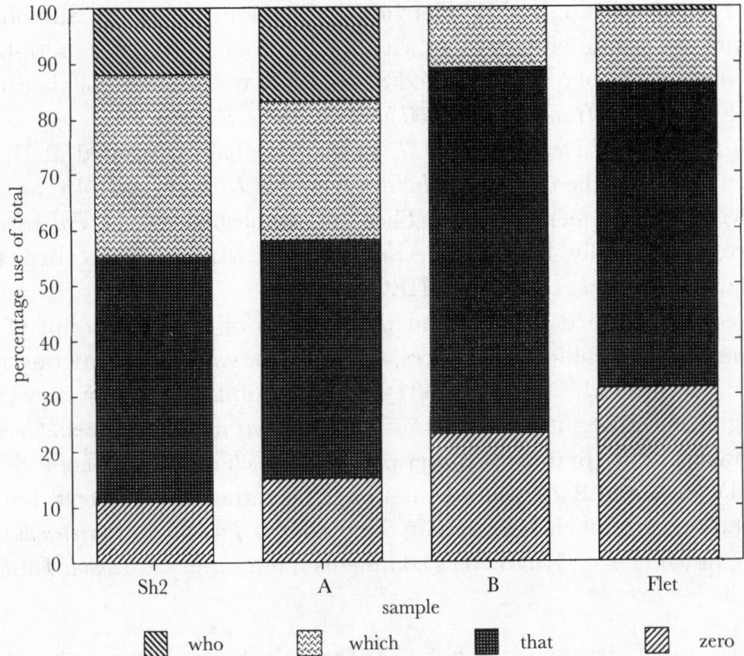


Graph 5.9 Relative marker use in *The Two Noble Kinsmen* sections A, B

below in the case of *Pericles* will show that texts containing material by two hands, but prepared by one of the collaborators, can show a uniform relativisation pattern; even when other linguistic features indicate the presence of two hands. This is because it is very much easier for one collaborator, producing a final fair copy of the whole play, to impose his own relative marker choices on the text, than it is for him to alter other linguistic features (such as auxiliary 'do'). The fact therefore that both *The Two Noble Kinsmen* and *Henry VIII* show distinct relativisation strategies in their Shakespearean and Fletcherian sections is evidence against any kind of final reworking of the plays by either of the collaborators.

*Summary*

Auxiliary 'do' and relativisation evidence confirm the generally accepted division of *The Two Noble Kinsmen* between Shakespeare and Fletcher. Relativisation evidence is against either of the collaborators having prepared a revised final version of the play text.

### *Double Falshood ('Cardenio')*

In 1612–13, the King's Men presented a play called 'Cardenna' or 'Cardenno' twice at court, and in 1653 Humphrey Moseley registered 'The

History of Cardenio, by Mr. Fletcher. & Shakespeare' in the Stationer's Register. The date of acting fits with the Stationer's Register ascription, since it dates the play to the period of Shakespeare's known collaboration with Fletcher on *Henry VIII* and *The Two Noble Kinsmen.*

On the 13th of December, 1727, Lewis Theobald presented at Drury Lane a play with the title *Double Falshood; or, The Distrest Lovers.* In the year following its first performance, Theobald published *Double Falshood* as 'Written Originally by W. SHAKESPEARE; And now Revised and Adapted to the Stage By Mr. THEOBALD'.

Theobald claimed to have had three copies of the manuscript of his 'original', and possible provenances, and fates, for two of them are traced in Freehafer 1969 and Hammond 1984. From the point of view of preservation of linguistic features it is worth stressing the point made by Freehafer and Kukowski (1990), that the manuscript Theobald claims to have come down from Downes and Betterton may not have been the 'original' text, but an adaptation of it, much as Davenant adapted *The Two Noble Kinsmen* as *The Rivals*, in which case Kukowski's comments might apply to *Double Falshood* as well:

> Davenant's revision of this play [*The Two Noble Kinsmen*] left not a line of the passages most confidently ascribed to Shakespeare intact, although several of Fletcher's passages survive with only minor alteration.
>
> (Kukowski 1990:81)

The circumstantial and external evidence therefore fits together in support of Theobald's claim that *Double Falshood* was based on an older text. H.C. Frazier excepted, twentieth century commentators have come to accept the identification of 'Cardenio' as the source-text for *Double Falshood.* Given this, debate has concentrated on the extent to which Fletcher and Shakespeare's work can be discerned in Theobald's text (see Frazier 1968 and 1974; Freehafer 1969; Kukowski 1990; Muir 1970; Bradford 1910; Schwartzstein 1954).

Studies using metrical tests and parallel passages have claimed to find two styles in *Double Falshood*, styles which can be related to those of Shakespeare and Fletcher. As has been pointed out, however, these types of evidence are problematic as determinants of authorship, especially in an adapted text as is alleged in the case of *Double Falshood.* Freehafer's use of parallels to establish that, whether mediated through 'Cardenio' or not, *Double Falshood* uses Shelton's translation of *Don Quixote* rather than a later one, is important, but given the tendency of both Fletcher and Theobald to echo Shakespeare, parallels can hardly be trusted as systematically indicative of authorship, or revealing anything about the textual predecessors of *Double Falshood.*

Work on *Double Falshood* thus gives us three possible explanations for its existence, cited here in order of likelihood:

(1) it is an adaptation of a Fletcher–Shakespeare manuscript (either a direct adaptation of 'Cardenio' by Theobald, or his adaptation of a restoration version)

(2) it is a Theobald adaptation of a wholly Shakespearean play (this is Theobald's claim in his preface to the first edition of *Double Falshood*; however, as Freehafer shows, changes made to this preface in the second edition suggest that Theobald may have come to accept Fletcher's part-authorship)

(3) it is a forgery by Theobald who, as Frazier points out, was steeped in Shakespeare, and who explicitly imitated his style in 'The Cave of Penury' and 'The Death of Hannibal' (*c.* 1739, 'attempted in imitation of Shakespeare's manner', now lost – see Seary 1990:204).

This study applies socio-historical linguistic evidence to the problem of *Double Falshood* in an attempt to provide evidence for or against each of the above possibilities from the text of the play itself.

### *The nature of the linguistic evidence in* Double Falshood

Before figures for the selected linguistic features in *Double Falshood* are presented and analysed, it is necessary to consider the nature of the evidence offered by the text of this play. Even if Theobald *did* own a manuscript of 'Cardenio', it would be wrong to treat figures from *Double Falshood* as if they were figures from an unaltered renaissance text, since Theobald admits that he revised his source, and this source may itself have been an adaptation. It therefore becomes necessary to address the question of the likely linguistic effects of a restoration adaptation of a renaissance text.

In previous studies, it has been established that auxiliary 'do' evidence is not affected by scribes or compositors, and probably not even by contemporary revision, because of the syntactic consequences of adding or removing auxiliary 'do' forms. Furthermore, although they are theoretically more liable to modernisation, no interference with relative markers has been found. The process of restoration adaptation, however, is another matter, and it cannot be assumed that this will leave even auxiliary 'do' forms intact.

Luckily evidence exists from which we can predict the likely consequences of Theobald 'adapting' a renaissance manuscript – in his own adaptation of Shakespeare's *Richard II*, and, with a view to the possibility that *Double Falshood* is based on a Fletcher–Shakespeare collaboration, possibly in a Davenant adaptation, in Davenant's adaptation of *The Two Noble Kinsmen*, *The Rivals*.

Theobald's adaptation of *Richard II* goes beyond simple cutting for production, and constitutes a total rewriting of the play, bringing it more into line with the unity of time, and reassigning, and reinterpreting, many speeches. It might be expected that such radical rewriting would totally disrupt the auxiliary 'do' evidence in the play, but in fact this seems not to happen. The overall regulation rate rises from 83 per cent in the Shakespeare version to 87 per cent in the Theobald, which suggests some degree of modernisation, but this is still below the regulation rate of Theobald's own play *The Persian Princess* (93 per cent).

When the individual sentence types are analysed, it becomes clear that Theobald does not modernise positive declarative sentences (89 per cent of which are regulated in Shakespeare, 90 per cent in Theobald's version), but does appear to modernise positive questions (26 per cent regulated in Shakespeare, 56 per cent in Theobald's version) and, to a lesser extent, negative declaratives (15 per cent in Shakespeare against 23 per cent in Theobald; however *The Persian Princess* has a 0 per cent regulation rate for negative declaratives).

Since positive declaratives make up such a large proportion of the sentences in any text, it can be assumed from this that a Theobald adaptation of a renaissance text would tend to increase the overall regulation rate slightly, but not to such a degree as to obscure the original evidence. Theobald's failure to modernise positive declarative auxiliary 'do' forms can be explained by their poetic register – it is interesting to note that unregulated positive questions do not seem to carry the same stylistic connotations.

Comparing *The Rivals* to *The Two Noble Kinsmen*, a different picture emerges, with the overall regulation rate of the Davenant adaptation actually lower than that of the original text (85 per cent against 91 per cent for Fletcher and Shakespeare's text). This is doubly surprising given Sprague's statement that Davenant chose to cut most of the Shakespeare sections from his adaptation – a practice which would be expected to *increase* the regulation rate of the play as a whole (the Shakespearean sections of *The Two Noble Kinsmen* have a regulation rate of 86 per cent, while the Fletcher sections have one of 95 per cent).

This low result can in fact be explained by two scenes in which Davenant introduces heroic couplets and consequently a large number of poetic positive declarative auxiliary 'do' forms (4.01 and 5.01). If these scenes are removed from the analysis, the regulation rate of the play rises to 90 per cent, still lower than that of the Fletcherian scenes of *The Two Noble Kinsmen*, and suggesting that Davenant actually introduces unregulated forms, particularly in positive declarative sentences. The regulation rate of positive declarative sentences in the Fletcher scenes of *The Two Noble Kinsmen* is 100 per cent (99.6 per cent), while that of the Shakespeare scenes is 91 per cent; the regulation rate of positive declarative sentences in Davenant's adaptation is 89 per cent.

The conclusions which can be drawn from this analysis of the effects of adaptation on auxiliary 'do' evidence are that, by and large, auxiliary 'do' evidence tends to survive adaptation. In neither Theobald's *Richard II* nor Davenant's *The Rivals* is there evidence for modernisation of the most important category of sentence: positive declarative. Davenant's tendency to introduce unregulated positive declaratives is not followed by Theobald (positive declaratives have a regulation rate of 89 per cent in Shakespeare's *Richard II*, and 90 per cent in Theobald's adaptation; Theobald's *The Persian Princess* shows a regulation rate of 99 per cent in positive declaratives).

As indicated above, relative markers are inherently more easily modernised than auxiliary 'do' forms, as changes involve simple substitution. Not only this, they are also the subject of much prescriptive comment by grammarians of the seventeenth and eighteenth centuries, and are certainly at the level of a conscious linguistic issue by Theobald's time, both in terms of the restrictive/non-restrictive distinction between 'that' and 'which', and the personal/non-personal distinction between 'who(m)' and 'which'.

During the compilation of the comparison sample, it was noted that although Fletcher does tend to adhere to the restrictive/non-restrictive rule more than Shakespeare, this tendency was not clearly enough marked for this to be used as an authorship tool. In the case of the 'who(m)'/'which' distinction, however, this was useful as an indicator of authorship, and it is therefore important to know what the effects of Theobald's adaptation of Shakespearean text will be on the relative markers. An educated guess would suggest that Theobald would be likely to 'correct' Shakespearean 'who(m)' and 'which' forms not in accordance with the personal/non–personal distinction. The statistical effect of such correction, since 'which' forms are more common in Shakespeare than 'who(m)' forms, would be to increase the percentage of 'who(m)' forms at the expense of 'which' forms.

When figures for relative markers in the Shakespeare and Theobald versions of *Richard II* are compared, this is exactly what we find to be the case: 'who(m)' forms increase from 9 per cent in Shakespeare to 18 per cent in Theobald, while 'which' forms decrease from 30 per cent to 17 per cent (these shifts can be clearly seen on graph 5.10). The following quotations illustrate the process of 'correction' taking place in contexts in which Theobald is otherwise following Shakespeare almost verbatim:

Shakespeare (*Richard II* 1.01. 172–3):

> The which no balme can cure but his heart bloud
> *Which* breathde this poyson

Theobald (*Richard II*, page 30):

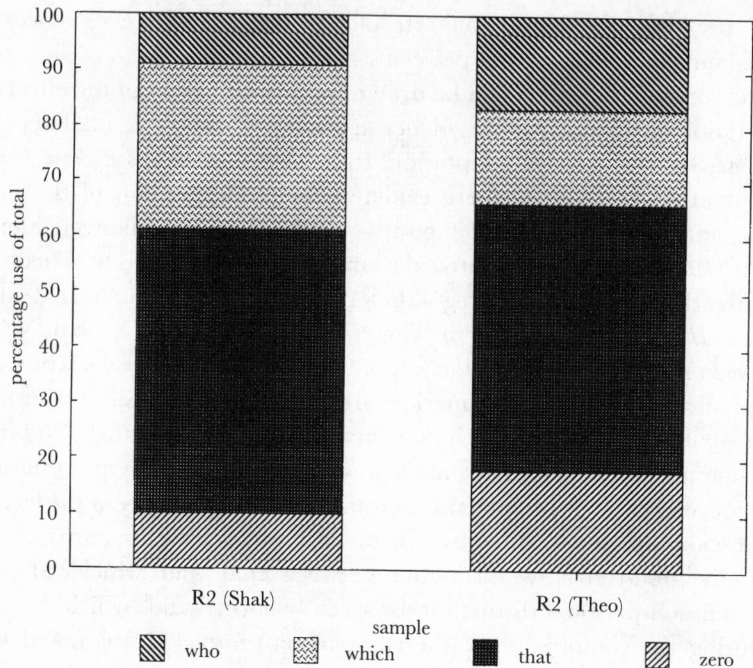


Graph 5.10 Relative marker use in the two versions of *Richard II*

> The which no Balm can cure, but his Heart's Blood,
> *Who* breath'd this Poison

Shakespeare (*Richard II* 5.01. 62–3):

> He shall thinke that thou *which* knowest the way
> To plant vnrightfull kings, wilt know againe

Theobald (*Richard II*, page 57):

> And He shall think, that Thou, *who* knew'st the way
> To plant unrightful Kings, wilt know again

Consideration of linguistic evidence in Davenant's *The Rivals*, Theobald's *The Persian Princess*, and Shakespeare and Theobald's versions of *Richard II* allows the following expectations to be stated about adaptation of renaissance texts by Davenant and Theobald:

In the case of auxiliary 'do', Theobald may tend to increase regulation slightly, but not in the case of positive declarative sentences, and not to the rates found in his unaided work. Davenant actually adds unregulated positive declaratives at one point – in neither is there evidence for systematic modernisation.

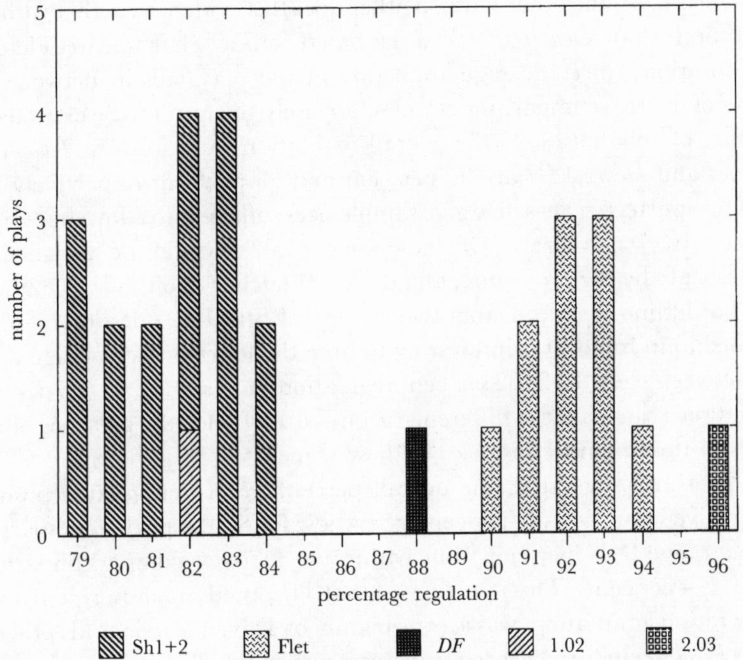


Graph 5.11 Auxiliary 'do' regulation in *Double Falshood*, and scenes 1.02, 2.03

In the case of relative markers it can be stated that Theobald will tend to increase the proportion of 'who(m)' forms at the expense of 'which' forms in a Shakespearean text, as a result of systematic modernisation of the forms according to their antecedents.

Having established the likely effects of restoration adaptation of a renaissance text, the socio-historical linguistic evidence afforded by *Double Falshood* can now be analysed.

### *Auxiliary 'do' evidence*

Graph 5.11 shows the auxiliary 'do' evidence for the authorship of *Double Falshood* (*DF* – the raw figures will be found in the Statistical Appendix). The overall regulation rate of this play is 88 per cent, four percentage points higher than the upper limit of the Shakespearean comparison sample (range 79–84 per cent) and two percentage points lower than the lower limit of the Fletcher comparison sample (range 90–4 per cent). This evidence is compatible with a number of hypotheses, depending on the presumed source of the text of *Double Falshood*. For instance, given the 4 per cent increase in the regulation rate of *Richard II* after it had passed through Theobald's hands, this evidence does not undermine the claim Theobald makes in his preface, that *Double Falshood* is based on a wholly Shakespearean manuscript. On the other hand, neither does this evidence conflict with the suggestion that *Double Falshood* is based on a Shakespeare–Fletcher collaboration, since the regulation rate of the play falls in between the ranges of the two comparison samples, precisely the result to be expected in the case of collaboration (the overall regulation rates for *The Two Noble Kinsmen* and *Henry VIII* are 91 per cent and 88 per cent respectively).

Of the fourteen scenes, five give sample sizes sufficient to allow analysis on a scene by scene basis. Of these, one (1.02) would be assigned to Shakespeare by the procedure, and three to Fletcher (2.03, 4.01, 5.02) with one borderline between the two (3.03). With the question of dual authorship in mind, it is interesting to note the fourteen percentage point gap between scene 1.02 (82 per cent regulation) and scene 2.03 (96 per cent regulation). Such a large difference argues strongly for the presence of two hands in the linguistic histories of these scenes.

As has been suggested, the overall percentage of unregulated positive declarative sentences at 3 per cent is very low for Shakespeare (comparison sample range 8–17 per cent) but within the Fletcher comparison sample range (1–4 per cent). This may suggest that Theobald's manuscript, if it was a restoration adaptation, was *not* one mainly by Davenant, since his practice in *The Rivals* seems to have been to increase unregulated positive declaratives. It does, however, support the notion, given Theobald's tendency to retain unregulated positive declarative forms when he adapts text containing them, that either Theobald, or an earlier adapter, cut the majority of Shakespeare's scenes from *Double Falshood*'s source text.

The auxiliary 'do' evidence tends to cast doubt on the theory that Theobald forged *Double Falshood*. The overall regulation rate of 88 per cent is about what we would expect of an adapted Shakespeare and Fletcher text, given Theobald's tendency not to modernise auxiliary 'do' forms to any substantial degree, and, as figures from *The Persian Princess* show, it is not consistent with Theobald's own usage.

It might be objected to this that Theobald, steeped in Shakespearean early Modern English, would have been careful to introduce unregulated auxiliary 'do' forms into his text, as they are (especially in positive declarative sentences) one of the stereotyped features of the language from that period. However, as socio-linguistics has often shown, it is very difficult to 'hit' a target usage exactly in terms of frequency, as can be seen from the regulation rate of William Henry Ireland's forged 'Shakespearean' play, *Vortigern*, which has a ridiculously low regulation rate of 66 per cent (Ireland hypercorrects unregulated forms in his attempt to reproduce early Modern English). It seems unlikely that Theobald, attempting to forge Shakespearean usage, would have erred on the side of modernity to produce linguistic evidence consistent with collaborative authorship between Shakespeare and Fletcher.

Even allowing Theobald to be a better forger than Ireland, he would be expected to focus on positive declaratives as a stereotyped marker of early Modern English. The high regulation rate of positive declarative sentences in *Double Falshood* (97 per cent) is therefore strong evidence against forgery.

Perhaps most telling of all against the forgery theory is the evidence cited above from the scene-by-scene analysis which suggests the presence of two hands in the text. Had Theobald been forging early Modern English, he would presumably have been careful to produce a text with a consistent rate of unregulated forms, not one which varied between patterns of regulation.

If it is accepted that *Double Falshood* is based on a Shakespeare–Fletcher collaboration, then auxiliary 'do' evidence would indicate that a Shakespearean original underlies 1.02, while Fletcherian originals underlie 2.03, 4.01, and 5.02. It would also imply that the early part of the play relies predominantly on Shakespearean material, while the latter part relies on Fletcherian. While any conclusions from this evidence as to the likely authorship of *Double Falshood*, and any manuscript which may underlie it, must be expressed with the utmost caution and qualification, it can be said that none of the auxiliary 'do' evidence conflicts with the theory that *Double Falshood* is a reasonably close adaptation of a play written in collaboration by Shakespeare and Fletcher, with the adapter tending to use more of the Fletcherian material than the Shakespearean.

### *Evidence from relative markers*

The evidence from relative markers in *Double Falshood* is shown in table 5.8. At first sight, on this evidence, *Double Falshood* seems unlikely to have been based on a wholly Shakespearean original. 'Who' usage at 16 per cent is just within the range of the late Shakespeare comparison sample (9–16 per cent). 'Which' usage is at 19 per cent here, but never below 28 per cent in the comparison sample. 'That' usage is 39 per cent here, just below the lower limit of the comparison sample (41 per cent). Zero relatives at 27 per cent here are very much more frequent than in the comparison sample (7–15 per cent). Furthermore, 'who' and 'which' are here distinguished on the basis of person, a non-Shakespearean feature.

The presence of this 'who'/'which' distinction might appear to be evidence against the presence of Shakespeare in any supposed original text; however, as was suggested earlier, it is probable that Theobald would have 'corrected' Shakespearean 'who' forms with non-personal antecedents, and 'which' forms with personal antecedents, in line with eighteenth-century prescriptive sensibilities. Such modernisation of Shakespearean relatives would none the less have preserved the high rate of 'who' and 'which' forms he displays elsewhere in contrast to Fletcher.

It can be predicted that any modernisation of 'who' and 'which' forms by Theobald would involve the creation of more 'who' forms than 'which',

Table 5.8 Relative marker choice in *Double Falshood*

| | | *restrictive* | | *non-restrictive* | | | | |
|---|---|---|---|---|---|---|---|---|
| | | *sub* | *obj* | *sub* | *obj* | *totals* | | *%* |
| who(m) | personal | 6 | 3 | 7 | 9 | 25 | 25 | 16 |
| | non-personal | 0 | 0 | 0 | 0 | 0 | | |
| which | personal | 0 | 1 | 0 | 0 | 1 | 30 | 19 |
| | non-personal | 1 | 18 | 6 | 4 | 29 | | |
| that | personal | 32 | 0 | 5 | 0 | 37 | 62 | 39 |
| | non-personal | 19 | 4 | 2 | 0 | 25 | | |
| zero | personal | 5 | 5 | 0 | 0 | 10 | 43 | 27 |
| | non-personal | 5 | 28 | 0 | 0 | 33 | | |
| | | | | | | N=160 | | |

since Shakespeare's use of 'which' with personal antecedents far exceeds his use of 'who' with non-personal ones. The effect of this can be seen in the figures for the two versions of *Richard II*, where Theobald's intervention results in an increase in the proportion of 'who' forms, and a decrease in the proportion of 'which' forms (see graph 5.10). Similarly, *Double Falshood* shows a higher proportion of 'who(m)' forms than *Henry VIII* and *The Two Noble Kinsmen* (16 per cent against 7–9 per cent), and a low proportion of 'which' forms (19 per cent against a range of 19–23 per cent in the collaborations). Similarly it can be seen from his version of *Richard II* that the effect of Theobald adapting Shakespearean text is to increase the proportion of zero relatives (which move from 10 per cent in the original to 18 per cent in the adaptation). This shifts the usage in the direction of Theobald's own usage of zero (23 per cent in *The Persian Princess*). The relatively high rate of zero forms in *Double Falshood* (27 per cent against 19–22 per cent in the collaborations) can be expected if we assume an increase in zero forms in Shakespeare-derived portions of the text, coupled with the high rates already likely to be present in the Fletcherian sections.

One piece of relativisation evidence which is difficult to fit into an assumed Theobald adaptation of a Shakespeare and Fletcher collaboration is the low rate of 'that' relativisation in *Double Falshood*: 39 per cent. This is

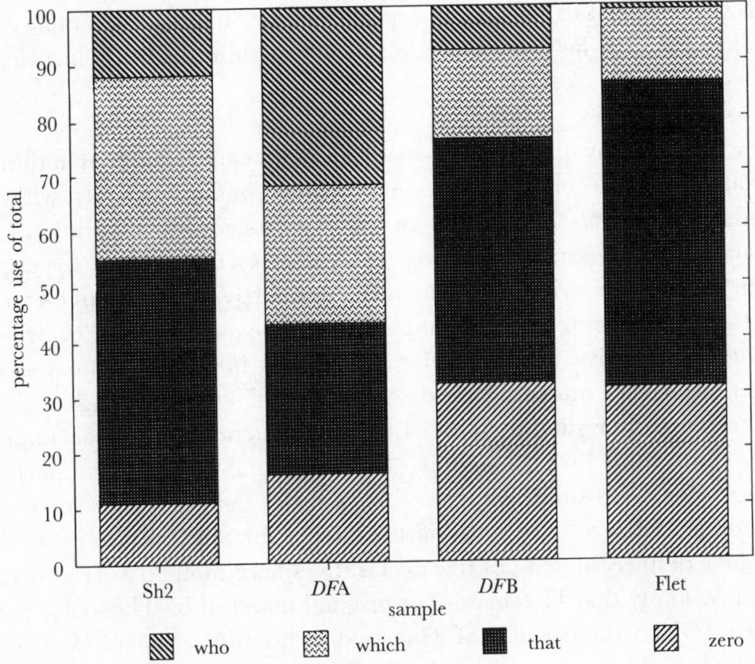


Graph 5.12 Relative marker use in *Double Falshood*

lower than the rates for 'that' in the collaborations, and in Theobald's *The Persian Princess* (52 per cent). Certainly, in his adaptation of *Richard II*, Theobald reduces the 'that' relativisation rate from 51 per cent to 48 per cent, but this slight shift is no evidence for a tendency on Theobald's part to alter Shakespearean 'that' forms systematically. Assuming that 'Cardenio', if it existed, would have had a 'that' relativisation rate similar to the other two Shakespeare–Fletcher collaborations, there is a 'drop' of about 10 per cent in the proportion of 'that' relatives from that expected in *Double Falshood* to that found. A possible, but highly speculative explanation, is that at some stage 'that' relatives have been replaced by zero forms – perhaps by a restoration adapter before Theobald trying to 'correct' Shakespeare and Fletcher's hypermetrical lines.

Graph 5.12 gives the evidence for a collaborative manuscript lying behind *Double Falshood*. Comparing the relative choices in the 'Shakespearean' (A) and 'Fletcherian' (B) sections suggested above, it will be seen that the results for these two sections do indeed suggest that there is evidence for there being two hands involved in the play – one of which has a markedly more formal relativisation strategy than the other. Comparing these sections to the Shakespeare and Fletcher comparison samples, it will be seen that section B shows a strikingly good fit to the Fletcher comparison sample, and even section A can be seen to depart from the Shakespeare sample in the predicted ways: 'who' forms increase, possibly at the expense of 'which' forms.

*Summary*

Stressing the many qualifications made above, it can be said that nothing in the auxiliary 'do' or relativisation evidence conflicts strongly with the notion that *Double Falshood* is an eighteenth-century adaptation of a collaboration between Shakespeare and Fletcher. Of the other two hypotheses given earlier, this evidence is much less supportive of the source-text for *Double Falshood* being solely by Shakespeare (the auxiliary 'do' evidence is strongly supportive of there being two hands in the play), and makes forgery look very unlikely indeed. Auxiliary 'do' evidence suggests that a Shakespearean original underlies 1.02, and Fletcherian originals underlie 2.03, 4.01, and 5.02. Generally, both types of evidence support the suggestion of most studies that the early parts of *Double Falshood* (up to and including 2.02) are those with most evidence for Shakespeare's presence. The lack of unregulated positive declaratives here though, as elsewhere in the play, imply that Fletcherian, or original material by Theobald, is also present. Given the practice of Theobald in adapting *Richard II*, it seems highly likely that most scenes in *Double Falshood* mix material from different scenes of any original text: we should not expect to be able to produce scene-by-scene ascriptions of *Double Falshood* to its putative grandparents.

## The Shakespeare–Middleton collaborations

In this section I consider two plays which have been linked with the names of Shakespeare and Middleton: *Timon of Athens* and *Macbeth*. The structure of each study is the same as that used in the previous section.

### *Timon of Athens*

There is now a considerable body of evidence which agrees that *Timon of Athens* is a collaboration between Shakespeare and Thomas Middleton (see summary in Wells *et al.* 1987:127–8 of work by Lake (1975), Jackson (1979), and Holdsworth (1982)). This study will examine the socio-historical linguistic evidence for and against collaboration in the play, and will specifically analyse Lake's suggested division.

*Auxiliary 'do' evidence*

The overall regulation rate for the play is 84 per cent – at the upper limit of, but not outside, the Shakespeare comparison sample. As is often the case, many scenes give too small a sample to be judged, but of those where N is greater than or equal to 50, 1.01 and 4.03a would be assigned to

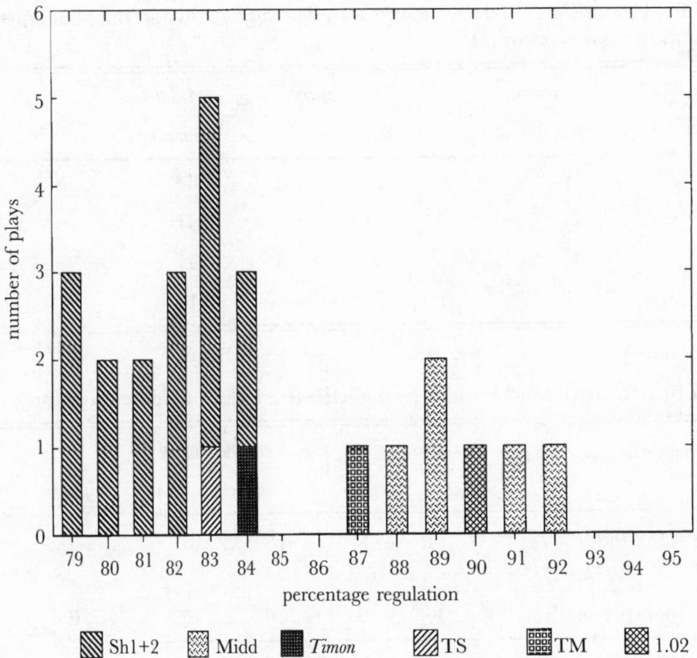


Graph 5.13 Auxiliary 'do' regulation in *Timon of Athens* and Lake's division

Shakespeare. Perhaps most significantly, 1.02 (90 per cent, N = 94) comes out as strongly unShakespearean and within the Middleton comparison sample range. This result is particularly marked because of the 82 per cent regulation shown by 1.01 (N = 111) – that two scenes of more or less equal length should vary by 8 per cent is strongly suggestive of there being two hands in the play (see graph 5.13).

The figures for the Shakespearean and Middletonian sections of the play as defined by Lake provide broad support for his division, with his claimed Middleton (TM) scenes having a regulation rate of 87 per cent (N = 303) and his Shakespearean (TS) 83 per cent (N = 467). A 4 per cent difference is not clinching evidence, even though 87 per cent regulation in a Shakespeare sample would seem very high when N = 303 – but as can be seen from graph 5.13, the Shakespeare and Middleton comparison samples are themselves only 4 per cent apart, suggesting that auxiliary 'do' differences between the two writers are not as great as they are between Shakespeare and Fletcher. None the less, the evidence from scene 1.02 remains strongly suggestive of there being a non-Shakespearean presence in the play – and there is nothing in the auxiliary 'do' evidence which would rule Middleton out from being that presence (raw totals and scene-by-scene figures for *Timon of Athens* can be found in the Statistical Appendix).

Table 5.9 Proportions of relative markers in *Timon of Athens* and the Shakespeare and Middleton comparison samples

| | Timon *whole text* | *Shakespeare Sample* | *Middleton Sample* |
|---|---|---|---|
| who | 16 | 12 | 8 |
| which | 27 | 33 | 13 |
| that | 47 | 44 | 55 |
| zero | 10 | 11 | 24 |

Table 5.10 Relative markers in *Timon of Athens* – Lake's Middleton claim

| | | *restrictive* | | *non-restrictive* | | | | |
|---|---|---|---|---|---|---|---|---|
| | | *sub* | *obj* | *sub* | *obj* | *totals* | | *%* |
| | personal | 1 | 0 | 3 | 1 | 5 | | |
| who(m) | | | | | | | 5 | 8 |
| | non-personal | 0 | 0 | 0 | 0 | 0 | | |
| | personal | 1 | 0 | 0 | 0 | 1 | | |
| which | | | | | | | 13 | 21 |
| | non-personal | 2 | 4 | 4 | 2 | 12 | | |
| | personal | 20 | 0 | 3 | 0 | 23 | | |
| that | | | | | | | 43 | 61 |
| | non-personal | 11 | 3 | 0 | 0 | 14 | | |
| | personal | 2 | 0 | 0 | 0 | 2 | | |
| zero | | | | | | | 6 | 10 |
| | non-personal | 2 | 2 | 0 | 0 | 4 | | |
| | | | | | | N=61 | | |

*Relative marker evidence*

As table 5.9 shows, relativisation in the whole text of *Timon of Athens* is closer to that of Shakespeare than Middleton – especially in the high values for 'who' and 'which', and the low rate of zero forms. As with auxiliary 'do', the overall results therefore do not necessitate a theory of collaboration at all.

However, also as with auxiliary 'do' evidence (for scenes 1.01 and 1.02) there is more detailed evidence which *does* support the theory of collaboration. This evidence is given in tables 5.10 and 5.11, which show detailed figures for relative markers in Lake's suggested divisions of *Timon of Athens*.

Table 5.11 Relative markers in *Timon of Athens* – Lake's Shakespeare claim

| | | *restrictive* | | *non-restrictive* | | | | |
|---|---|---|---|---|---|---|---|---|
| | | *sub* | *obj* | *sub* | *obj* | *totals* | | *%* |
| who(m) | personal | 1 | 7 | 7 | 5 | 20 | 22 | 20 |
| | non-personal | 1 | 0 | 0 | 1 | 2 | | |
| which | personal | 5 | 0 | 1 | 0 | 6 | 32 | 30 |
| | non-personal | 10 | 6 | 5 | 5 | 26 | | |
| that | personal | 18 | 1 | 5 | 0 | 24 | 43 | 40 |
| | non-personal | 13 | 2 | 4 | 0 | 19 | | |
| zero | personal | 2 | 0 | 0 | 0 | 2 | 11 | 10 |
| | non-personal | 3 | 6 | 0 | 0 | 9 | | |
| | | | | | | N=108 | | |

The key feature here is the fact that the 'who'/'which' distinction is almost fully observed in the Middleton scenes, but not in the Shakespearean – which is what the comparison samples would lead us to expect in a Shakespeare–Middleton collaboration. However, there may also be grounds for altering some of Lake's ascriptions as the percentage for 'which' use is rather high for Middleton at 21 per cent (against 17 per cent in his highest play), and that for zero is so low (10 per cent as against 18 per cent in his lowest sampled play.

As both of these abnormalities involve a shift towards Shakespearean usage, this either indicates that Middleton is accommodating, or that some Shakespeare scenes have been included in Lake's Middleton section. This latter suggestion is in accord with the 87 per cent regulation rate for Lake's Middleton section, which is high for Shakespeare, but perhaps not high enough for Middleton. In both cases therefore, the evidence shows a shift in the direction of Shakespearean usages.

This can be further seen in graph 5.14, which shows Lake's suggested divisions plotted against the Shakespeare and Middleton comparison samples respectively. Lake's suggested Shakespeare scenes are clearly more like the Shakespeare sample than they are like Middleton's plays; his Middleton scenes show much less similarity to their proposed author.

I do not consider this poor separation in graph 5.14 to be evidence against

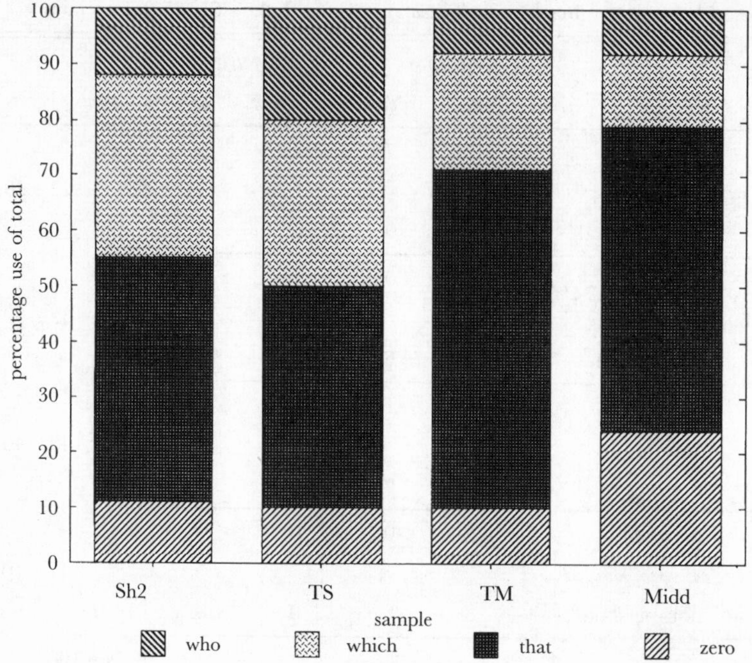


Graph 5.14 Relative marker use in *Timon of Athens*

the collaborative nature of *Timon of Athens*. Either it suggests that there is room for further work to improve the precise division of the play, or it is evidence for a final revision by Shakespeare which involved the alteration of Middleton's relative markers (as has been noted above, this is textually possible).

*Summary*

Auxiliary 'do' and relativisation evidence give broad support for the notion that *Timon of Athens* is a collaboration between Shakespeare and Middleton. Relativisation evidence may suggest that some of the scenes identified by Lake as Middleton's are in fact Shakespeare's, or that Shakespeare prepared the final copy text of the play.

### *Macbeth*

The second play in the Shakespeare canon associated with Middleton is *Macbeth*. The basis for this association is the fact that the two songs called for in the folio text of *Macbeth* can be found in Middleton's play *The Witch*. Since *Macbeth* is short when compared to most of Shakespeare's plays (auxiliary 'do' N for *Macbeth* = 783, against 900–1000 in most of the other plays), and the 'additions' are obviously disposable, it is generally thought that Middleton's presence in this play is probably as an adapter for the stage, rather than as a collaborator (see Wells *et al.* 1987:128–9).

Unfortunately, the suggested additions to *Macbeth* are rather short, and this coupled with the nature of Middleton's supposed role in *Macbeth*, makes it unlikely that socio-historical linguistic evidence will be able to throw much light on the subject. The additions themselves give N values of twenty-two for auxiliary 'do', and three for relatives, and even including the scenes in which the additions appear does not yield significant samples (N = 73 and 14 respectively). Nevertheless, I have included an analysis of *Macbeth* for the sake of completeness, and to illustrate the limitations of the use of this type of evidence.

*Auxiliary 'do' evidence*

The whole text of the play shows a regulation rate of 84 per cent, acceptably Shakespearean, and below the range of any of the other sampled playwrights. Only a few scenes give samples where N is greater than, or equal to, fifty:

1.03 N = 64 75%
2.03 N = 55 86%
3.01 N = 50 80%
4.03 N = 89 85%

but none of these has been claimed as Middleton's, and none looks unShakespearean on this evidence.

Evidence from the two scenes containing the 'additions' (3.05 and 4.01) is based on very small samples, and should therefore be treated carefully. The two scenes together have a regulation rate of 88 per cent (N = 73), which makes them look less 'Shakespearean' than the play as a whole, but not conclusively so on such a small sample.

Removing the 'additions' from these scenes does make them appear more 'Shakespearean': the scenes without the additions have a regulation rate of 86 per cent (N = 51); the additions themselves have a rate of 91 per cent (but N = 22). This is what I would expect, if the additions were by Middleton, but the samples are too small for this to carry much weight.

*Relative marker evidence*

As a whole, the relativisation strategy in *Macbeth* is as would be expected from a Shakespearean play of this date. Since N = 3 for the additions and N = 14 for the scenes in which they appear, relativisation evidence can have nothing to say about the authorship of these scenes.

# Chapter 6

# The Shakespeare apocrypha

## The 1664 folio plays

This section considers the plays which were added to the second issue of the third Shakespeare folio (first issue 1663, second issue 1664): *Pericles*, *The London Prodigal*, *Thomas Lord Cromwell*, *Sir John Oldcastle*, *The Puritan*, *A Yorkshire Tragedy*, and *Locrine*.

### *Pericles*

*Pericles* was first published in 1608 as 'By William Shakespeare', but did not appear in the 1623 first folio. By the time it appeared in the third folio it had gone through six quarto editions. The text we have is highly problematic, and is almost certainly a memorial reconstruction – which of course raises problems for the application of linguistic evidence. Taylor (Wells *et al.* 1987:558) suggests that the reconstruction may have been by George Wilkins, alleged to have collaborated on the play with Shakespeare.

Much recent stylometric work on *Pericles* has tended to strengthen the case for Wilkins as the author of the early part of the play (Chorus 1 to scene 2.05 in the Arden edition), and Shakespeare of the later part (chorus 3 to Epilogue) – see Smith 1987, 1988, 1989, 1992; Jackson 1991, 1993a, 1993b; Wells *et al.* 1987:130 (who doubt Shakespeare's presence in the Epilogue and their scene 18); caution and dissent are sounded by Merriam (1992b) and Sams (1991) respectively. For this reason I include here figures for auxiliary 'do' use and relative marker choice from Wilkins' only unaided play, *The Miseries of Enforced Marriage*.

#### *Auxiliary 'do' evidence*

Graph 6.1 shows the auxiliary 'do' evidence for *Pericles* plotted against the results from the Shakespeare comparison samples. *Pericles* tests as showing 85 per cent regulation; 1 per cent above the highest plays in the comparison samples. Given the present state of knowledge about the significance (or otherwise) of small shifts in regulation rate, even on large samples like these, it is difficult to judge how much weight to put on this result. Of the sixteen

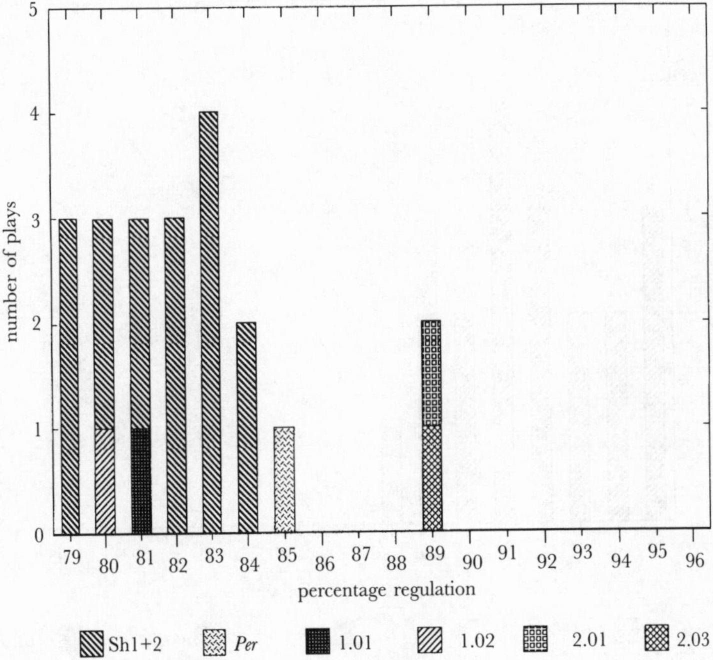


Graph 6.1 Auxiliary 'do' use in *Pericles*

plays in the Shakespeare comparison samples, none is over 84 per cent overall regulation, while of the Shakespearean collaborations studied in the course of this work, all show regulation rates above, or at the top end of, the Shakespeare range. I think this result can therefore be taken as an indication of *some* abnormality in the textual or authorial history of *Pericles*. Given that we know the play to be textually corrupt however, this overall regulation rate cannot on its own be sufficient evidence on which to build a case for the play being collaborative.

Also plotted on graph 6.1 is a selection of those scenes in *Pericles* where N is greater than or equal to 50 (1.01, 1.02, 2.01, 2.03). Those scenes which show high regulation rates do so on N values which are too low to allow confident ascriptions of authorship to be made.

As has been said, much recent work on *Pericles* has tended towards confirming the division of the play into two sections: section A (chorus 1 – 2.05), and section B (chorus 3 to end). Increasingly, section A is ascribed to George Wilkins, and B to Shakespeare. This division and the ascription accord with impressionistic judgements (e.g. that of Northrop Frye 1965:38).

Graph 6.2 shows the regulation rates for sections A and B (*Per*A, *Per*B) plotted against those for the Shakespeare comparison samples, *Pericles* as a

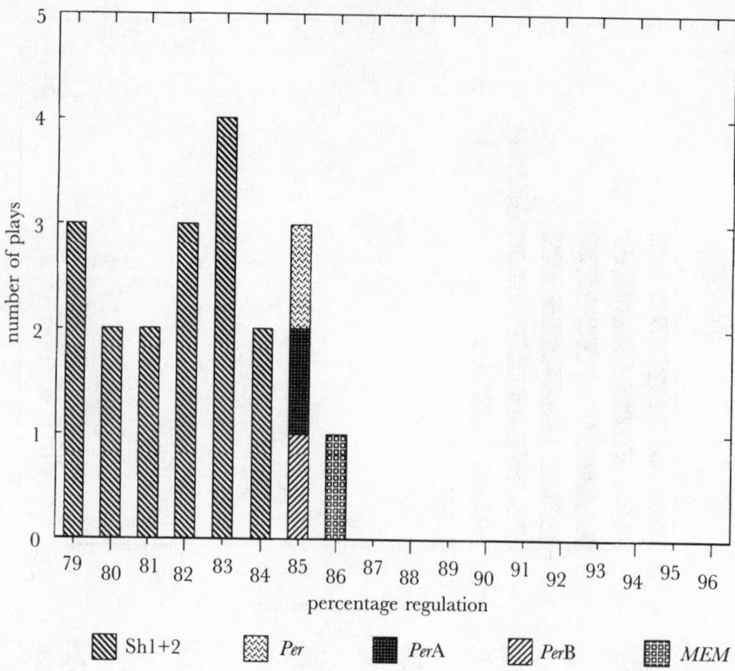


Graph 6.2 Auxiliary 'do' use in *Pericles* sections A and B, and *The Miseries of Enforced Marriage*

whole, and Wilkins' *The Miseries of Enforced Marriage* (*MEM*). Strikingly, it will be noticed that both sections of *Pericles* show regulation rates of 85 per cent, exactly that of the play as a whole. This is initially surprising given the repeated findings of other tests that sections A and B differ linguistically, but this is explained by the result for *The Miseries of Enforced Marriage*, which at 86 per cent regulation is only 1 per cent above the rate of *Pericles*, 2 per cent above the upper limit of the Shakespeare sample. Given this result, it is clear that we should not expect auxiliary 'do' evidence to be able to disentangle the hands of Shakespeare and Wilkins: their usages are too similar.

Auxiliary 'do' can only distinguish between writers if their usages are sufficiently distinct. If, as here, candidates for the authorship of a play have similar usages, then other tests have to be used. The results of this study therefore, which found *Pericles* to lie close to the Shakespeare comparison samples, and to be textually uniform as far as auxiliary 'do' was concerned, do not conflict with the many published studies suggesting that the play is collaborative: if Wilkins *is* Shakespeare's collaborator here, then this is precisely the result we should expect.

On a broader note, this illustrates the necessity for authorship studies to

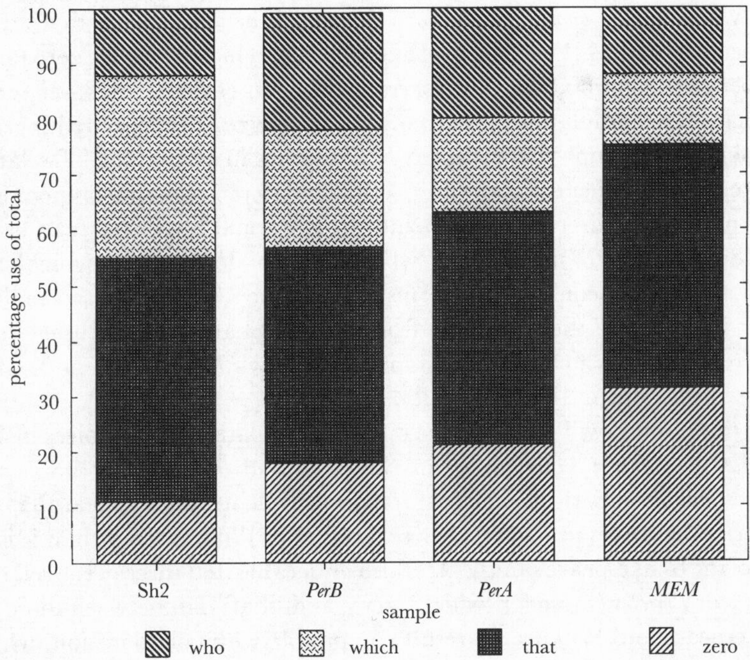


Graph 6.3 Relative marker use in *Pericles* and *The Miseries of Enforced Marriage*

be cumulative, for cases to be built on a variety of independent tests, rather than just one type of evidence.

*Relative marker evidence*

Graph 6.3 shows the relative marker evidence from *Pericles* (sections A and B shown separately) plotted against the result for the late Shakespeare sample and Wilkins' *The Miseries of Enforced Marriage*. Immediately it will be seen that the two sections are more like each other than either is like Shakespeare sample 2. This is surprising, given that section B is supposed to be by Shakespeare, and might seem to tell against collaboration in this text – in terms of socio-historical linguistic evidence, sections A and B of *Pericles* are linguistically similar. Where the auxiliary 'do' evidence for *Pericles* as a whole was very close to normal Shakespearean usage however, the overall relative marker evidence is obviously deviant from the Shakespeare comparison sample.

If we were considering the whole text of *Pericles* as a Shakespearean play, it would have the highest percentage of 'who' forms in either sample (21 per cent against 16 per cent in *The Tempest*); the equal second-lowest 'which' result (19 per cent with *The Two Gentlemen of Verona*, beaten only by the highly unusual *A Comedy of Errors* at 7 per cent); the joint lowest 'that' result (41 per cent with *A Winter's Tale*); and the second highest rate of zero forms (20 per cent, again behind the aberrant *A Comedy of Errors* at 23 per cent).

Such an accumulation of extreme results suggests that something has interfered to disrupt the expected Shakespearean patterning of relative marker choice: either collaboration, scribal interference, or oral or memorial corruption. The direction of the 'shift' from normal Shakespearean usage may be significant – increases in 'who' and zero, decreases in 'which' and 'that'. This is not consistent in terms of Romaine's hierarchy of formality, but it is similar to the departure from normal Shakespearean usage in *A Comedy of Errors*, which also shows increases in 'who' and zero – in theory, opposed in terms of their formality.

At this point it will be useful to consider the relativisation choices in *The Miseries of Enforced Marriage* against those in both *Pericles* and the second Shakespeare comparison sample. From graph 6.3, it would appear that the pattern of relatives in *Pericles* is closer to that of Wilkins' play than it is to that of the Shakespeare sample. It is also noticeable that three of the relative values for *Pericles* (those for 'which', zero, and 'that') fall between those for Shakespeare and Wilkins – a result compatible with collaboration, which would tend to produce an overall average usage midway between those of the collaborators.

The confused textual history of *Pericles* may account for the very high 'who' result, since relative markers are open to corruption during textual transmission (as has been explained, auxiliary 'do' evidence would not be affected by this process, but relative markers could be more easily substituted for each other). As with *Double Falshood*, there may be a case for suspecting that personal 'which' forms have been altered to 'who' since only three out of forty-nine 'which' forms in the play are personal (Shakespeare's later plays average seven or eight personal 'which' forms per play).

Looking at the relativisation evidence in more detail (tables 6.1 and 6.2), there is more evidence in support of there being two hands in the text of *Pericles*. The figures show that the 'who'/'which' distinction is more firmly in place in section B than in section A, which is particularly marked by a series of non-personal 'who' forms – six forms in scenes 1.01, 1.02, and 1.04. Although non-personal 'who' is normally taken to be a feature of Shakespeare's idiolect, this usage is much higher than his usual frequency: only eight non-personal 'who' forms appear in the five plays of sample one; and twenty in sample two. Here there are six in three scenes.

Looking at table 6.3, however, it can be seen that there are seven non-personal 'who' forms in *The Miseries of Enforced Marriage* – supporting the suggestion that section A may be by Wilkins.

A further piece of relativisation evidence separates the early scenes of

Table 6.1 Relatives in *Pericles* – section A (chorus 1 – 2.05)

| | | *restrictive* | | *non-restrictive* | | | | |
|---|---|---|---|---|---|---|---|---|
| | | *sub* | *obj* | *sub* | *obj* | *totals* | | *%* |
| who(m) | personal | 6 | 2 | 9 | 4 | 21 | 27 | 20 |
| | non-personal | 1 | 0 | 5 | 0 | 6 | | |
| which | personal | 2 | 0 | 0 | 0 | 2 | 23 | 17 |
| | non-personal | 3 | 3 | 9 | 6 | 21 | | |
| that | personal | 22 | 0 | 8 | 0 | 30 | 56 | 42 |
| | non-personal | 14 | 6 | 6 | 0 | 26 | | |
| zero | personal | 5 | 1 | 0 | 0 | 6 | 28 | 21 |
| | non-personal | 9 | 8 | 4 | 1 | 22 | | |
| | | | | | | N=134 | | |

Table 6.2 Relatives in *Pericles* – section B (chorus 3 – epilogue)

| | | *restrictive* | | *non-restrictive* | | | | |
|---|---|---|---|---|---|---|---|---|
| | | *sub* | *obj* | *sub* | *obj* | *totals* | | *%* |
| who(m) | personal | 4 | 1 | 14 | 7 | 26 | 26 | 21 |
| | non-personal | 0 | 0 | 0 | 0 | 0 | | |
| which | personal | 0 | 0 | 1 | 0 | 1 | 26 | 21 |
| | non-personal | 6 | 2 | 10 | 7 | 25 | | |
| that | personal | 24 | 2 | 3 | 0 | 29 | 48 | 39 |
| | non-personal | 12 | 5 | 2 | 0 | 19 | | |
| zero | personal | 4 | 1 | 0 | 0 | 5 | 22 | 18 |
| | non-personal | 5 | 12 | 0 | 0 | 17 | | |
| | | | | | | N=122 | | |

Table 6.3 Relatives in *The Miseries of Enforced Marriage*

| | | *restrictive* | | *non-restrictive* | | | |
|---|---|---|---|---|---|---|---|
| | | *sub* | *obj* | *sub* | *obj* | *totals* | *%* |
| who(m) | personal | 1 | 6 | 13 | 5 | 25 | |
| | | | | | | | 32 12 |
| | non-personal | 1 | 1 | 5 | 0 | 7 | |
| which | personal | 1 | 0 | 0 | 0 | 1 | |
| | | | | | | | 35 13 |
| | non-personal | 3 | 8 | 14 | 9 | 34 | |
| that | personal | 49 | 4 | 24 | 0 | 77 | |
| | | | | | | | 116 44 |
| | non-personal | 15 | 11 | 12 | 1 | 39 | |
| zero | personal | 21 | 4 | 6 | 0 | 31 | |
| | | | | | | | 83 31 |
| | non-personal | 10 | 40 | 2 | 0 | 52 | |
| | | | | | | N=266 | |

*Pericles* from the rest of the play and links them to Wilkins: the syntactic function of zero forms. In the early scenes of section A there are, arguably, up to five non-restrictive zero forms (in the following quotations, zero is represented by (0)):

> Bad child, worse father, to intice his owne
> To euill, (0) should be done by none[. . .]
>
> (Chorus 1, 27–8)

> For Vice repeated, is like the wandring Wind,
> (0) Blowes dust in others eyes to spread it selfe[. . .]
>
> (1.01.96–7)

> I sought the purchase of a glorious beautie,
> From whence an issue I might propogate,
> (0) Are armes to Princes, and bring ioies to subiects[. . .]
>
> (1.02.72–4)

> And these our Ships (0) you happily may thinke,
> Are like the Troian Horse, (0) was stuft within
> With bloody veines expecting ouerthrow[. . .]
>
> (1.04.92–4)

This is a highly marked form – and it is completely absent from either Shakespeare comparison sample (indeed, it is a very rare form indeed – only occurring in the Massinger and Fletcher comparison samples). The concentration of so many of these forms in such a short section of the play, and their absence from the rest of the play, looks significant – even more so when it is known that *The Miseries of Enforced Marriage* has eight such forms (table 6.3).

There are then two small pieces of relativisation evidence which distinguish the early part of *Pericles* from the later part, and which conform to the usage of Wilkins more than to the usage of Shakespeare. Of the two, I would place much more weight on the use of non-restrictive zero forms as an indicator of non-Shakespearean material, since the distinction in use of non-personal 'who' is a matter of degree only.

The overall relativisation evidence however suggests that the proposed sections of *Pericles* have a non-Shakespearean influence in common – that is, that sections A *and* B have unShakespearean relatives – and this is confirmed by further analysis of the pattern of zero forms in the play.

In the comparison samples, Shakespeare's zero forms show a consistent preference for the object position: in each sample, only 17 per cent of zero forms appear in the subject position. It will be remembered that the use of zero forms is eventually grammatically conditioned, so that in Present-day Standard English the use of zero in the subject position is very rare indeed (although it is in fact quite common in most non-standard varieties). *Pericles* has a very high rate of zero forms in the subject position – 54 per cent overall – and this is true for both sections (section A= 64 per cent; section B=41 per cent). *The Miseries of Enforced Marriage* shows a subject zero rate of 47 per cent.

### *Summary*

Because of the similarity of Shakespeare and Wilkins' usages, auxiliary 'do' evidence can tell us little about the authorship of *Pericles*. Relativisation evidence however, supports the notion that *Pericles* is a collaboration between Wilkins and Shakespeare, with Wilkins' influence most evident in the early part of the play. Certain non-Shakespearean features of the relativisation pattern are consistent across the proposed division of the play however, and I take this to be evidence supporting Taylor's suggestion that Wilkins was responsible for the reconstruction of the text. The differences between section B and Shakespeare's normal relativisation strategies mean that we must posit some kind of textual interference between it, and a supposed Shakespearean original: memorial reconstruction by Wilkins of a Shakespearean original is consistent with the evidence I have presented here.

### The London Prodigal

*The London Prodigal* was published in a quarto in 1605 ascribed on the title page to 'William Shakespeare', and then appeared in the 1664 folio. As Taylor states, 'No serious scholar has taken the attribution seriously' (Wells *et al.* 1987:138). Dekker, Wilkins, and Middleton have been mentioned as possible authors, but the most rigorous work on the authorship of the play appears in a doctoral dissertation by Thomas Merriam (currently under examination). It would be unfair to discuss the details of Merriam's work in advance of its publication, but in his thesis he makes a serious linguistic and thematic case for John Fletcher as a possible author of the play.

*Auxiliary 'do' evidence*

Graph 6.4 shows the auxiliary 'do' evidence for *The London Prodigal* (*LP*: see the Statistical Appendix for raw figures and a scene by scene analysis). Considering the play as a whole first, it will be seen that the overall regulation rate is 86 per cent – slightly higher than the Shakespeare comparison sample, and much lower than the Fletcher comparison sample. This makes Fletcherian authorship of the whole text very unlikely, and supports the lack of belief in the title page ascription.

At 86 per cent, the play falls within the comparison samples of two of the authors who have been suggested as possible candidates: Dekker and

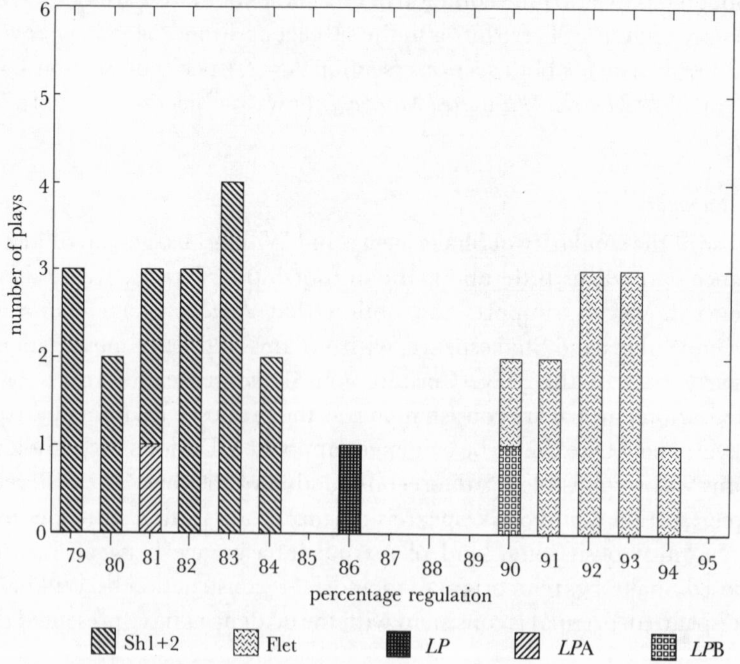


Graph 6.4 Auxiliary 'do' regulation in *The London Prodigal*

Wilkins (*Miseries of Enforced Marriage*). However, I do not propose to follow-up these potential ascriptions (which are not supported by relativisation evidence), since auxiliary 'do' evidence is strongly supportive of there being two hands present in this play. The raw figures for unregulated positive declarative forms in the play are as follows:

| 1.01 | 1.02 | 2.01 | 2.02 | 2.03 | 2.04 | 3.01 | 3.02 | 3.03 |
|---|---|---|---|---|---|---|---|---|
| 0 | 0 | 1 | 0 | 2 | 1 | 0 | 10 | 10 |

| 4.01 | 4.02 | 4.03 | 5.01 |
|---|---|---|---|
| 0 | 3 | 3 | 7 |

and the apparent shift in usage in scenes 3.02, 3.03, and 5.01 is confirmed by the overall percentage rates given for these scenes (termed section *LP*A – 81 per cent) against the remainder of the play (section *LP*B – 90 per cent) shown on graph 6.4.

This division of the play clearly shows two auxiliary 'do' strategies at work in the text of the play: one highly regulated, the other much less so. On this division at least, section B certainly could be by Fletcher, and section A by Shakespeare.

### *Relative marker evidence*

Shakespeare scholars will probably be relieved to discover that the relativisation evidence from *The London Prodigal* makes it unlikely that he wrote the section A scenes, since the 'who' and 'which' rates for these scenes, and indeed the whole play, are far below his usual rates (these figures are given in the Statistical Appendix and plotted onto graph 6.5).

Relativisation evidence from this text does not conflict with the possibility of Fletcherian authorship, given the low incidence of 'who' usage. Nor, though, can it be used to rule out either Middleton (whose usages are quite close to those found in *The London Prodigal*) or Dekker (whose relatives are so unpredictable that he could never be ruled out of the authorship of a play on their basis alone).

Although the sample sizes are small (N = 55 and 49 respectively), it may be worth noting that there are no differences in terms of relativisation between sections A and B. Given the gap between them in terms of auxiliary 'do' evidence, I would not want to question the dual authorship of these sections, but it may be the case that one of the collaborators 'corrected' his partner's relatives in a final version.

### *Summary*

On the basis of auxiliary 'do' evidence, there would appear to be two hands in *The London Prodigal* – one highly regulated, the other unregulated. This would conflict with Merriam's claim that the play is wholly Fletcherian.

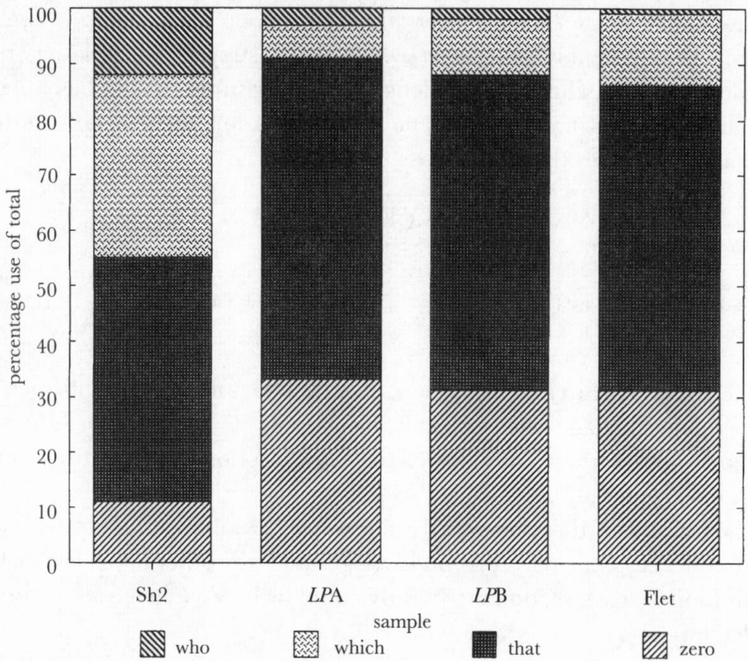


Graph 6.5 Relative marker use in *The London Prodigal*

From those sampled in this study, the author of the regulated section B scenes *could* have been Fletcher, Middleton, or Dekker. The section A scenes fall within the Shakespearean comparison sample, but Shakespeare is ruled out as author by relativisation evidence. As was the case with *Pericles*, inconsistent auxiliary 'do' usage across proposed divisions of the play, and consistent relativisation, may suggest a final revision by one of the collaborators.

### *Thomas, Lord Cromwell*

*Thomas, Lord Cromwell* was first published in 1602 and was, according to the title page of the quarto, 'Written by W.S.'. The play was included in the 1664 folio, but as Taylor reports, 'no one this century has supported the attribution to Shakespeare' (Wells *et al.* 1987:135).

#### *Auxiliary 'do' evidence*

The auxiliary 'do' evidence from *Thomas, Lord Cromwell* (*TLC*) is plotted onto graph 6.6 (raw figures are given in the Statistical Appendix). From the graph it will be seen that the whole text of *Thomas, Lord Cromwell* gives a regulation rate of only 77 per cent. In terms of the plays sampled for this

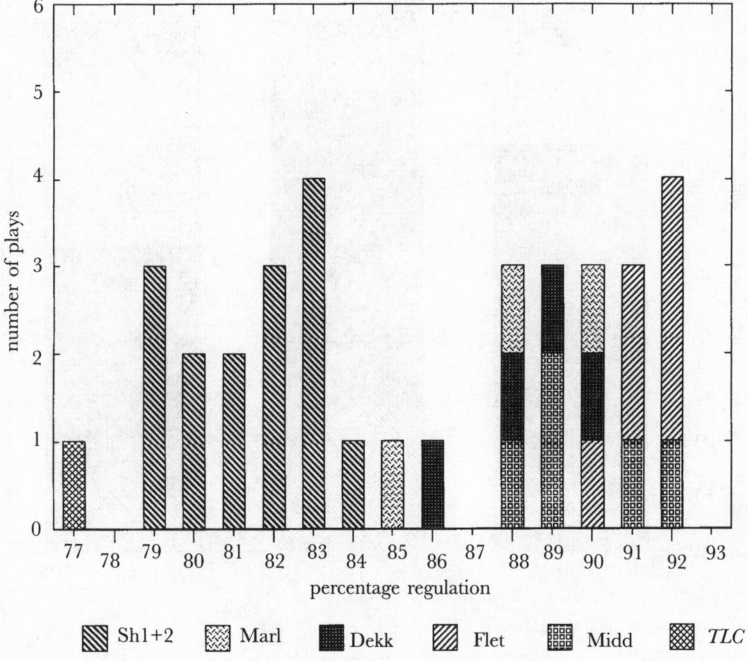


Graph 6.6 Auxiliary 'do' regulation in *Thomas, Lord Cromwell* and samples

study, this is an extraordinary result: it is the least regulated play yet found, and of the named playwrights sampled, only Shakespeare comes anywhere close to this rate. Given the consistency of usage in the sixteen Shakespeare plays sampled though, this result (2 per cent below the lower limit of the Shakespeare sample) makes *Thomas, Lord Cromwell* look unShakespearean. If the whole text was written by one writer, that writer probably does not appear in any of the other comparison samples.

A scene-by-scene analysis does not support suggestions that the play is collaborative: there is no clear difference in auxiliary 'do' use between scenes which give significant samples (see Statistical Appendix). This could merely mean, of course, that any collaborators shared equally unregulated usages, but given the extremely unregulated nature of the text I think this is unlikely. Judging by the idiolects sampled so far, the chances are that of any two collaborators, one will have a regulation rate which is at least in the mid-eighties. Pairing such a writer with an extremely unregulated one will tend to produce a play with an overall regulation rate which falls between the usages of both writers (as happens with Shakespeare and Fletcher in their collaborations). Thus the effect of collaboration is likely to be to reduce extreme linguistic usage – and any play which manifests this is unlikely to be collaborative.

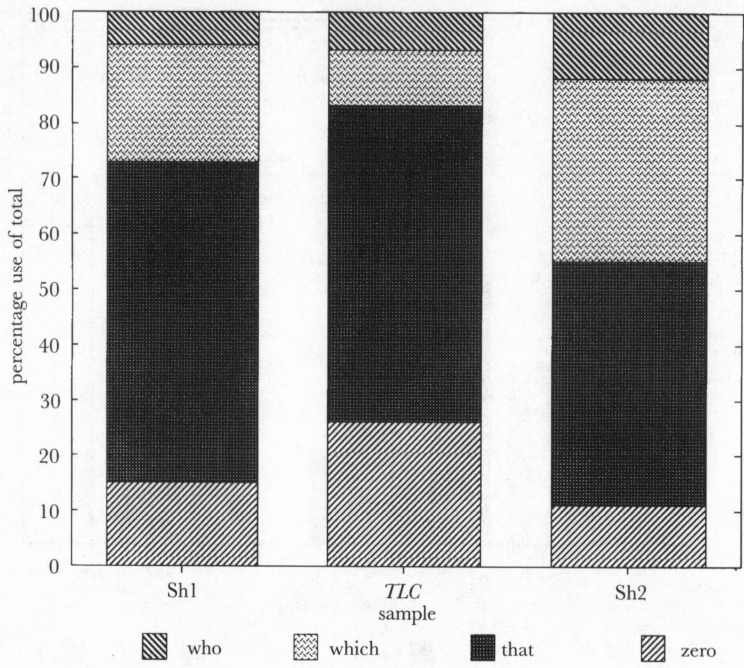


Graph 6.7 Relative marker use in *Thomas, Lord Cromwell*

*Relative marker evidence*

Evidence from relative markers tends to confirm that from auxiliary 'do': Shakespeare is unlikely to have been the author of this play because the 'who'/'which' distinction is fully in place, 'which' usage is too low, and zero usage too high (see graph 6.7 and the Statistical Appendix). The fact that the 'who'/'which' distinction is fully in place throughout the text tends to confirm the suggestion that the play is not collaborative. Given the auxiliary 'do' result, there is little point in comparing the relatives here to those in any of the other comparison samples.

From a historical linguistic point of view however, it is worth noting that highly unregulated auxiliary 'do' usage is here accompanied by 'standardised' use of 'who' and 'which': as was found with Shakespeare and Fletcher, it is not possible to predict relativisation strategies from auxiliary 'do' use.

*Summary*

Auxiliary 'do' evidence suggests that *Thomas, Lord Cromwell* is not by Shakespeare or any other of the writers sampled in this study. The play is by a writer with an extraordinarily unregulated usage of auxiliary 'do'.

Auxiliary 'do' evidence does not support the suggestion that this play is collaborative – and the extreme result makes this unlikely, since the effect of collaboration is to dilute extreme usage and make it appear less so. This finding is supported by relativisation evidence, which also supports the finding that the play is probably not by Shakespeare.

Given the extreme nature of the auxiliary 'do' result here, if there are any extant plays by the writer of *Thomas, Lord Cromwell*, and they are sampled at some point in the future, it should be relatively easy to identify him or her.

## *Sir John Oldcastle*

*Sir John Oldcastle* exists in two quarto editions, both dated 1600, although the second was in fact printed for Thomas Pavier in 1619. In this second edition the play was ascribed to Shakespeare, which presumably accounts for its appearance in the 1664 folio. Alone amongst the 1664 plays we have contemporary evidence for the true authorship of the play: *Henslowe's Diary* records that it is a collaboration between Anthony Munday, Michael Drayton, Robert Wilson, and Richard Hathway (Wells *et al.* 1987:140).

### *Auxiliary 'do' evidence*

The auxiliary 'do' evidence from *Sir John Oldcastle* is shown in table 6.4. Although the overall regulation rate of 85 per cent would not in fact rule out Shakespearean authorship, it can clearly be seen from the results for individual scenes such as 1.03 and 3.01 that auxiliary 'do' evidence supports the contemporary record that the play is collaborative. In all, seven scenes give significant samples, and these fall into a highly regulated group (1.03, 2.01, 4.01, 4.02 – 88–94 per cent) and an unregulated group (1.02, 3.01, 5.11 – 70–81 per cent). Thus, even if we did not have Henslowe's evidence, auxiliary 'do' evidence would lead us to assume that there were at least two hands in the play.

### *Relative marker evidence*

Evidence for relative markers in the play is given in table 6.5. With four hands at work in the play, it is not possible to disentangle distinct relativisation strategies since relative markers are too infrequent for patterns to emerge except over very long stretches of text. I have analysed the relatives in the two groups of scenes identified above, but even here no clear pattern emerges, suggesting that the two groups contain work by more than two writers.

Table 6.4 Auxiliary 'do' use in *Sir John Oldcastle*

| | *P* | *1.01* | *1.02* | *1.03* | *2.01* | *2.02* | *2.03* | *3.01* | *3.02* | *3.03* | *3.04* | *4.01* | *4.02* | *4.03* | *4.04* | *4.05* | *5.01* | *5.04* |
|---|---|---|---|---|---|---|---|---|---|---|---|---|---|---|---|---|---|---|
| reg | 5 | 20 | 35 | 69 | 58 | 14 | 30 | 58 | 26 | 14 | 28 | 68 | 53 | 33 | 19 | 16 | 12 | 6 |
| unreg | 0 | 5 | 15 | 8 | 4 | 2 | 9 | 14 | 1 | 0 | 7 | 7 | 7 | 8 | 2 | 2 | 3 | 0 |
| N = | 5 | 25 | 50 | 77 | 62 | 16 | 39 | 72 | 27 | 14 | 35 | 75 | 60 | 41 | 21 | 18 | 15 | 6 |
| %reg | 100 | 80 | 70 | 90 | 94 | 88 | 77 | 81 | 96 | 100 | 80 | 91 | 88 | 81 | 91 | 89 | 80 | 100 |

| | *5.05* | *5.06* | *5.07* | *5.08* | *5.02* | *5.03* | *5.09* | *5.10* | *5.11* | *total* |
|---|---|---|---|---|---|---|---|---|---|---|
| reg | 8 | 1 | 4 | 20 | 8 | 5 | 29 | 11 | 44 | 694 |
| unreg | 1 | 0 | 0 | 4 | 0 | 0 | 8 | 1 | 13 | 121 |
| N = | 9 | 1 | 4 | 24 | 8 | 5 | 37 | 12 | 57 | 815 |
| %reg | 89 | 100 | 100 | 83 | 100 | 100 | 78 | 92 | 77 | 85 |

Table 6.5 Relatives in *Sir John Oldcastle*

| | | restrictive | | non-restrictive | | | | |
|---|---|---|---|---|---|---|---|---|
| | | *sub* | *obj* | *sub* | *obj* | *totals* | | % |
| who(m) | personal | 1 | 0 | 8 | 8 | 17 | 18 | 10 |
| | non-personal | 0 | 0 | 0 | 1 | 1 | | |
| which | personal | 1 | 0 | 3 | 1 | 5 | 28 | 16 |
| | non-personal | 3 | 5 | 4 | 11 | 23 | | |
| that | personal | 45 | 1 | 6 | 2 | 54 | 78 | 45 |
| | non-personal | 16 | 7 | 1 | 0 | 24 | | |
| zero | personal | 9 | 5 | 2 | 0 | 16 | 50 | 29 |
| | non-personal | 10 | 24 | 0 | 0 | 34 | | |
| | | | | | | N=174 | | |

## *The Puritan; or, The Widow of Watling Street*

Published in 1607 as by 'W.S.', *The Puritan* subsequently appeared in the 1664 folio, but modern commentators, most significantly Lake (1975) and Jackson (1979), ascribe the play to Middleton (Wells *et al.* 1987:140).

### *Auxiliary 'do' evidence*

Graph 6.8 shows the auxiliary 'do' evidence for *The Puritan* (*Pur*). At 93 per cent regulation for the whole text, the play is certainly not by Shakespeare, and this result puts it one percentage point above the upper limit of the Middleton comparison sample – an acceptable variation given that this sample consists of five plays, rather than the sixteen of the Shakespeare sample. There is no suggestion from the scene-by-scene analysis that the play is collaborative (see the table of raw figures in the Statistical Appendix).

### *Relative marker evidence*

Table 6.6 shows the relativisation evidence from *The Puritan*. From this it will be seen that the 'who'/'which' distinction is observed in this play – which conforms to Middletonian, rather than Shakespearean, practice.

Graph 6.9 shows the results from *The Puritan* plotted against those for the

Table 6.6 Relativisation in *The Puritan*

| | | *restrictive* | | *non-restrictive* | | | | |
|---|---|---|---|---|---|---|---|---|
| | | *sub* | *obj* | *sub* | *obj* | *totals* | | *%* |
| who(m) | personal | 3 | 2 | 1 | 3 | 9 | 9 | 10 |
| | non-personal | 0 | 0 | 0 | 0 | 0 | | |
| which | personal | 1 | 0 | 0 | 0 | 1 | 22 | 24 |
| | non-personal | 4 | 6 | 7 | 4 | 21 | | |
| that | personal | 35 | 2 | 5 | 0 | 42 | 55 | 60 |
| | non-personal | 7 | 6 | 0 | 0 | 13 | | |
| zero | personal | 4 | 0 | 0 | 0 | 4 | 6 | 7 |
| | non-personal | 1 | 1 | 0 | 0 | 2 | | |
| | | | | | | N=92 | | |

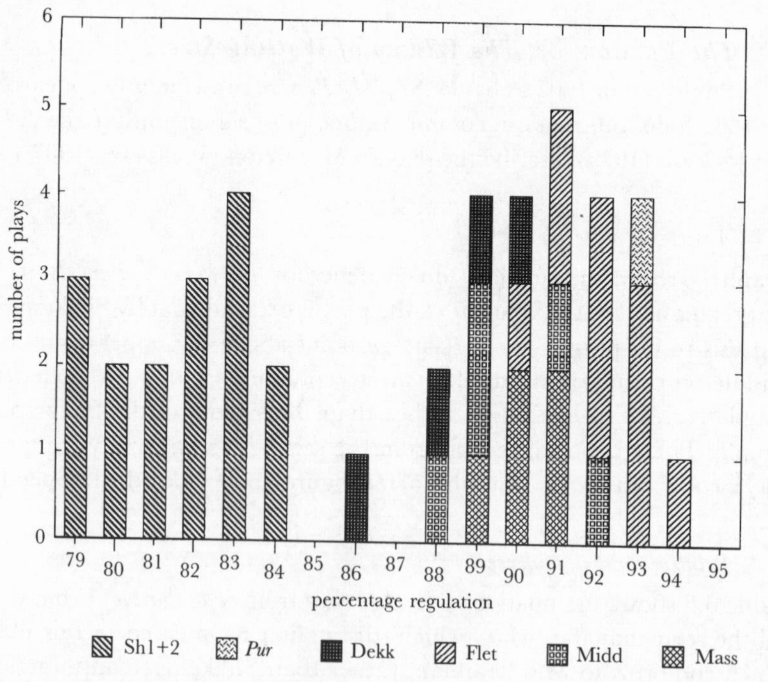


Graph 6.8 Auxiliary 'do' use in *The Puritan* and samples

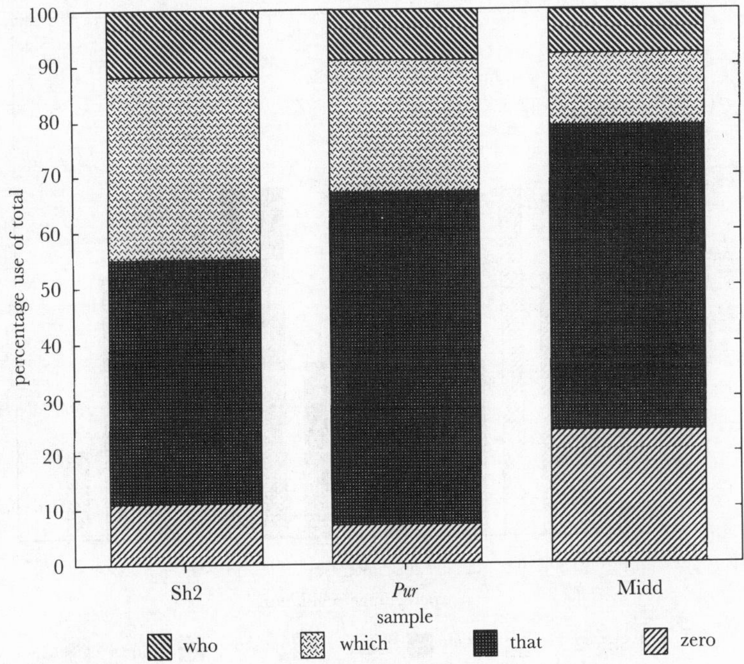


Graph 6.9 Relative marker use in *The Puritan*

second Shakespeare and Middleton comparison samples. Although relativisation evidence in general does not conflict with the ascription of *The Puritan* to Middleton, neither is it strongly in support of that ascription. As might be expected given the auxiliary 'do' evidence, three out of four markers give results outside the range of the late Shakespeare sample. When *The Puritan* is compared to the Middleton sample however, it will be seen that the rate of zero usage in this play is very low compared with Middleton's normal usage. Given the textual instability of relatives, and the fact that all of the other relatives give results within the range of the Middleton comparison sample, this result can not be conclusive against Middleton's presence in the play, but it does perhaps throw some doubt on either the ascription, or the textual history of the play.

### *Summary*

Auxiliary 'do' evidence is strongly against Shakespearean authorship of *The Puritan*, and is not inconsistent with the ascription to Middleton. Relativisation evidence does not conflict directly with this ascription, but any theory which would ascribe the play to Middleton needs to account for the lack of zero forms in the text.

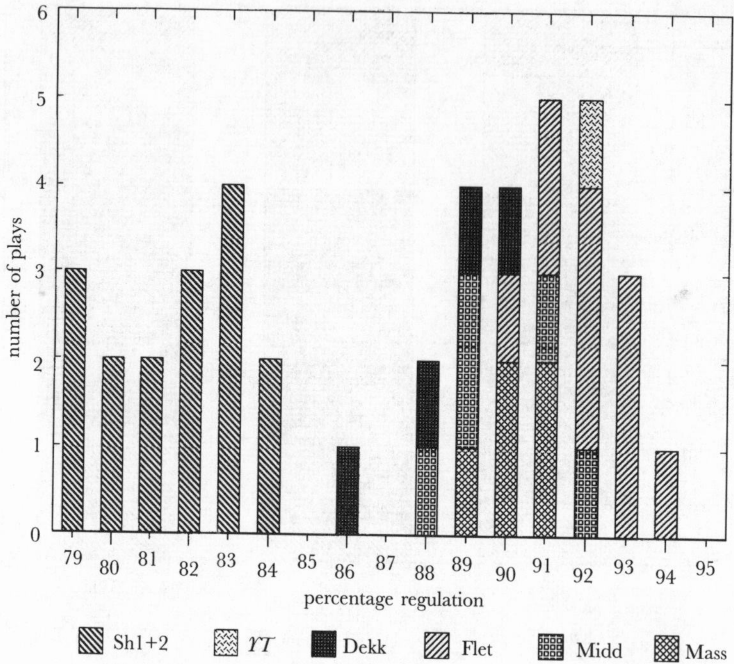


Graph 6.10 Auxiliary 'do' regulation in *A Yorkshire Tragedy* and samples

## *A Yorkshire Tragedy*

*A Yorkshire Tragedy* was registered and published as Shakespeare's in 1608. From the head title of the quarto, and the brevity of the play itself, it is clear that the piece would have been presented with three other plays, and it is possible that one of the other plays was by Shakespeare, thus giving rise to the attribution (Taylor in Wells *et al.* 1987:141). Lake (1975) ascribes the play to Middleton, although he suggests that Shakespeare might have supplied the first scene. Jackson (1979) and Holdsworth (1982) concur in assigning the whole play to Middleton.

### *Auxiliary 'do' evidence*

Graph 6.10 shows the auxiliary 'do' evidence for the authorship of *A Yorkshire Tragedy* (*YT*). The overall regulation rate of this play is 92 per cent, eight percentage points higher than the upper limit of the Shakespeare comparison sample (range 79–84 per cent), but within the range of the Middleton sample (88–92 per cent). On a sample where N = 263, this result almost certainly rules out Shakespearean authorship of this play. Only scene 2 gives a significant sample size, and its rate of regulation is, in

Table 6.7 Relative marker choice in *A Yorkshire Tragedy*

| | | *restrictive* | | *non-restrictive* | | | | |
|---|---|---|---|---|---|---|---|---|
| | | *sub* | *obj* | *sub* | *obj* | *totals* | | *%* |
| who(m) | personal | 1 | 2 | 2 | 2 | 7 | 7 | 12 |
| | non-personal | 0 | 0 | 0 | 0 | 0 | | |
| which | personal | 0 | 0 | 0 | 0 | 0 | 12 | 20 |
| | non-personal | 2 | 2 | 5 | 3 | 12 | | |
| that | personal | 6 | 1 | 6 | 0 | 13 | 20 | 33 |
| | non-personal | 6 | 1 | 0 | 0 | 7 | | |
| zero | personal | 2 | 2 | 0 | 0 | 4 | 21 | 35 |
| | non-personal | 7 | 9 | 1 | 0 | 17 | | |
| | | | | | | | N=60 | |

fact, acceptably Shakespearean (84 per cent – see below on the use of relatives in this scene though).

### *Relative marker evidence*

Table 6.7 shows the results for *A Yorkshire Tragedy*, which are plotted against the second Shakespeare comparison sample and the Middleton sample in graph 6.11. As with *The Puritan*, another play printed as Shakespeare's in the 1664 folio, but now thought to be Middleton's, the 'who'/'which' distinction is in place.

The figures in table 6.7 compare with the comparison samples in the following ways:

(a) The 'who'/'which' personal/non-personal distinction is observed – this corresponds to the Middleton comparison sample, but not to usage in the Shakespeare sample.
(b) 'Who' usage: at 12 per cent this rate is within the range of both samples.
(c) 'Which' usage: at 20 per cent this is low for the Shakespeare sample (28–38 per cent) and slightly high for the Middleton sample (10–17 per cent).
(d) 'That' usage: at 33 per cent this is low for the Shakespeare sample (41–7 per cent) and very low for the Middleton sample (49–60 per cent).

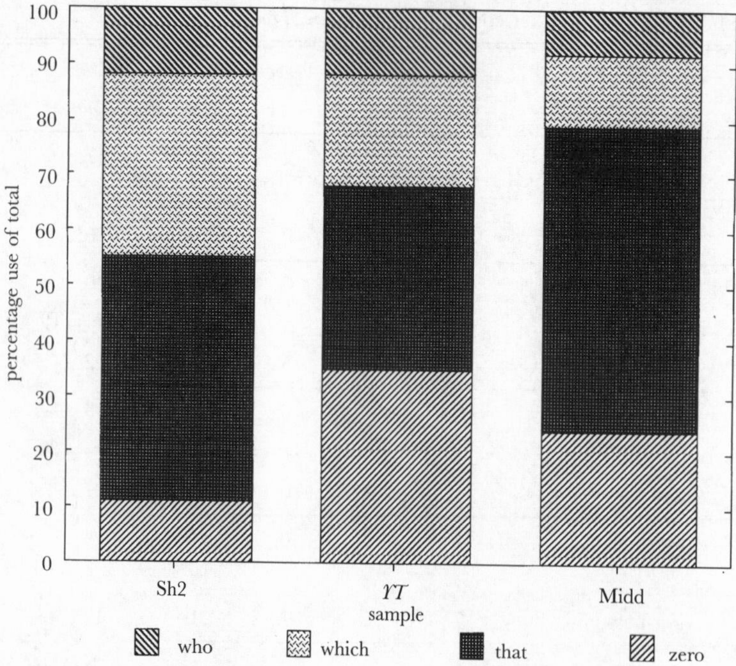


Graph 6.11 Relative marker use in *A Yorkshire Tragedy*

(e) Zero: at 35 per cent this is high for the Shakespeare sample (7–15 per cent) and just above the range of the Middleton sample (18–31); it is also notable that scene 2, acceptably Shakespearean on auxiliary 'do' evidence, contains a high number of zero relatives – a non-Shakespearean feature.

As graph 6.11 shows, relativisation in *A Yorkshire Tragedy* does not conform to either the late Shakespeare or Middleton comparison samples. In terms of its relatives, *A Yorkshire Tragedy* looks less Middletonian than *The Puritan*.

*Summary*

Overall this evidence would support the attribution of *A Yorkshire Tragedy* to Middleton rather than Shakespeare. However, as was the case with *The Puritan*, the relativisation evidence as it stands is not entirely Middletonian, perhaps again suggesting textual interference.

### *Locrine*

*Locrine* was published in 1595 as being 'Newly set foorth, ouerseene and corrected, By W.S.', and was included in the 1664 folio. Taylor, citing Maxwell 1956, notes that it 'has clearly been revised' (Wells *et al.* 1987:138).

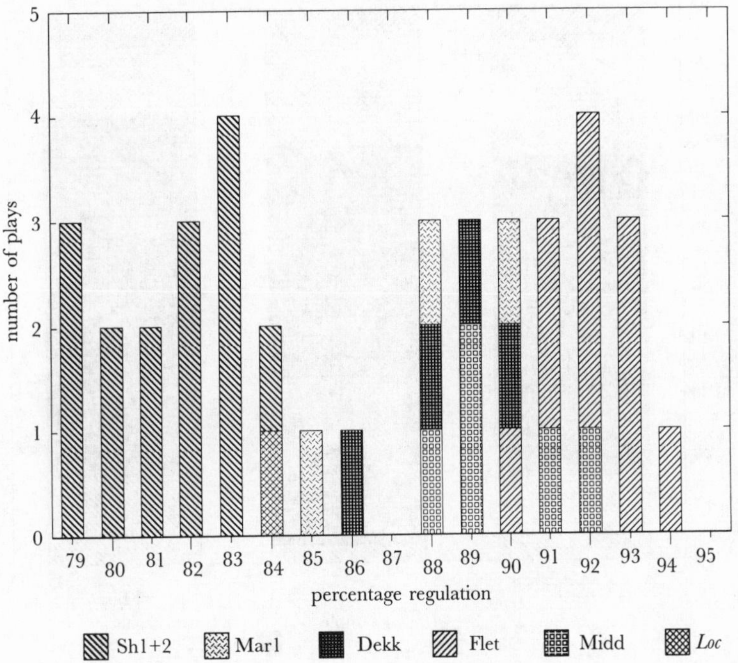


Graph 6.12 Auxiliary 'do' regulation in *Locrine* and samples

*Auxiliary 'do' evidence*

The auxiliary 'do' evidence from *Locrine* (*Loc*) can be found plotted on graph 6.12. Given the unregulated nature of the play (84 per cent), of the sampled playwrights, only Shakespeare, Marlowe, or Dekker can be considered serious candidates for its authorship.

Only two scenes in the play give significant sample sizes – 1.02 (N = 86, 88 per cent), 4.02 (N = 67, 81 per cent) – and these are not far enough apart to imply collaborative authorship.

*Relative marker evidence*

The relativisation evidence for *Locrine* is shown in graph 6.13 (see also Statistical Appendix). The most striking result from this is that the play shows two features which can be associated with Marlowe: very high 'that' usage, and observance of the 'who' distinction, but not the 'which'.

However, the rate of zero forms in this play is far too low for Marlowe – indeed, 3 per cent is the lowest result for any play sampled in the course of this study, suggesting the possibility that at some point in the history of the text, perhaps Taylor's mooted revision, zero forms have been changed to

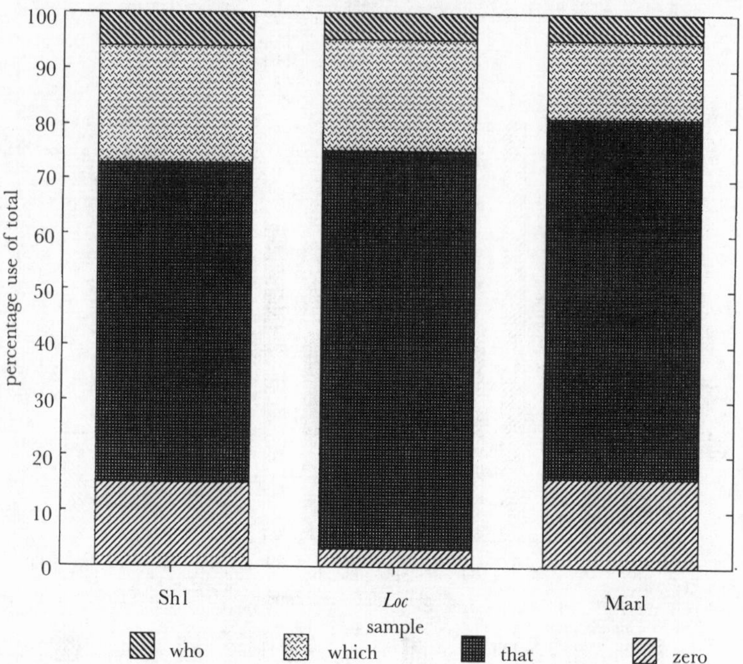


Graph 6.13 Relative marker use in *Locrine*

'that' forms. Under this scenario, the original author would have had a usage of 'that' forms less extreme than Marlowe, and of zero forms higher than is currently found in the text.

## Other apocryphal plays

This section considers five plays not included in the 1664 folio, but which have been ascribed to Shakespeare at various times. A large number of plays would fit into this category – these have been selected either because particularly strong cases for Shakespeare's presence have been made recently, or because socio-historical linguistic evidence seems likely to throw some light on the authorship issue.

### *Arden of Faversham*

*Arden of Faversham* was entered in the Stationer's Register on 3 April 1592, and two editions appear to have been published in that year. The play was not ascribed to Shakespeare until 1770, when Edward Jacob presented a case based on parallel passages, which he included in his edition of the text.

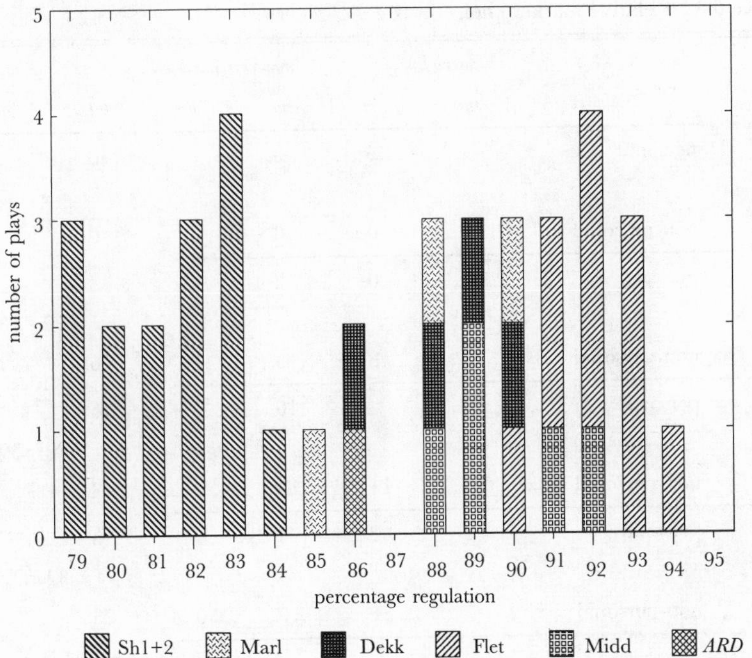


Graph 6.14 Auxiliary 'do' regulation in *Arden of Faversham* and samples

*Auxiliary 'do' evidence*

Graph 6.14 shows the auxiliary 'do' evidence for the authorship of *Arden of Faversham* (*Ard*). The overall regulation rate of this play is 86 per cent, two percentage points higher than the upper limit of the Shakespeare comparison sample (range 79–84 per cent). On a sample where N = 851, this result makes Shakespearean authorship unlikely, although it does not rule it out. Nor does this result rule out Shakespearean authorship of parts of the play: four of the six scenes which give significant sample sizes show acceptably Shakespearean regulation rates (2.02, 3.05, 3.06, 5.01); of the remaining two, 4.04 at 92 per cent regulation looks unShakespearean, while 1.01, at 88 per cent, might be said to be borderline, although the large sample (N = 230) makes this also look high for Shakespeare. Overall, the auxiliary 'do' evidence for this play suggests that its author has a more regulated usage than Shakespeare's.

*Relative marker evidence*

The evidence from relative marker choice in *Arden of Faversham* is shown in table 6.8 and graph 6.15.

Table 6.8 Relative marker choice in *Arden of Faversham*

| | | *restrictive* | | *non-restrictive* | | | |
|---|---|---|---|---|---|---|---|
| | | *sub* | *obj* | *sub* | *obj* | *totals* | *%* |
| who(m) | personal | 1 | 3 | 5 | 1 | 10 | |
| | | | | | | 10 | 7 |
| | non-personal | 0 | 0 | 0 | 0 | 0 | |
| which | personal | 0 | 0 | 2 | 1 | 3 | |
| | | | | | | 19 | 13 |
| | non-personal | 2 | 8 | 5 | 1 | 16 | |
| that | personal | 33 | 2 | 10 | 0 | 45 | |
| | | | | | | 88 | 59 |
| | non-personal | 24 | 14 | 5 | 0 | 43 | |
| zero | personal | 3 | 2 | 1 | 0 | 6 | |
| | | | | | | 32 | 22 |
| | non-personal | 2 | 24 | 0 | 0 | 26 | |
| | | | | | | N=149 | |

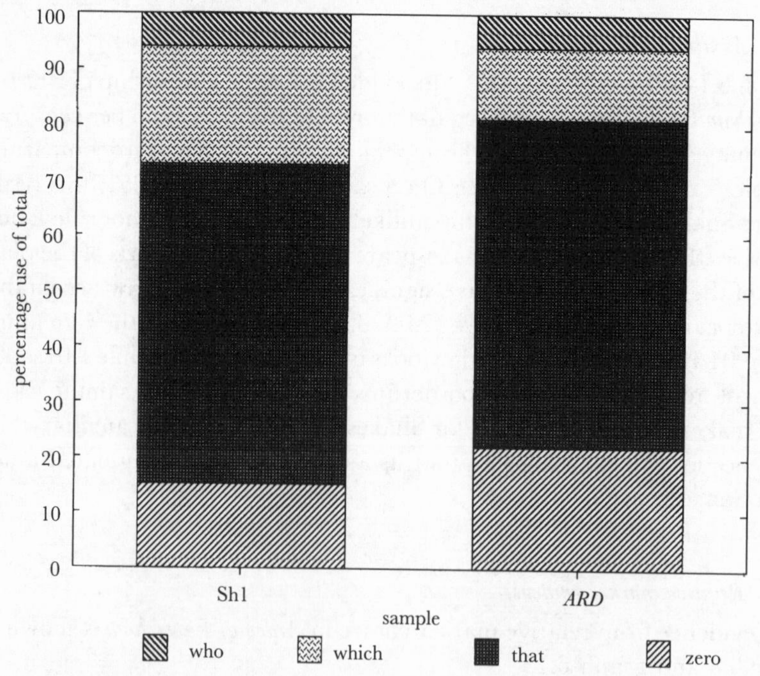


Graph 6.15 Relative marker use in *Arden of Faversham*

Comparison with the early Shakespeare relativisation comparison sample gives a reasonably good fit:

(a) The personal/non-personal distinction is in place, certainly with 'who', if not entirely with 'which' – this is a non-Shakespearean feature.
(b) 'Who' usage: at 7 per cent, this is acceptably within the bounds of the early Shakespeare comparison sample (4–11 per cent).
(c) 'Which' usage: at 13 per cent this is low for Shakespeare excepting the aberrant *Comedy of Errors* (comparison sample range 7–30 per cent).
(d) 'That' usage: at 59 per cent of the total this is within the range of the comparison sample (51–64 per cent).
(e) Zero forms: a rate of 22 per cent is also high for Shakespeare, again excepting the aberrant *Comedy of Errors* (compare a range of 6–23 per cent per cent in the comparison sample).

*Summary*

Although Shakespearean authorship of *Arden of Faversham* is unlikely, given the high auxiliary 'do' result and the restriction of 'who', socio-historical linguistic evidence is not conclusive in ruling it out. Nor though, would these results rule out Marlowe as a candidate for the authorship of the play – since his idiolect includes restriction of 'who', but not 'which', as observed here.

### *The Birth of Merlin*

*The Birth of Merlin* was published in 1662 – according to the title page a collaboration between Shakespeare and William Rowley. Dominik's case for Shakespeare's presence in the play (1985) is essentially based on parallels and, as Gary Taylor points out (Wells *et al.* 1987:135), the assumption of an 'unparalleled' type of collaboration between Shakespeare and Rowley in which work by both authors is mixed throughout the text.

*Auxiliary 'do' evidence*

Graph 6.16 shows the auxiliary 'do' evidence for the authorship of *The Birth of Merlin* (*BoM*). The overall regulation rate of this play is 88 per cent, four percentage points higher than the upper limit of the Shakespeare comparison sample (range 79–84 per cent). On a sample where N = 738, this result makes Shakespearean authorship unlikely. Eight scenes give significant sample sizes (including 1.01 where N = 49), of which three have acceptable Shakespearean regulation rates (2.01, 3.02, 4.01).

The auxiliary 'do' evidence for this play does not support Shakespearean authorship of the whole play. Collaboration can not be ruled out on this evidence, but Shakespeare almost certainly did not write 1.02, 3.01, 4.05, and probably not 2.03.

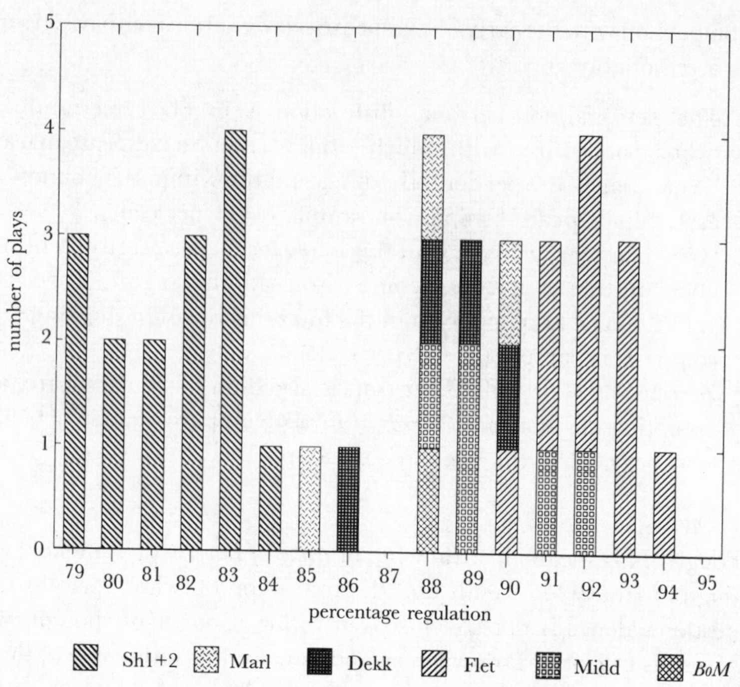


Graph 6.16 Auxiliary 'do' regulation in *The Birth of Merlin* and samples

### *Relative marker evidence*

Table 6.9 and graph 6.17 show the relative marker evidence in *The Birth of Merlin.*

These figures compare with the comparison sample in the following ways:

(a) The personal/non-personal distinction in 'who' and 'which' is not fully observed.
(b) 'Who' usage: at 10 per cent this is within the range of the early and late Shakespearean comparison samples.
(c) 'Which' usage: at 18 per cent this is very low for later Shakespeare, who does not fall below 28 per cent in the comparison sample, but within the range of the early comparison sample (7–28 per cent).
(d) 'That' usage: at 39 per cent this is just below the lower limit of the late Shakespearean comparison sample (range 41–7 per cent), and further below the limit of the early sample (51–64 per cent).
(e) Zero: at 32 per cent this is very high for Shakespeare who never rises above 15 per cent zero forms in the late comparison sample and 23 per cent in the early one.

Although (a), (b), (c), and (d) are not inconsistent with possible

Table 6.9 Relative marker choice in *The Birth of Merlin*

| | | *restrictive* | | *non-restrictive* | | | | |
|---|---|---|---|---|---|---|---|---|
| | | *sub* | *obj* | *sub* | *obj* | *totals* | | *%* |
| | personal | 2 | 2 | 10 | 2 | 16 | | |
| who(m) | | | | | | | 18 | 10 |
| | non-personal | 0 | 0 | 2 | 0 | 2 | | |
| | personal | 0 | 1 | 2 | 0 | 3 | | |
| which | | | | | | | 32 | 18 |
| | non-personal | 3 | 7 | 10 | 9 | 29 | | |
| | personal | 22 | 2 | 12 | 0 | 36 | | |
| that | | | | | | | 68 | 39 |
| | non-personal | 20 | 9 | 3 | 0 | 32 | | |
| | personal | 8 | 7 | 0 | 0 | 15 | | |
| zero | | | | | | | 56 | 32 |
| | non-personal | 18 | 21 | 1 | 1 | 41 | | |
| | | | | | | N=174 | | |

Shakespearean authorship, (e) emphatically is. Overall, relativisation evidence is against Shakespearean authorship of *The Birth of Merlin.*

*Summary*

Both types of evidence are against Shakespearean authorship of *The Birth of Merlin*, although he is not ruled out as a collaborator on some scenes. Taylor (Wells *et al.* 1987:135) reports that Fletcher can be ruled out as a possible author, and I would concur with this: regulation of auxiliary 'do' is too low for Fletcher, and use of 'who' too high. This evidence would not, however, rule out any of the other sampled playwrights.

### *Edward III*

*Edward III*, now that *The Two Noble Kinsmen* can be said to have entered the canon, is commonly regarded by reputable commentators as the next best candidate for inclusion. John Kerrigan refers to this 'fine play, partly or wholly by Shakespeare' (1990:47) and cites it extensively in his edition of *The Sonnets* (1986:293–5). G.R. Proudfoot calls it 'the sole remaining "doubtful play" which continues, on substantial grounds, to win

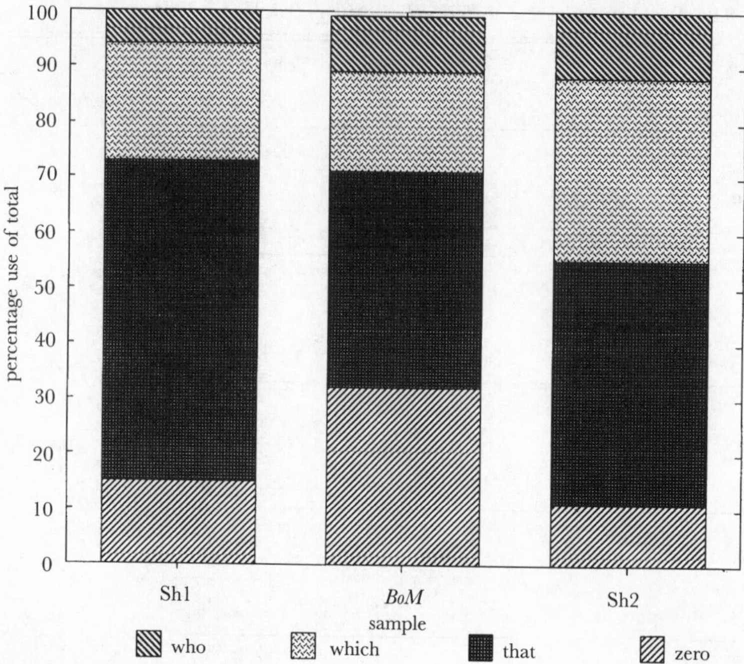


Graph 6.17 Relative marker use in *The Birth of Merlin*

the support of serious investigators as arguably the work of Shakespeare', and suggests that the burden of proof should shift from those who would include it in the collected works to those who would exclude it (1985:185). Taylor (Wells *et al.* 1987:136) states that 'of all the non-canonical plays [it] has the strongest claim to inclusion in the Complete Works', and goes on to say that 'if we had attempted a thorough reinvestigation of candidates for inclusion in the early dramatic canon, it would have begun with *Edward III*' (page 137). Recent work by M.W.A. Smith confirms the possibility of Shakespearean authorship (1993:204–5).

The play itself was registered at the end of 1595, and published anonymously in 1596. The first ascription to Shakespeare is in a publisher's catalogue of 1656, which would also have him as author of *Edward II* (Marlowe's) and *Edward IV* (Heywood's). The most notable study in support of Shakespeare's authorship is probably that of Slater (1988 – but see also Smith and Calvert 1989) – others are summarised in Proudfoot 1985. See also Smith 1991.

*Auxiliary 'do' evidence*

Graph 6.18 shows the auxiliary 'do' evidence for the authorship of *Edward III* (*Ed3*). The overall regulation rate of this play is 84 per cent, within the

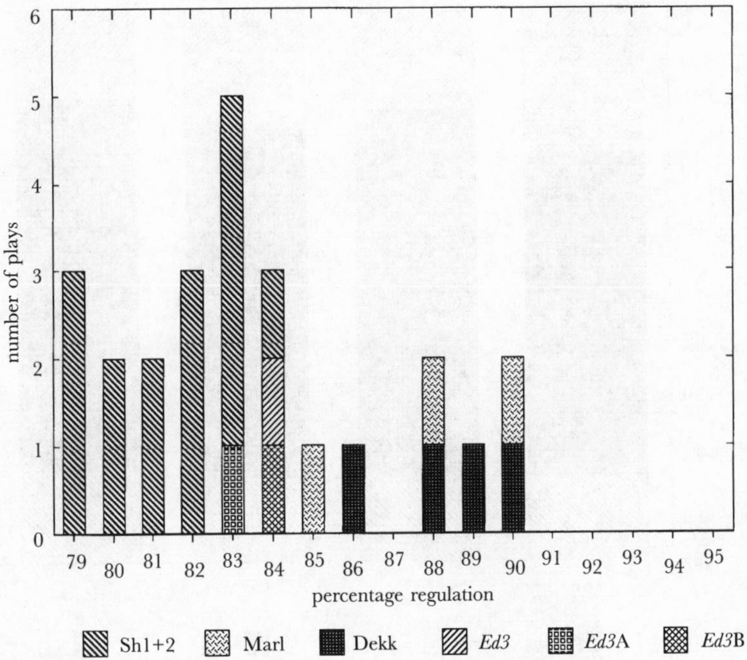


Graph 6.18 Auxiliary 'do' regulation in *Edward III* and samples

upper limit of the Shakespeare comparison sample (range 79–84 per cent). Shakespearean authorship of the whole play is therefore not ruled out by this evidence.

Seven scenes give significant sample sizes, four of which have acceptably Shakespearean regulation rates (2.01, 3.03, 4.04, 5.01). Of the remaining three (1.02: 91 per cent, N = 54; 2.02: 90 per cent, N = 68; 3.01: 89 per cent, N = 63), none is categorically non-Shakespearean, given the relatively low regulation rates and sample sizes. Thus the auxiliary 'do' evidence for this play is compatible with Shakespearean authorship.

Graph 6.18 also shows plots of figures for acts 1–2 (*Ed3*A) and acts 3–5(*Ed3*B), since it has been suggested that the play is collaborative, with Shakespeare contributing the early acts. These figures give no support to this hypothesis, as the sections do not differ significantly.

*Relative marker evidence*

Detailed figures for relativisation evidence in *Edward III* are given in the Statistical Appendix. They are shown here in graph 6.19.

Taking the evidence for divided authorship first, the similarity in the proportions of relative markers between the proposed sections of the play would seem to diminish the case for divided authorship. However, acts 3–5

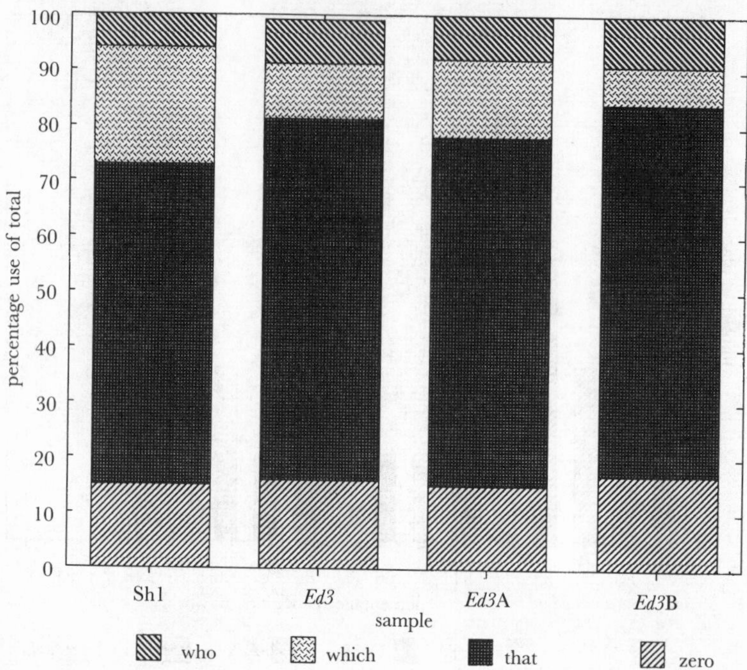


Graph 6.19 Relative marker use in *Edward III*

show observance of the 'who'/'which' personal/non-personal distinction, whereas acts 1–2 do not, albeit on a small sample. This would accord with the suggestion that Shakespeare wrote acts 1–2 but not acts 3–5.

Acts 3–5 also display a further non-Shakespearean feature – zero in non-restrictive clauses (see table A6.17 in the Statistical Appendix). Quite how much weight should be placed on this distinction given the tendency for some clauses to be ambiguous in their restriction is uncertain. There is certainly no clear cut relativisation evidence for the presence of two hands in this play.

The figures for the whole text compare with the early Shakespeare comparison sample in the following ways:

(a) The 'who'/'which' personal/non-personal distinction is observed more closely than is usual in the comparison sample plays.
(b) 'Who' usage: at 8 per cent this is within the range of the comparison sample (4–11 per cent).
(c) 'Which' usage: at 10 per cent this is within the range of the comparison sample, but only because of the aberrant *Comedy of Errors* – 7–30 per cent with *Comedy of Errors*; 19–30 per cent without it. Both halves of the play are low (acts 1–2 = 14 per cent; acts 3–5 = 7 per cent), and the

samples are too small for the differences between the halves to be significant.

(d) 'That' usage: at 65 per cent is only just outside the upper limit of the comparison sample (51–64 per cent).

(e) Zero forms: at 16 per cent the rate of zero forms is within the range of the Shakespearean comparison sample (6–23 per cent).

Apart from (a), where the difference is one of degree, the relativisation evidence is generally supportive of the notion of Shakespearean authorship of *Edward III*.

*Summary*

Nothing in the findings of this study offers a serious challenge to the status of *Edward III* as the best candidate from the apocryphal plays for inclusion in the canon.

### *Edmond Ironside*

Preserved only in an undated, anonymous manuscript in the British Library (MS Egerton 1994), the play was first attributed to Shakespeare in Everitt 1954. This position has been vigorously defended by Sams (1985), in an edition which he calls 'avowedly polemical and anything but diplomatic' (page 1) and which Kerrigan calls 'dotty' (1986:21). Sams' tone, which savours, for those who have read them, of the monomania of the nineteenth- and early twentieth-century Baconians, has discouraged serious work on the play. Taylor states rightly, however, that irritation at this tone 'and the erratic conduct of his argument should not obscure the real verbal similarities between *Ironside* and Shakespeare's early work. The whole subject merits further investigation' (Wells *et al.* 1987:138). Smith 1993 charts Sams' battles with the reviewers of his edition and gives stylometric evidence which makes Shakespearean authorship look unlikely.

*Auxiliary 'do' evidence*

Graph 6.20 shows the auxiliary 'do' evidence for the authorship of *Edmond Ironside* (*EdIrn*). The overall regulation rate of this play is 80 per cent, within the range of the Shakespeare comparison sample (range 79–84 per cent). Five scenes give significant sample sizes, and all show regulation rates which are acceptably Shakespearean. Thus the auxiliary 'do' evidence for this play is entirely consistent with Shakespearean authorship.

*Relative marker evidence*

The evidence from relativisation in *Edmond Ironside* is shown in table 6.10 and graph 6.21.

Table 6.10 Relative marker choice in *Edmond Ironside*

| | | *restrictive* | | *non-restrictive* | | | | |
|---|---|---|---|---|---|---|---|---|
| | | *sub* | *obj* | *sub* | *obj* | *totals* | | *%* |
| who(m) | personal | 3 | 0 | 6 | 0 | 9 | 10 | 9 |
| | non-personal | 0 | 0 | 1 | 0 | 1 | | |
| which | personal | 0 | 0 | 0 | 0 | 0 | 34 | 32 |
| | non-personal | 5 | 7 | 14 | 8 | 34 | | |
| that | personal | 35 | 0 | 4 | 0 | 39 | 51 | 47 |
| | non-personal | 9 | 2 | 1 | 0 | 12 | | |
| zero | personal | 0 | 0 | 0 | 0 | 0 | 13 | 12 |
| | non-personal | 1 | 12 | 0 | 0 | 13 | | |
| | | | | | | N=108 | | |

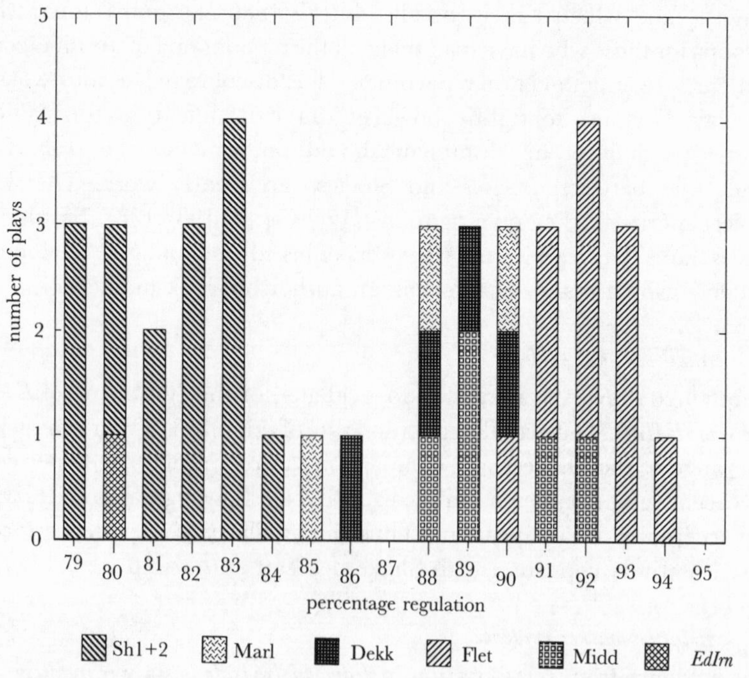


Graph 6.20 Auxiliary 'do' regulation in *Edmond Ironside* and samples

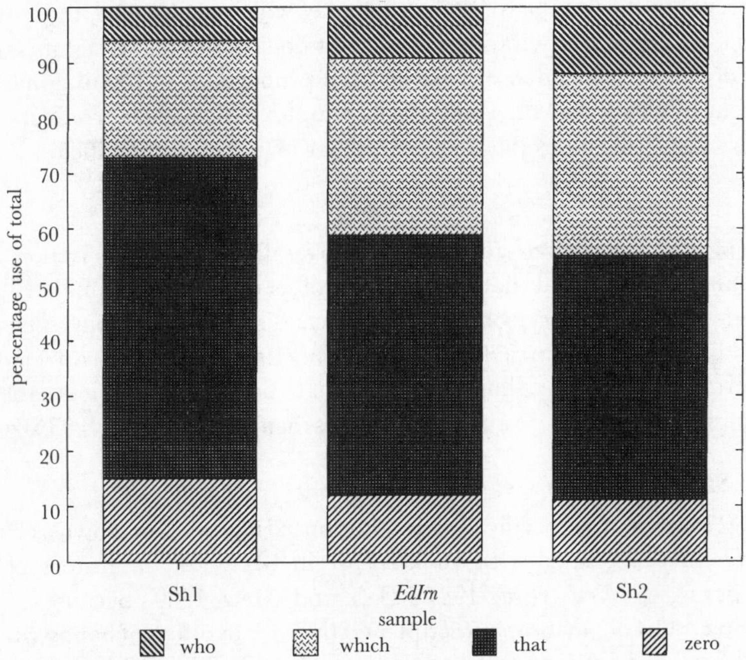


Graph 6.21 Relative marker use in *Edmond Ironside*

These figures compare with the Shakespeare comparison samples in the following ways:

(a) The 'who'/'which' personal/non-personal distinction is observed more fully than in the comparison samples.
(b) 'Who' usage: 9 per cent is within both of the Shakespearean comparison sample ranges (4–9 per cent and 9–16 per cent).
(c) 'Which' usage: 32 per cent is within the late Shakespearean comparison sample range (28–38 per cent) and just above the range for the early sample (7–30 per cent).
(d) 'That' usage: 47 per cent is within the late Shakespearean comparison sample range (41–7 per cent) and below the early sample range (51–64 per cent).
(e) Zero forms: 12 per cent is within both Shakespearean comparison sample ranges (7–15 per cent and 6–23 per cent).

It will be noted that (b), (c), (d), and (e) are consistent with Shakespearean authorship; only (a) is against it. These figures, however, are thrown into question by the striking lack of use of relativisation in the play: N = 108 against an average of N = 278 in the comparison sample (there is no great difference in the number of lines in the play which might account for this). This low rate of relativisation may have to be considered as significant as any of the correspondences between the proportions of relative markers used in this play and the comparison samples. Given the current state of knowledge, it is impossible to say whether or not this is justified.

*Summary*

Taking the reservations about the low overall rate of relativisation into account, it can be said that, on the basis of its relatives and auxiliary 'do' evidence, *Edmond Ironside* looks a very strong candidate for further investigation. The different tests carried out by Smith (1993), however, do tend to undermine the case for Shakespeare. As his article points out, it is easier to establish a negative case in authorship studies than a positive one (1993:204–5).

### *Sir Thomas More*

This play, and specifically the additions to it in what is known as Hand D, was first associated with Shakespeare in 1871. For the history of the ascription see Wells *et al.* 1987:124–5 and Metz 1989. Because of the multiple additions to the manuscript, and the various different handwritings, the textual and authorship debates surrounding *Sir Thomas More* are highly complex. There is space here only to address certain problems: is there evidence to support or cast doubt on the ascription to Shakespeare of Addition IID and Addition III; is there evidence to support or cast doubt on Merriam's conjecture that the whole play is by Shakespeare (1982); is there evidence to support or cast doubt on the suggestion that the original scenes (1–17) are collaborative?

*Auxiliary 'do' evidence*

Analysis of the figures given in the Statistical Appendix (table A6.19) and plotted on graph 6.22 is inconclusive with regard to Shakespeare's hand in Addition IID and/or Addition III, as these sections of text, even when taken together, do not give a significant sample size for the tests. The overall regulation rate of 86 per cent is slightly high for Shakespeare, but does not rule him out of authorship of the whole play. Of the four scenes which give significant sample sizes, three (2, 9, Addition IV hand C 8ii) have regulation rates within the Shakespearean range, while scene 13 shows a regulation rate of 91 per cent on a sample where N = 61. This result makes Shakespearean authorship of this scene unlikely, but does not rule it out.

Most telling against Merriam's suggestion that the whole play is by Shakespeare is good evidence that the original seventeen scenes are collaborative. This is based on differing rates in the use of unregulated

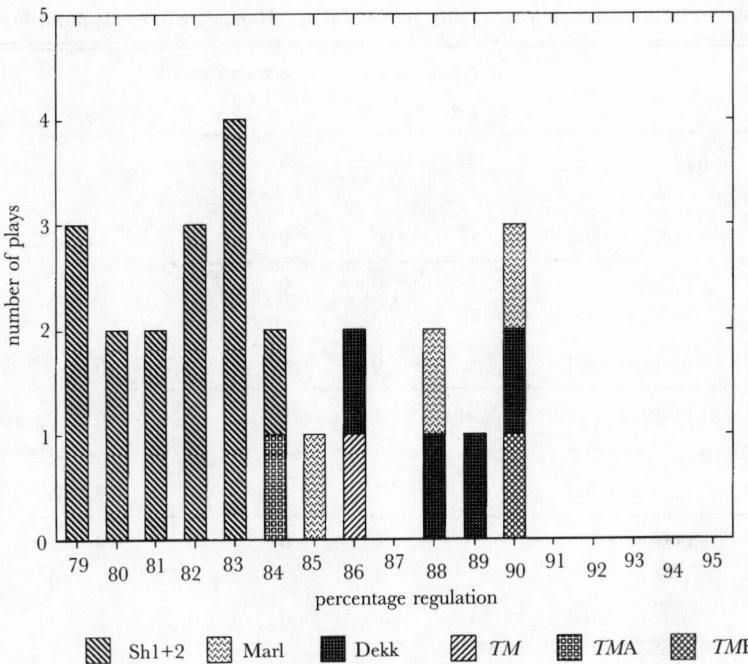


Graph 6.22 Auxiliary 'do' regulation in *Sir Thomas More* and samples

positive declarative sentences: there appears to be a set of scenes in the original part of the play which show an increased use of unregulated positive declaratives when compared with other scenes in this section of the play. There is not space here to attempt a detailed division of this section of the play, which would require a consideration of what the minimum significant sample size is for using the percentage of unregulated positive declaratives as an indicator of authorship, but an experimental division, with scenes 3, 7, 8b, 9, and 10 in 'section a' (*TM*A) and the remaining scenes in 'section b' (*TM*B), allows an overall regulation rate for each section to be calculated on the basis of significant samples (graph 6.22).

These regulation rates show a marked separation: 'section a' at 84 per cent regulation, and 'section b' at 90 per cent. This therefore seems to be a strong indication that the original scenes of the play are collaborative between one author with a highly regulated usage, and one with a relatively unregulated usage. It should be stressed here that the division offered is purely experimental: there is a case for considering scenes such as 4, 6, 11, 14, and 16, which all have relatively high rates of unregulated positive declarative sentences, although on very small samples, for inclusion in 'section a'.

Table 6.11 Relative marker choice in *Sir Thomas More* (Addition II, hand D)

| | | *restrictive* | | *non-restrictive* | | | |
|---|---|---|---|---|---|---|---|
| | | *sub* | *obj* | *sub* | *obj* | *totals* | |
| who(m) | personal | 1 | 0 | 0 | 0 | 1 | 1 |
| | non-personal | 0 | 0 | 0 | 0 | 0 | |
| which | personal | 0 | 0 | 0 | 0 | 0 | 5 |
| | non-personal | 0 | 0 | 3 | 2 | 5 | |
| that | personal | 5 | 1 | 0 | 0 | 6 | 8 |
| | non-personal | 1 | 1 | 0 | 0 | 2 | |
| zero | personal | 0 | 0 | 0 | 0 | 0 | 5 |
| | non-personal | 1 | 4 | 0 | 0 | 5 | |
| | | | | | | N=19 | |

*Evidence from relative markers*

Tables 6.11–14 show the evidence from relative markers in *Sir Thomas More.*

The relative marker evidence for Shakespeare as the author of Addition II, hand D is inconclusive, as the addition does not give a large enough sample (N = 19). It is noteworthy, however, that this section of the text does not show the avoidance of zero forms found elsewhere in the play (for example in 'section a'), which suggests the presence of a different author to much of the rest of the play. Avoidance of zero to the extent found in 'section a', and the hand C scenes, is a non-Shakespearean characteristic.

Also noteworthy is the fact that, while the 'who'/'which' personal/ non-personal distinction is strictly speaking in place, the 'who' form recorded falls into the less personal category: 'what rebell captaine/ . . . can still the rout who will obay a traytor' (Addition II, hand D, lines 237–9). It can be said then that there is nothing in the relative evidence which weakens the case for Shakespeare's hand in this addition to the play, and that in one respect the scene looks more Shakespearean than other parts of the play.

Unfortunately the inclusion of Addition III in the figures for relativisation does not increase the sample greatly, as there are only four relative markers in this section of the play.

Table 6.12 Relative marker choice in *Sir Thomas More* (complete text of play)

| | | restrictive | | non-restrictive | | | |
|---|---|---|---|---|---|---|---|
| | | *sub* | *obj* | *sub* | *obj* | *totals* | *%* |
| who(m) | personal | 4 | 1 | 3 | 4 | 12 | |
| | | | | | | 12 | 7 |
| | non-personal | 0 | 0 | 0 | 0 | 0 | |
| which | personal | 0 | 0 | 0 | 0 | 0 | |
| | | | | | | 34 | 19 |
| | non-personal | 1 | 4 | 17 | 12 | 34 | |
| that | personal | 56 | 5 | 10 | 0 | 71 | |
| | | | | | | 115 | 64 |
| | non-personal | 27 | 14 | 3 | 0 | 44 | |
| zero | personal | 4 | 1 | 0 | 0 | 5 | |
| | | | | | | 19 | 11 |
| | non-personal | 3 | 11 | 0 | 0 | 14 | |
| | | | | | | N = 180 | |

Table 6.12 gives the relativisation evidence from the complete text of the play to allow an assessment of Merriam's suggestion that the whole play is Shakespearean. These figures compare with the Shakespeare comparison samples in the following ways:

(a) The 'who'/'which' personal/non-personal distinction is observed – this does not correspond to usage in the Shakespeare samples (but see comments on Addition II, hand D above).
(b) 'Who' usage: at 7 per cent this rate is below the range of the late Shakespeare sample (9–16 per cent), but within that of the early sample (4–11 per cent).
(c) 'Which' usage: at 19 per cent this is low for the late Shakespeare sample (28–38 per cent) but within the range of the early sample (7–30 per cent).
(d) 'That' usage: at 64 per cent this is high for the late Shakespeare sample (41–7 per cent) but within the range of the early sample (51–64 per cent).
(e) Zero: at 11 per cent this is within the ranges of both samples (late: 7–15 per cent; early 6–23 per cent); the play contains no zero relatives in non-restrictive clauses – this conforms with usage in the Shakespeare comparison samples.

Table 6.13 Relative marker choice in *Sir Thomas More* ('section a')

| | | *restrictive* | | *non-restrictive* | | | | |
|---|---|---|---|---|---|---|---|---|
| | | *sub* | *obj* | *sub* | *obj* | *totals* | | *%* |
| who(m) | personal | 2 | 0 | 1 | 1 | 4 | 4 | 9 |
| | non-personal | 0 | 0 | 0 | 0 | 0 | | |
| which | personal | 0 | 0 | 0 | 0 | 0 | 8 | 18 |
| | non-personal | 1 | 1 | 6 | 0 | 8 | | |
| that | personal | 21 | 0 | 1 | 0 | 22 | 31 | 69 |
| | non-personal | 4 | 4 | 1 | 0 | 9 | | |
| zero | personal | 0 | 0 | 0 | 0 | 0 | 2 | 4 |
| | non-personal | 1 | 1 | 0 | 0 | 2 | | |
| | | | | | | N=45 | | |

Table 6.14 Relative marker choice in *Sir Thomas More* ('section b')

| | | *restrictive* | | *non-restrictive* | | | | |
|---|---|---|---|---|---|---|---|---|
| | | *sub* | *obj* | *sub* | *obj* | *totals* | | *%* |
| who(m) | personal | 1 | 1 | 1 | 2 | 5 | 5 | 6 |
| | non-personal | 0 | 0 | 0 | 0 | 0 | | |
| which | personal | 0 | 0 | 0 | 0 | 0 | 9 | 11 |
| | non-personal | 0 | 1 | 2 | 6 | 9 | | |
| that | personal | 20 | 3 | 6 | 0 | 29 | 55 | 68 |
| | non-personal | 16 | 9 | 1 | 0 | 26 | | |
| zero | personal | 4 | 1 | 0 | 0 | 5 | 12 | 15 |
| | non-personal | 1 | 6 | 0 | 0 | 7 | | |
| | | | | | | N=81 | | |

Overall, while the proportions of relatives conform to usage in the early Shakespeare sample, the observance of the 'who'/'which' distinction tends to tell against Shakespearean authorship.

Tables 6.13 and 6.14 show the relativisation evidence for sections 'a' and 'b' respectively, allowing an assessment of the evidence for collaboration in the original script of *Sir Thomas More*. As will be seen from the similar proportions of relative markers used in the sections, relativisation evidence is not as strongly in favour of collaboration as auxiliary 'do' evidence. One marked difference between the sections is the avoidance of zero in 'section a' (4 per cent compared with 15 per cent in 'section b'), which is particularly interesting given that the division of scenes into sections 'a' and 'b' was made on the basis of auxiliary 'do' evidence alone.

# PART III

# CONCLUSION

# Chapter 7

# Summary of findings

### The use and limitations of socio-historical linguistic evidence

This book has shown that it is possible to use the varying rates of standardisation in the work of early Modern dramatists as evidence in authorship studies. Socio-historical linguistic evidence can be used to its fullest effect in cases where the investigator wishes to divide a play between two named candidates, for each of whom there exists a group of non-controversial plays suitable for use as a comparison sample. This is the case in the Shakespeare–Fletcher collaborations, where marked differences in linguistic usage between Shakespeare and Fletcher allow detailed comments on the likely authorship of individual scenes to be made. In such cases, knowledge of the minimum significant sample size, gained from tests on plays of known authorship, allows an assessment of the relative certainty of any ascription to be made. In some cases however, the linguistic usages of collaborators may be so similar as to preclude the use of this type of evidence in authorship work.

Even where specific candidates for authorship have not been agreed upon, or where there are not comparison samples available for all candidates, it is still possible for this type of evidence to make limited contributions to the authorship debates surrounding texts. Where suitable comparison samples exist for only one suggested collaborator in a play, for example, it may be possible to rule that writer out of certain portions of the play, or indicate the relative likelihood of their having written other sections. Where plays are anonymous, socio-historical linguistic evidence can be used to rule certain playwrights out of consideration, or give an indication of whether the play is collaborative.

Given the fact that suitable comparison samples could never be compiled for every potential authorship candidate, socio-historical linguistic evidence will never be able to give a categorically positive attribution for an anonymous play – it can, though, confirm that a named author for whom a comparison sample exists could have written a play. This might allow the application of more specific types of evidence – and the creation of a cumulative case for the authorship of a play from different types of evidence.

The aim of this book has been to establish a methodology for socio-historical linguistics, and show it at work on a number of texts. I would hope that there are still considerable advances to be made in that methodology: most immediately in using the auxiliary 'do' regulation rates of individual sentence types, rather than all sentences; and in a more detailed analysis of relativisation strategies. I would also hope that other linguistic variables can be found which will function as socio-historical linguistic evidence.

## Summary of authorship findings

### *The Shakespeare–Fletcher collaborations*

#### *Henry VIII*

My study of the authorship of *Henry VIII* has the following conclusions:

(i) the play is certainly a collaboration
(ii) of the playwrights sampled in this study, Shakespeare and Fletcher are the best candidates for the authorship of the play
(iii) in his division of the play, Cyrus Hoy has been lead by his lack of a positive indicator for Shakespeare to over-estimate Shakespeare's presence in the play
(iv) my division of the play is as follows (scenes marked * are reassigned from Hoy's study)

Shakespeare: 1.01, 1.02, 2.03, 2.04, 3.02a, 5.01
Fletcher: P, 1.03, 1.04, 2.01*, 2.02*, 3.01, 3.02b*, 4.01*, 4.02*, 5.02, 5.03, 5.04, E

#### *The Two Noble Kinsmen*

Like *Henry VIII*, *The Two Noble Kinsmen* is shown by socio-historical linguistic evidence to be a collaborative play – and once again, Shakespeare and Fletcher are the best candidates for the authorship of it. My results confirm those of most previous studies (including Hoy) in assigning the play as follows:

Shakespeare: 1.01, 1.02, 1.03, 1.04, 1.05, 2.01, 3.01, 3.02, 5.01b, 5.03, 5.04
Fletcher: P, 2.02, 2.03, 2.04, 2.05, 2.06, 3.03, 3.04, 3.05, 3.06, 4.01, 4.02, 4.03, 5.01a, 5.02, E

#### *Double Falshood ('Cardenio')*

As I explain above, the textual history of *The Double Falshood* makes authorship work on this play highly speculative. However, certain indications as to likely authorship can be given:

(i) socio-historical linguistic evidence is against the play being a forgery by Theobald, as there is no evidence of hypercorrection of salient features as found in other attempted forgeries of Shakespeare

(ii) (also counting against forgery) there is some evidence in the text of the play for the presence of two distinct auxiliary 'do' regulation strategies – strategies which conform to those of Shakespeare and Fletcher

(iii) if the play is assumed to be based on a Shakespeare–Fletcher collaboration, then the scenes up to and including 2.02 appear to be more 'Shakespearean', while the later ones are more 'Fletcherian' – however, given Theobald's practice in his adaptation of *Richard II*, it seems unlikely that a more clear separation of Shakespearean and Fletcherian sections will be possible

## The Shakespeare–Middleton collaborations

### *Timon of Athens*

The results of my study of *Timon of Athens* give broad support to the position of Lake (1975:279-86), who finds evidence for a non-Shakespearean presence in sections of the play, possibly with subsequent Shakespearean revision of those sections. This is mainly provided by scene 1.02, which is unlikely to be by Shakespeare, and tests on the conventional division given by Lake (which ascribes to Middleton scenes 1.02, 3.01, 3.02, 3.03, 3.04, 3.05, 3.06, 4.02b, 4.03b). These tests show that the 'Middleton' scenes are not quite as Middletonian as might be expected if he were the author of all of them.

The main conclusions to be drawn from this are that there is almost certainly a non-Shakespearean presence in *Timon of Athens*, but that it has not yet been precisely isolated, either because subsequent Shakespearean revision has blurred the evidence, or because more careful work is needed.

### *Macbeth*

The 'additions' to *Macbeth* do not provide sufficiently large samples for the application of socio-historical linguistic evidence.

## The Shakespeare apocrypha

### *Pericles*

The authorship of *Pericles* is currently a vexed question in the field of authorship studies, following work by Merriam and Smith, and a rather cantankerous article by Sams (1991). Up to Sams 1991, a consensus was developing which supported the notion that acts 1 and 2 of the play were by Wilkins, and the rest by Shakespeare, although probably put in their final form by Wilkins.

The results of my study provide support for this consensus, and would tend to undermine Sams' suggestion that acts 1 and 2 represented work by the young Shakespeare. The evidence for this comes from relativisation strategies in the play: acts 1 and 2 are notable for the use of zero relative markers in non-restrictive clauses, a highly unusual feature absent from Shakespeare's work (in both the early and late periods) but present in Wilkins' play *The Miseries of Enforced Marriage*. Furthermore, both sections of the play show a high rate of zero relatives in the subject position – a non-Shakespearean feature – which may indicate a final draft of the manuscript by someone other than Shakespeare.

The evidence presented in my study does not conflict with the hypothesis that the text of *Pericles* as we have it is a final draft by Wilkins of a collaboration between him and Shakespeare in which Wilkins contributed more to acts 1 and 2 than in the remainder of the play.

### *The London Prodigal*

As noted above, Thomas Merriam has recently suggested that *The London Prodigal* may be by John Fletcher. On thematic grounds, such an ascription would certainly be a possibility. However, socio-historical linguistic evidence indicates that such an ascription can only be partially accurate, since auxiliary 'do' evidence suggests strongly that the play is a collaboration. My study shows that scenes 3.02, 3.03, 5.01 are strikingly less regulated than the rest of the play (1.01, 1.02, 2.01, 2.02, 2.03, 2.04, 3.01, 4.01, 4.02, 4.03).

The three unregulated scenes cannot be by Fletcher, while the rest of the play certainly could be (although Middleton and Dekker are also possible candidates on this evidence). Relativisation evidence would not rule Fletcher out as a candidate for the authorship of these scenes.

### *Thomas, Lord Cromwell*

In terms of auxiliary 'do' evidence, *Thomas, Lord Cromwell* is the most unusual play sampled in the course of this study. It shows a regulation rate below the lower limit of the Shakespeare comparison sample – the only play to do so. Two firm conclusions can be drawn from this:

(i) the play is not collaborative
(ii) the play was not written by Shakespeare, or any of the other writers sampled in the course of this study

### *Sir John Oldcastle*

As would be expected in the light of evidence from *Henslowe's Diary* that *Sir John Oldcastle* is by Munday, Drayton, Wilson, and Hathway, socio-historical linguistic evidence suggests that this play is collaborative. Without samples of unaided work by the proposed collaborators, a detailed division can not be attempted, but on auxiliary 'do' evidence the play falls into a highly regulated section (1.03, 2.01, 4.01, 4.02) and an unregulated section (1.02, 3.01, 5.11). Relativisation evidence suggests that these sections themselves contain work by more than one hand.

*The Puritan*

Auxiliary 'do' evidence puts this play well beyond the possibility of Shakespearean authorship, and does not suggest that the play is collaborative. Middleton is currently the strongest candidate for the authorship of this play, and auxiliary 'do' evidence would not conflict with this ascription. Relativisation evidence however, is less supportive of Middleton's undiluted presence, raising the possibility of alternative authorship, or textual interference.

*A Yorkshire Tragedy*

Auxiliary 'do' evidence rules Shakespeare out as the author of the whole text of this play. As with *The Puritan*, Middleton is confirmed as a possible candidate for authorship. However, again as with *The Puritan*, relativisation evidence is not entirely Middletonian, leaving the possibility that the play may be by a third hand, or that a final revision of the manuscript took place by someone other than Middleton.

*Locrine*

The auxiliary 'do' result for *Locrine* would allow only Shakespeare, Marlowe, or Dekker of the sampled authors as candidates for authorship. There is no suggestion from this study that the play is collaborative. Interestingly, relativisation evidence may link the play with Marlowe – but this evidence is not consistent, merely suggestive. Relativisation evidence in the play would tend to tell against Shakespearean authorship.

*Arden of Faversham*

Auxiliary 'do' evidence is not strongly supportive of Shakespeare's presence in this play. The play as a whole is unlikely to be by Shakespeare, and scenes 4.04 and 1.01 are clearly not by him. Relativisation evidence is similarly unsupportive of Shakespearean authorship. In neither case though, are my findings so clear-cut as to rule Shakespeare out. As with *Locrine*, relativisation evidence may suggest the possibility of Marlowe as a candidate for authorship. In all cases however, the evidence is inconclusive given the current state of knowledge.

### *The Birth of Merlin*

Auxiliary 'do' evidence is strongly against Shakespearean authorship of the whole play (although he would not be ruled out of scenes 2.01, 3.02, 4.01). Collaboration is a possibility, with scenes 1.02, 3.01, 4.05 highly regulated. Relativisation evidence is against Shakespeare's authorship of the play.

### *Edward III*

The auxiliary 'do' regulation rate for *Edward III* places it within the range of the Shakespeare comparison sample: of all the plays sampled in the course of this study, only three non-canonical plays fall into this range (*Edmond Ironside, Locrine*, and *Edward III*). No individual scene would be ruled out of possible Shakespearean authorship on the basis of the tests applied here.

While auxiliary 'do' evidence gives no support to the frequent suggestion that *Edward III* is collaborative, with Shakespeare contributing the first two acts, relativisation evidence may offer some slight support for this. Evidence from relatives is not as reliable as that from auxiliary 'do' however, and there is no overwhelming case for viewing the play as collaborative.

Nothing in the findings of this study offers a serious challenge to the status of *Edward III* as the best candidate from the apocryphal plays for inclusion in the canon.

### *Edmond Ironside*

As has been stated, *Edmond Ironside* is one of only three non-canonical plays to fall within the range of the Shakespearean comparison sample for auxiliary 'do' use. No individual scene in the play gives an unShakespearean result, and the auxiliary 'do' evidence is entirely compatible with Shakespearean authorship of the whole text of the play. However, one piece of socio-historical linguistic evidence which may throw Shakespearean authorship of this play into doubt is the very low overall frequency of relativisation (less than half that of the Shakespearean sample). I have as yet done no work on the significance or otherwise of this result – but *Edmond Ironside* certainly stands as a strong candidate for further detailed examination of possible Shakespearean authorship (Smith 1993, however, finds stylometric evidence which is not in accord with Shakespearean authorship).

### *Sir Thomas More*

The textual history, and manuscript, of *Sir Thomas More* are so complex as to necessitate a book-length study for any firm conclusions to be reached. I have restricted myself here to consideration of the likely authorship of the additions commonly ascribed to Shakespeare, and to Merriam's 1982 suggestion that the whole play may be by Shakespeare.

Unfortunately, the additions are too short to provide sufficient evidence for the application of socio-historical linguistic tests. Of Merriam's suggestion however, it is possible to say that socio-historical linguistic evidence suggests that there are at least two hands at work in the original scenes of the play (1–17) – with scenes 3, 7, 8b, 9, 10 apparently representing the work of a less regulated author or authors. This experimental division is supported to a limited degree by relativisation evidence, which would also discriminate between these and the other original scenes.

# Statistical appendix

## *Chapter 2 Auxiliary 'do'*

Table A2.1 Shakespeare sample 1 (early plays)

| *play* | | *TG* | *CE* | *LL* | *R2* | *MSN* | *MV* |
|---|---|---|---|---|---|---|---|
| R | | 657 | 666 | 718 | 745 | 536 | 755 |
| N | | 791 | 797 | 896 | 903 | 683 | 940 |
| %reg | | 83 | 84 | 80 | 83 | 79 | 80 |
| R | | | 4077 | | | | |
| N | total | | 5010 | | | | |
| % | regulation | | 81 | | | | |

Table A2.2 Shakespeare sample 2 (late plays)

| *play* | *TC* | *MM* | *O* | *AW* | *KL* | *AC* | *CO* | *CY* | *WT* | *T* |
|---|---|---|---|---|---|---|---|---|---|---|
| R | 928 | 696 | 899 | 866 | 905 | 851 | 825 | 825 | 684 | 507 |
| N | 1120 | 857 | 1135 | 1026 | 1099 | 1034 | 1019 | 993 | 830 | 640 |
| %reg | 83 | 81 | 79 | 84 | 82 | 82 | 81 | 83 | 82 | 79 |
| R | | | | 7986 | | | | | | |
| N | | total | | 9753 | | | | | | |
| % | regulation | | | 82 | | | | | | |

Table A2.3 Marlowe sample

| *play* | *T1* | *T2* | *E2* |
|---|---|---|---|
| R | 566 | 559 | 724 |
| N | 642 | 622 | 857 |
| %reg | 88 | 90 | 85 |
| R | | | 1849 |
| N | total | | 2121 |
| % | regulation | | 87 |

Table A2.4 Dekker sample

| *play* | *SH* | *WB* | *IF* | *ML* |
|---|---|---|---|---|
| R | 589 | 939 | 778 | 744 |
| N | 684 | 1048 | 887 | 839 |
| %reg | 86 | 90 | 88 | 89 |
| R | | | 3050 | |
| N | total | | 3458 | |
| % | regulation | | 88 | |

Table A2.5 Fletcher sample

| *play* | *MT* | *WP* | *V* | *ML* | *LS* | *HL* | *B* | *IP* | *WG* | *P* |
|---|---|---|---|---|---|---|---|---|---|---|
| R | 733 | 830 | 720 | 872 | 674 | 988 | 1038 | 873 | 857 | 774 |
| N | 794 | 914 | 783 | 954 | 730 | 1058 | 1105 | 935 | 921 | 856 |
| %reg | 93 | 91 | 91 | 92 | 93 | 94 | 92 | 93 | 90 | 93 |
| R | | | | 8359 | | | | | | |
| N | total | | | 9050 | | | | | | |
| % | regulation | | | 92 | | | | | | |

Table A2.6 Middleton sample

| *play* | *PH* | *MT* | *MW* | *TC* | *FG* |
|---|---|---|---|---|---|
| R | 728 | 762 | 667 | 626 | 728 |
| N | 802 | 852 | 725 | 702 | 828 |
| %reg | 91 | 89 | 92 | 89 | 88 |
| R | | | 3511 | | |
| N | total | | 3909 | | |
| % | regulation | | 90 | | |

Table A2.7 Massinger sample

| *play* | *MH* | *DM* | *BM* | *RG* | *UC* |
|---|---|---|---|---|---|
| R | 581 | 673 | 748 | 708 | 620 |
| N | 638 | 743 | 830 | 791 | 682 |
| %reg | 91 | 91 | 90 | 90 | 89 |
| R | | | 3330 | | |
| N | total | | 3684 | | |
| % | regulation | | 90 | | |

Table A2.8 Scene by scene regulation in *All's Well that Ends Well*

| | *1.01* | *1.02* | *1.03* | *2.01* | *2.02* | *2.03* | *2.04* | *2.05* | *3.01* | *3.02* | *3.03* |
|---|---|---|---|---|---|---|---|---|---|---|---|
| R | 61 | 32 | 95 | 64 | 15 | 81 | 15 | 21 | 10 | 42 | 2 |
| N | 76 | 37 | 112 | 72 | 18 | 97 | 17 | 33 | 10 | 51 | 2 |
| % | 80 | 87 | 85 | 89 | 83 | 84 | 88 | 64 | 100 | 82 | 100 |

| | *3.04* | *3.05* | *3.06* | *3.07* | *4.01* | *4.02* | *4.03* | *4.04* | *4.05* | *5.01* | *5.02* |
|---|---|---|---|---|---|---|---|---|---|---|---|
| R | 11 | 39 | 25 | 17 | 15 | 23 | 77 | 7 | 31 | 8 | 18 |
| N | 13 | 44 | 33 | 19 | 19 | 28 | 89 | 8 | 34 | 12 | 20 |
| % | 85 | 89 | 76 | 90 | 54 | 79 | 87 | 88 | 91 | 67 | 90 |

| | *5.03* |
|---|---|
| R | 153 |
| N | 182 |
| % | 84 |

N = total number of tokens; R = regulated tokens; % = percentage regulation

Table A2.9 Scene by scene regulation in *The Wild Goose Chase*

| | *1.01* | *1.02* | *1.03* | *2.01* | *2.02* | *2.03* | *3.01* | *4.01* | *4.02* | *4.03* | *5.01* |
|---|---|---|---|---|---|---|---|---|---|---|---|
| R | 45 | 22 | 74 | 79 | 64 | 46 | 145 | 51 | 39 | 68 | 8 |
| N | 50 | 26 | 80 | 85 | 69 | 50 | 167 | 60 | 45 | 72 | 8 |
| % | 90 | 85 | 93 | 93 | 93 | 92 | 87 | 85 | 87 | 94 | 100 |

| | *5.02* | *5.03* | *5.04* | *5.05* | *5.06* |
|---|---|---|---|---|---|
| R | 41 | 16 | 20 | 8 | 56 |
| N | 43 | 17 | 21 | 10 | 61 |
| % | 95 | 94 | 95 | 80 | 92 |

N = total number of tokens; R = regulated tokens; % = percentage regulation

Table A2.10 Scenes in *All's Well that Ends Well* and *The Wild Goose Chase* where N = 50 and over

*All's Well that Ends Well*

| *1.01* | *1.03* | *2.01* | *2.03* | *3.02* | *4.03* | *5.03* |
|---|---|---|---|---|---|---|
| R 61 | 95 | 64 | 81 | 42 | 77 | 153 |
| N 76 | 112 | 72 | 97 | 51 | 89 | 182 |
| % 80 | 85 | 89 | 84 | 82 | 87 | 84 |

*The Wild Goose Chase*

| *1.01* | *1.03* | *2.01* | *2.02* | *2.03* | *3.01* | *4.01* | *4.03* | *5.06* |
|---|---|---|---|---|---|---|---|---|
| R 45 | 74 | 79 | 64 | 46 | 145 | 51 | 68 | 56 |
| N 50 | 80 | 85 | 69 | 50 | 167 | 60 | 72 | 61 |
| % 90 | 93 | 93 | 93 | 92 | 87 | 85 | 94 | 92 |

## Chapter 3 Relative markers

*Proportions of relative markers in individual plays in the comparison samples (see graphs in main text)*

Table A3.1 Shakespeare sample 1

| *play* | *TG* | *CE* | *LL* | *R2* | *MSN* | *MV* |
|---|---|---|---|---|---|---|
| who(m) | 5 | 11 | 4 | 9 | 5 | 9 |
| which | 19 | 7 | 28 | 30 | 27 | 23 |
| that | 64 | 59 | 62 | 51 | 52 | 52 |
| zero | 13 | 23 | 6 | 10 | 16 | 17 |

Table A3.2 Shakespeare sample 2

| *play* | *AC* | *CO* | *CY* | *WT* | *T* |
|---|---|---|---|---|---|
| who(m) | 9 | 14 | 13 | 10 | 16 |
| which | 37 | 30 | 28 | 38 | 34 |
| that | 42 | 47 | 44 | 41 | 43 |
| zero | 12 | 9 | 15 | 12 | 7 |

Table A3.3 Marlowe sample

| *play* | *T1* | *T2* | *E2* |
|---|---|---|---|
| who(m) | 4 | 5 | 6 |
| which | 12 | 19 | 10 |
| that | 70 | 55 | 71 |
| zero | 14 | 21 | 14 |

Table A3.4 Dekker sample

| *play* | *SH* | *WB* | *IF* | *ML* |
|---|---|---|---|---|
| who(m) | 8 | 6 | 20 | 4 |
| which | 20 | 20 | 17 | 24 |
| that | 45 | 60 | 35 | 33 |
| zero | 27 | 14 | 28 | 39 |

Table A3.5 Fletcher sample

| *play* | *MT* | *WP* | *B* | *V* | *ML* |
|---|---|---|---|---|---|
| who(m) | 1 | 1 | 2 | 3 | 1 |
| which | 23 | 16 | 12 | 9 | 8 |
| that | 45 | 53 | 58 | 60 | 55 |
| zero | 31 | 31 | 27 | 29 | 35 |

Table A3.6 Middleton sample

| *play* | *PH* | *MT* | *MW* | *TC* | *FG* |
|---|---|---|---|---|---|
| who(m) | 14 | 10 | 5 | 4 | 7 |
| which | 17 | 11 | 15 | 10 | 13 |
| that | 51 | 56 | 58 | 60 | 49 |
| zero | 18 | 22 | 22 | 25 | 31 |

Table A3.7 Massinger sample

| *play* | *MH* | *DM* | *BM* | *RG* | *UC* |
|---|---|---|---|---|---|
| who(m) | 8 | 4 | 4 | 3 | 3 |
| which | 21 | 15 | 25 | 20 | 24 |
| that | 49 | 61 | 49 | 50 | 49 |
| zero | 22 | 20 | 22 | 26 | 25 |

*Effect of animateness of antecedent and restriction on relative marker choice in the comparison samples*

Table A3.8 Shakespeare

(a) animateness

| | *who* | *which* | *that* | *zero* |
|---|---|---|---|---|
| Shakespeare sample 1 | | | | |
| Personal | 86 | 10 | 54 | 19 |
| Non-personal | 15 | 90 | 46 | 82 |
| Shakespeare sample 2 | | | | |
| Personal | 88 | 8 | 57 | 22 |
| Non-personal | 12 | 92 | 43 | 79 |

(b) restriction

| | *who* | *which* | *that* | *zero* |
|---|---|---|---|---|
| Shakespeare sample 1 | | | | |
| Restrictive | 35 | 49 | 91 | 100 |
| Non-restrictive | 66 | 51 | 9 | 0 |
| Shakespeare sample 2 | | | | |
| Restrictive | 33 | 53 | 88 | 100 |
| Non-restrictive | 67 | 47 | 12 | 0 |

Table A3.9 Marlowe sample

| | *who* | *which* | *that* | *zero* |
|---|---|---|---|---|
| animateness: | | | | |
| Personal | 100 | 11 | 60 | 17 |
| Non-personal | 0 | 89 | 40 | 83 |
| restriction: | | | | |
| Restrictive | 21 | 43 | 82 | 100 |
| Non-restrictive | 79 | 57 | 18 | 0 |

Table A3.10 Dekker sample

| | *who* | *which* | *that* | *zero* |
|---|---|---|---|---|
| animateness: | | | | |
| Personal | 97 | 3 | 56 | 31 |
| Non-personal | 3 | 97 | 44 | 69 |
| restriction: | | | | |
| Restrictive | 72 | 83 | 99 | 100 |
| Non-restrictive | 28 | 17 | 2 | 0 |

Table A3.11 Fletcher sample

| | *who* | *which* | *that* | *zero* |
|---|---|---|---|---|
| animateness | | | | |
| Personal | 94 | 4 | 59 | 20 |
| Non-personal | 6 | 96 | 41 | 80 |
| restriction: | | | | |
| Restrictive | 25 | 27 | 91 | 99 |
| Non-restrictive | 75 | 74 | 9 | 1 |

Table A3.12 Middleton sample

| | *who* | *which* | *that* | *zero* |
|---|---|---|---|---|
| animateness: | | | | |
| Personal | 98 | 6 | 71 | 50 |
| Non-personal | 2 | 94 | 29 | 50 |
| restriction: | | | | |
| Restrictive | 48 | 45 | 94 | 100 |
| Non-restrictive | 52 | 55 | 6 | 0 |

Table A3.13 Massinger sample

| | *who* | *which* | *that* | *zero* |
|---|---|---|---|---|
| animateness: | | | | |
| Personal | 98 | 1 | 49 | 12 |
| Non-personal | 2 | 99 | 52 | 88 |
| restriction: | | | | |
| Restrictive | 30 | 45 | 82 | 98 |
| Non-restrictive | 71 | 55 | 18 | 2 |

## Chapter 5

Table A5.1 Auxiliary 'do' use in *Henry VIII*

| | *P* | *1.01* | *1.02* | *1.03* | *1.04* | *2.01* | *2.02* | *2.03* | *2.04* | *3.01* |
|---|---|---|---|---|---|---|---|---|---|---|
| reg | 13 | 96 | 58 | 17 | 26 | 68 | 47 | 26 | 65 | 67 |
| unreg | 0 | 17 | 11 | 0 | 1 | 3 | 4 | 7 | 21 | 7 |
| N= | 13 | 113 | 69 | 17 | 27 | 71 | 51 | 33 | 76 | 74 |
| %reg | 100 | 85 | 84 | 100 | 96 | 96 | 92 | 79 | 86 | 91 |

| | *3.02a* | *3.02b* | *4.01* | *4.02* | *5.01* | *5.02* | *5.03* | *5.04* | *E* |
|---|---|---|---|---|---|---|---|---|---|
| reg | 58 | 95 | 47 | 67 | 58 | 65 | 33 | 16 | 7 |
| unreg | 22 | 4 | 2 | 6 | 13 | 6 | 5 | 0 | 0 |
| N= | 80 | 99 | 49 | 73 | 71 | 71 | 38 | 16 | 7 |
| %reg | 73 | 96 | 96 | 92 | 82 | 92 | 87 | 100 | 100 |

| | *total* | *section A* | *section B* | *section C* |
|---|---|---|---|---|
| reg | 929 | 361 | 244 | 324 |
| unreg | 129 | 91 | 19 | 19 |
| N= | 1058 | 452 | 263 | 343 |
| %reg | 88 | 80 | 93 | 95 |

Table A5.2 Proportions of relative markers in *Henry VIII*

| | *A* | *B* | *C* |
|---|---|---|---|
| who | 14 | 5 | 8 |
| which | 38 | 14 | 16 |
| that | 33 | 57 | 49 |
| zero | 15 | 25 | 28 |

Table A5.3 Auxiliary 'do' use in *The Two Noble Kinsmen*

| | *P* | *1.01* | *1.02* | *1.03* | *1.04* | *1.05* | *2.01* | *2.02* | *2.03* | *2.04* |
|---|---|---|---|---|---|---|---|---|---|---|
| reg | 16 | 62 | 40 | 33 | 12 | 5 | 18 | 76 | 21 | 19 |
| unreg | 0 | 7 | 14 | 5 | 1 | 0 | 2 | 3 | 3 | 1 |
| N= | 16 | 69 | 54 | 38 | 13 | 5 | 20 | 79 | 24 | 20 |
| %reg | 100 | 90 | 74 | 87 | 92 | 100 | 90 | 96 | 88 | 95 |

| | *2.05* | *2.06* | *3.01* | *3.02* | *3.03* | *3.04* | *3.05* | *3.06* | *4.01* | *4.02* |
|---|---|---|---|---|---|---|---|---|---|---|
| reg | 22 | 12 | 39 | 13 | 15 | 6 | 51 | 118 | 81 | 60 |
| unreg | 0 | 1 | 4 | 3 | 2 | 0 | 2 | 4 | 4 | 3 |
| N= | 22 | 13 | 43 | 16 | 17 | 6 | 53 | 122 | 85 | 63 |
| %reg | 100 | 92 | 91 | 81 | 88 | 100 | 96 | 97 | 95 | 95 |

| | *4.03* | *5.01a* | *5.01b* | *5.02* | *5.03* | *5.04* | *E* | *total* | *section A* | *section B* |
|---|---|---|---|---|---|---|---|---|---|---|
| reg | 27 | 12 | 46 | 43 | 39 | 65 | 6 | 957 | 372 | 585 |
| unreg | 3 | 0 | 6 | 3 | 11 | 7 | 2 | 91 | 60 | 31 |
| N= | 30 | 12 | 52 | 46 | 50 | 72 | 8 | 1048 | 432 | 616 |
| %reg | 90 | 100 | 89 | 94 | 78 | 90 | 75 | 91 | 86 | 95 |

Table A5.4 Proportions of relative markers in *The Two Noble Kinsmen*

| | *A* | *B* |
|---|---|---|
| who | 17 | 0 |
| which | 25 | 11 |
| that | 43 | 66 |
| zero | 15 | 23 |

Table A5.5 Auxiliary 'do' use in *Double Falshood*

| | *1.01* | *1.02* | *1.03* | *2.01* | *2.02* | *2.03* | *2.04* | *3.01* | *3.02* | *3.03* |
|---|---|---|---|---|---|---|---|---|---|---|
| reg | 16 | 63 | 27 | 14 | 12 | 69 | 14 | 11 | 31 | 51 |
| unreg | 3 | 14 | 3 | 1 | 5 | 3 | 6 | 2 | 9 | 7 |
| N= | 19 | 77 | 30 | 15 | 17 | 72 | 20 | 13 | 40 | 58 |
| %reg | 84 | 82 | 90 | 93 | 71 | 96 | 70 | 85 | 78 | 88 |

Table A5.5 (*cont*).

| | *4.01* | *4.02* | *5.01* | *5.02* | *total* |
|---|---|---|---|---|---|
| reg | 97 | 38 | 31 | 95 | 569 |
| unreg | 12 | 1 | 3 | 11 | 80 |
| N= | 109 | 39 | 34 | 106 | 649 |
| %reg | 89 | 97 | 91 | 90 | 88 |

Table A5.6 Auxiliary 'do' use in *Timon of Athens*

| | *1.01* | *1.02* | *2.01* | *2.02* | *3.01* | *3.02* | *3.03* | *3.04* | *3.05* | *3.06* |
|---|---|---|---|---|---|---|---|---|---|---|
| reg | 91 | 85 | 17 | 67 | 17 | 28 | 14 | 29 | 31 | 33 |
| unreg | 20 | 9 | 1 | 11 | 2 | 2 | 1 | 4 | 7 | 10 |
| N= | 111 | 94 | 18 | 78 | 19 | 30 | 15 | 33 | 38 | 43 |
| %reg | 82 | 90 | 94 | 86 | 90 | 93 | 93 | 88 | 82 | 77 |

| | *4.01* | *4.02a* | *4.02b* | *4.03a* | *4.03b* | *5.01* | *5.02* | *5.03* | *5.04* |
|---|---|---|---|---|---|---|---|---|---|
| reg | 3 | 6 | 4 | 107 | 22 | 71 | 8 | 1 | 16 |
| unreg | 0 | 2 | 1 | 32 | 4 | 11 | 2 | 0 | 1 |
| N= | 3 | 8 | 5 | 139 | 26 | 82 | 10 | 1 | 17 |
| %reg | 100 | 75 | 80 | 77 | 85 | 87 | 80 | 100 | 94 |

| | *total* | *Lake's M* | *Lake's S* |
|---|---|---|---|
| reg | 650 | 263 | 387 |
| unreg | 120 | 40 | 80 |
| N= | 770 | 303 | 467 |
| %reg | 84 | 87 | 83 |

Table A5.7 Relatives in *Timon of Athens* – whole text

| | | *restrictive* | | *non-restrictive* | | | |
|---|---|---|---|---|---|---|---|
| | | *sub* | *obj* | *sub* | *obj* | *totals* | *%* |
| who(m) | personal | 2 | 7 | 10 | 6 | 25 | |
| | | | | | | 27 | 16 |
| | non-personal | 1 | 0 | 0 | 1 | 2 | |
| which | personal | 6 | 0 | 1 | 0 | 7 | |
| | | | | | | 45 | 27 |
| | non-personal | 12 | 10 | 9 | 7 | 38 | |
| that | personal | 38 | 1 | 8 | 0 | 47 | |
| | | | | | | 80 | 47 |
| | non-personal | 24 | 5 | 4 | 0 | 33 | |
| zero | personal | 4 | 0 | 0 | 0 | 4 | |
| | | | | | | 17 | 10 |
| | non-personal | 5 | 8 | 0 | 0 | 13 | |
| | | | | | | N=169 | |

Table A5.8 Auxiliary 'do' use in *Macbeth*

| | *1.01* | *1.02* | *1.03* | *1.04* | *1.05* | *1.06* | *1.07* | *2.01* | *2.02* | *2.03* |
|---|---|---|---|---|---|---|---|---|---|---|
| reg | 2 | 32 | 48 | 16 | 23 | 10 | 14 | 31 | 31 | 47 |
| unreg | 0 | 5 | 16 | 1 | 5 | 1 | 5 | 2 | 9 | 8 |
| N= | 2 | 37 | 64 | 17 | 28 | 11 | 19 | 33 | 40 | 55 |
| %reg | 100 | 87 | 75 | 94 | 82 | 91 | 74 | 94 | 78 | 86 |

| | *2.04* | *3.01* | *3.02* | *3.03* | *3.04* | *3.05a* | *3.05b* | *3.06* | *4.01a* | *4.01b* |
|---|---|---|---|---|---|---|---|---|---|---|
| reg | 11 | 40 | 16 | 6 | 40 | 7 | 17 | 19 | 37 | 3 |
| unreg | 3 | 10 | 1 | 3 | 7 | 0 | 0 | 3 | 7 | 2 |
| N= | 14 | 50 | 17 | 9 | 47 | 7 | 17 | 22 | 44 | 5 |
| %reg | 79 | 80 | 94 | 67 | 85 | 100 | 100 | 86 | 84 | 60 |

| | *4.02* | *4.03* | *5.01* | *5.02* | *5.03* | *5.04* | *5.05* | *5.06* | *5.07* |
|---|---|---|---|---|---|---|---|---|---|
| reg | 26 | 76 | 16 | 10 | 13 | 9 | 21 | 1 | 33 |
| unreg | 7 | 13 | 4 | 5 | 3 | 0 | 5 | 1 | 2 |
| N= | 33 | 89 | 20 | 15 | 16 | 9 | 26 | 2 | 35 |
| %reg | 79 | 85 | 80 | 67 | 81 | 100 | 81 | 50 | 94 |

Table A5.8 (*cont*).

| | *totals* | *adds* | *3.05+4.01* |
|---|---|---|---|
| reg | 655 | 20 | 64 |
| unreg | 128 | 2 | 9 |
| N= | 783 | 22 | 73 |
| %reg | 84 | 91 | 88 |

## *Chapter 6*

Table A6.1 Auxiliary 'do' use in *Pericles*

| | *Ch.1* | *1.01* | *1.02* | *1.03* | *1.04* | *Ch.2* | *2.01* | *2.02* | *2.03* | *2.04* |
|---|---|---|---|---|---|---|---|---|---|---|
| reg | 13 | 59 | 49 | 13 | 46 | 16 | 54 | 19 | 46 | 21 |
| unreg | 4 | 14 | 12 | 3 | 4 | 1 | 7 | 1 | 6 | 3 |
| N= | 17 | 73 | 61 | 16 | 50 | 17 | 61 | 20 | 52 | 24 |
| %reg | 77 | 81 | 80 | 81 | 92 | 94 | 89 | 95 | 89 | 88 |

| | *2.05* | *Ch.3* | *3.01* | *3.02* | *3.03* | *3.04* | *Ch.4* | *4.01* | *4.02* | *4.03* |
|---|---|---|---|---|---|---|---|---|---|---|
| reg | 26 | 18 | 14 | 38 | 14 | 6 | 12 | 36 | 43 | 21 |
| unreg | 7 | 2 | 2 | 5 | 0 | 1 | 3 | 4 | 6 | 6 |
| N= | 33 | 20 | 16 | 43 | 14 | 7 | 15 | 40 | 49 | 27 |
| %reg | 79 | 90 | 88 | 88 | 100 | 86 | 80 | 90 | 88 | 78 |

| | *4.04* | *4.05* | *4.06* | *Ch.5* | *5.01* | *5.02* | *5.03* | *E* |
|---|---|---|---|---|---|---|---|---|
| reg | 20 | 2 | 39 | 18 | 72 | 5 | 33 | 5 |
| unreg | 3 | 0 | 9 | 0 | 25 | 0 | 6 | 0 |
| N= | 23 | 2 | 48 | 18 | 97 | 5 | 39 | 5 |
| %reg | 87 | 100 | 81 | 100 | 74 | 100 | 85 | 100 |

| | *totals* | *ch.1-2.05* | *ch.3-Ep* |
|---|---|---|---|
| reg | 758 | 362 | 396 |
| unreg | 134 | 62 | 72 |
| N= | 892 | 424 | 468 |
| %reg | 85 | 85 | 85 |

Table A6.2 Auxiliary 'do' use in *The Miseries of Enforced Marriage*

| scene | 01 | 02 | 03 | 04 | 05 | 06 | 07 | 08 | 09 | 10 | 11 | 12 | total |
|---|---|---|---|---|---|---|---|---|---|---|---|---|---|
| reg | 121 | 40 | 39 | 87 | 37 | 89 | 22 | 36 | 81 | 48 | 104 | 77 | 781 |
| unreg | 12 | 5 | 6 | 24 | 11 | 10 | 3 | 5 | 6 | 11 | 21 | 9 | 123 |
| N= | 133 | 45 | 45 | 111 | 48 | 99 | 25 | 41 | 87 | 59 | 125 | 86 | 904 |
| %reg | 91 | 89 | 87 | 78 | 77 | 90 | 88 | 88 | 93 | 81 | 83 | 90 | 86 |

Table A6.3 Auxiliary 'do' use in *The London Prodigal*

| | *1.01* | *1.02* | *2.01* | *2.02* | *2.03* | *2.04* | *3.01* | *3.02* | *3.03* | *4.01* | *4.02* | *4.03* | *5.01* |
|---|---|---|---|---|---|---|---|---|---|---|---|---|---|
| reg | 85 | 33 | 29 | 12 | 15 | 31 | 27 | 33 | 61 | 15 | 12 | 16 | 105 |
| unreg | 5 | 3 | 3 | 2 | 2 | 7 | 1 | 13 | 16 | 0 | 3 | 5 | 18 |
| N= | 90 | 36 | 32 | 14 | 17 | 38 | 28 | 46 | 77 | 15 | 15 | 21 | 123 |
| %reg | 94 | 92 | 91 | 86 | 88 | 82 | 96 | 72 | 79 | 100 | 80 | 76 | 85 |

| | *total* | *A*<br>*scenes 3.02, 3.03, 5.01* | *B*<br>*remainder of play* |
|---|---|---|---|
| reg | 474 | 199 | 275 |
| unreg | 78 | 47 | 31 |
| N= | 552 | 246 | 123 |
| %reg | 86 | 81 | 90 |

Table A6.4 Relativisation evidence in *The London Prodigal*

| | | *restrictive* | | *non-restrictive* | | | |
|---|---|---|---|---|---|---|---|
| | | *sub* | *obj* | *sub* | *obj* | *totals* | *%* |
| who(m) | personal | 1 | 1 | 0 | 0 | 2 | |
| | | | | | | 3 | 3 |
| | non-personal | 0 | 0 | 0 | 1 | 1 | |
| which | personal | 1 | 0 | 0 | 1 | 2 | |
| | | | | | | 8 | 8 |
| | non-personal | 0 | 1 | 3 | 2 | 6 | |
| that | personal | 32 | 2 | 4 | 1 | 39 | |
| | | | | | | 60 | 58 |
| | non-personal | 8 | 11 | 1 | 1 | 21 | |
| zero | personal | 10 | 4 | 0 | 1 | 15 | |
| | | | | | | 33 | 32 |
| | non-personal | 3 | 15 | 0 | 0 | 18 | |
| | | | | | | N=104 | |

Table A6.5 Proportions of relative marker by section in *The London Prodigal*

| | *who* | *which* | *that* | *zero* |
|---|---|---|---|---|
| section A | 4 | 6 | 58 | 33 |
| section B | 2 | 10 | 57 | 31 |

Table A6.6 Auxiliary 'do' use in *Thomas, Lord Cromwell*

| | *1.01* | *1.02* | *1.03* | *1.04* | *1.05* | *1.06* | *1.07* | *1.08* | *1.09* | *1.10* | *1.11* | *1.12* |
|---|---|---|---|---|---|---|---|---|---|---|---|---|
| reg | 5 | 34 | 37 | 1 | 14 | 39 | 16 | 27 | 25 | 40 | 8 | 30 |
| unreg | 1 | 12 | 8 | 1 | 5 | 7 | 2 | 9 | 10 | 18 | 3 | 7 |
| N= | 6 | 46 | 45 | 2 | 19 | 46 | 18 | 36 | 35 | 58 | 11 | 37 |
| %reg | 83 | 74 | 82 | 50 | 74 | 85 | 89 | 75 | 71 | 69 | 73 | 81 |

| | *1.13* | *1.14* | *1.15* | *1.16* | *1.17* | *1.18* | *1.19* | *1.20* | *1.21* | *1.22* | *1.23* | *total* |
|---|---|---|---|---|---|---|---|---|---|---|---|---|
| reg | 4 | 31 | 51 | 8 | 10 | 44 | 11 | 1 | 18 | 5 | 45 | 504 |
| unreg | 3 | 4 | 9 | 2 | 5 | 14 | 4 | 2 | 4 | 5 | 12 | 147 |
| N= | 7 | 35 | 60 | 10 | 15 | 58 | 15 | 3 | 22 | 10 | 57 | 651 |
| %reg | 57 | 89 | 85 | 80 | 67 | 76 | 73 | 33 | 82 | 50 | 79 | 77 |

Table A6.7 Relative marker choice in *Thomas, Lord Cromwell*

| | | *restrictive* | | *non-restrictive* | | | | |
|---|---|---|---|---|---|---|---|---|
| | | *sub* | *obj* | *sub* | *obj* | *totals* | | *%* |
| who(m) | personal | 1 | 1 | 6 | 3 | 11 | 11 | 8 |
| | non-personal | 0 | 0 | 0 | 0 | 0 | | |
| which | personal | 0 | 0 | 0 | 0 | 0 | 15 | 10 |
| | non-personal | 1 | 4 | 5 | 5 | 15 | | |
| that | personal | 37 | 2 | 10 | 1 | 50 | 83 | 57 |
| | non-personal | 14 | 18 | 1 | 0 | 33 | | |
| zero | personal | 8 | 2 | 0 | 0 | 10 | 38 | 26 |
| | non-personal | 4 | 24 | 0 | 0 | 28 | | |
| | | | | | | N = 147 | | |

Table A6.8 Auxiliary 'do' use in *The Puritan*

| *scene* | *1* | *2* | *3* | *4* | *5* | *6* | *7* | *8* | *9* | *10* | *11* | *12* |
|---|---|---|---|---|---|---|---|---|---|---|---|---|
| reg | 48 | 33 | 10 | 65 | 86 | 19 | 14 | 83 | 76 | 6 | 90 | 6 |
| unreg | 3 | 0 | 1 | 9 | 4 | 1 | 3 | 5 | 4 | 0 | 10 | 1 |
| N= | 51 | 33 | 11 | 74 | 90 | 20 | 17 | 88 | 80 | 6 | 100 | 7 |
| %reg | 94 | 100 | 91 | 88 | 96 | 95 | 82 | 94 | 95 | 100 | 90 | 86 |

| | *13* | *14* | *15* | *totals* |
|---|---|---|---|---|
| reg | 5 | 8 | 28 | 577 |
| unreg | 0 | 0 | 6 | 47 |
| N= | 5 | 8 | 34 | 624 |
| %reg | 100 | 100 | 82 | 93 |

Table A6.9 Auxiliary 'do' use in *A Yorkshire Tragedy*

| *scene* | *.01* | *.02* | *.03* | *.04* | *.05* | *.06* | *.07* | *.08* | *.09* | *.10* | *totals* |
|---|---|---|---|---|---|---|---|---|---|---|---|
| reg | 33 | 64 | 32 | 42 | 11 | 2 | 12 | 9 | 13 | 23 | 241 |
| unreg | 0 | 12 | 1 | 4 | 1 | 0 | 1 | 1 | 10 | 2 | 22 |
| N= | 33 | 76 | 33 | 46 | 12 | 2 | 13 | 10 | 23 | 25 | 263 |
| %reg | 100 | 84 | 97 | 91 | 92 | 100 | 92 | 90 | 57 | 92 | 92 |

Table A6.10 Auxiliary 'do' use in *Locrine*

| | *1.01* | *1.02* | *1.03* | *1.04* | *2.01* | *2.02* | *2.03* | *2.04* | *2.05* | *2.06* | *2.07* | *3.01* |
|---|---|---|---|---|---|---|---|---|---|---|---|---|
| reg | 11 | 76 | 21 | 3 | 8 | 26 | 16 | 20 | 2 | 33 | 6 | 7 |
| unreg | 2 | 10 | 3 | 0 | 1 | 8 | 2 | 7 | 3 | 6 | 1 | 2 |
| N= | 13 | 86 | 24 | 3 | 9 | 34 | 18 | 27 | 5 | 39 | 7 | 9 |
| %reg | 85 | 88 | 88 | 100 | 89 | 77 | 89 | 74 | 40 | 85 | 86 | 78 |

| | *3.02* | *3.03* | *3.04* | *3.05* | *3.06* | *4.01* | *4.02* | *4.03* | *4.04* | *4.05* | *5.01* | *5.02* |
|---|---|---|---|---|---|---|---|---|---|---|---|---|
| reg | 23 | 22 | 6 | 12 | 19 | 8 | 54 | 35 | 11 | 6 | 5 | 26 |
| unreg | 4 | 5 | 2 | 2 | 3 | 1 | 13 | 1 | 0 | 1 | 0 | 7 |
| n= | 27 | 27 | 8 | 14 | 22 | 9 | 67 | 36 | 11 | 7 | 5 | 33 |
| %reg | 85 | 82 | 75 | 86 | 86 | 89 | 81 | 97 | 100 | 86 | 100 | 79 |

| | *5.03* | *5.04* | *5.05* | *total* |
|---|---|---|---|---|
| reg | 16 | 2 | 25 | 541 |
| unreg | 5 | 2 | 3 | 101 |
| N= | 21 | 4 | 28 | 642 |
| %reg | 76 | 50 | 89 | 84 |

Table A6.11 Relative marker evidence in *Locrine*

| | | *restrictive* | | *non-restrictive* | | | |
|---|---|---|---|---|---|---|---|
| | | *sub* | *obj* | *sub* | *obj* | *totals* | *%* |
| who(m) | personal | 3 | 1 | 2 | 2 | 8 | |
| | | | | | | 8 | 5 |
| | non-personal | 0 | 0 | 0 | 0 | 0 | |
| which | personal | 2 | 1 | 0 | 0 | 3 | |
| | | | | | | 32 | 20 |
| | non-personal | 5 | 4 | 4 | 6 | 29 | |
| that | personal | 62 | 0 | 14 | 0 | 76 | |
| | | | | | | 114 | 72 |
| | non-personal | 32 | 3 | 3 | 0 | 38 | |
| zero | personal | 0 | 0 | 0 | 0 | 0 | |
| | | | | | | 4 | 3 |
| | non-personal | 0 | 4 | 0 | 0 | 4 | |
| | | | | | | N=158 | |

Table A6.12 Auxiliary 'do' use in *Arden of Faversham*

| | *1.01* | *2.01* | *2.02* | *3.01* | *3.02* | *3.03* | *3.04* | *3.05* | *3.06* | *4.01* | *4.02* | *4.03* |
|---|---|---|---|---|---|---|---|---|---|---|---|---|
| reg | 202 | 29 | 44 | 38 | 18 | 24 | 10 | 56 | 60 | 35 | 8 | 19 |
| unreg | 28 | 5 | 12 | 4 | 2 | 2 | 2 | 14 | 9 | 5 | 1 | 4 |
| N= | 230 | 34 | 56 | 42 | 20 | 26 | 12 | 70 | 69 | 40 | 9 | 23 |
| %reg | 88 | 85 | 79 | 91 | 90 | 92 | 83 | 80 | 87 | 88 | 89 | 83 |

| | *4.04* | *5.01* | *5.02* | *5.03* | *5.04* | *5.05* | *E* | *total* |
|---|---|---|---|---|---|---|---|---|
| reg | 57 | 99 | 7 | 13 | 2 | 8 | 3 | 730 |
| unreg | 5 | 23 | 0 | 1 | 0 | 3 | 1 | 121 |
| N= | 62 | 122 | 7 | 14 | 2 | 12 | 4 | 851 |
| %reg | 92 | 81 | 100 | 93 | 100 | 67 | 75 | 86 |

Table A6.13 Auxiliary 'do' use in *The Birth of Merlin*

| | *1.01* | *1.02* | *2.01* | *2.02* | *2.03* | *3.01* | *3.02* | *3.03* | *3.04* | *3.05* | *3.06* | *4.01* |
|---|---|---|---|---|---|---|---|---|---|---|---|---|
| reg | 46 | 81 | 61 | 30 | 74 | 70 | 45 | 4 | 36 | 9 | 27 | 64 |
| unreg | 3 | 7 | 11 | 3 | 10 | 6 | 11 | 1 | 4 | 0 | 5 | 14 |
| N= | 49 | 88 | 72 | 33 | 84 | 76 | 56 | 5 | 40 | 9 | 32 | 78 |
| %reg | 88 | 92 | 85 | 91 | 88 | 92 | 80 | 80 | 90 | 100 | 84 | 82 |

| | *4.02* | *4.03* | *4.04* | *4.05* | *5.01* | *5.02* | *total* |
|---|---|---|---|---|---|---|---|
| reg | 10 | 7 | 4 | 52 | 11 | 18 | 649 |
| unreg | 2 | 2 | 1 | 1 | 4 | 1 | 89 |
| N= | 12 | 9 | 5 | 53 | 15 | 19 | 738 |
| %reg | 83 | 78 | 80 | 98 | 73 | 95 | 88 |

Table A6.14 Auxiliary 'do' use in *Edward III*

| | *1.01* | *1.02* | *2.01* | *2.02* | *3.01* | *3.02* | *3.03* | *3.04* | *3.05* | *4.01* | *4.02* | *4.03* |
|---|---|---|---|---|---|---|---|---|---|---|---|---|
| reg | 34 | 49 | 107 | 61 | 56 | 30 | 53 | 4 | 28 | 10 | 15 | 14 |
| unreg | 9 | 5 | 32 | 7 | 7 | 6 | 9 | 1 | 2 | 1 | 2 | 5 |
| N= | 43 | 54 | 139 | 68 | 63 | 36 | 62 | 5 | 30 | 11 | 17 | 19 |
| %reg | 79 | 91 | 77 | 90 | 89 | 83 | 86 | 80 | 93 | 91 | 88 | 74 |

| | *4.04* | *4.05* | *4.06* | *4.07* | *4.08* | *4.09* | *5.01* | *total* | *acts 1-2* | *acts 3-5* |
|---|---|---|---|---|---|---|---|---|---|---|
| reg | 57 | 37 | 2 | 11 | 3 | 14 | 58 | 643 | 251 | 392 |
| unreg | 10 | 10 | 4 | 1 | 2 | 2 | 14 | 127 | 53 | 74 |
| N= | 67 | 47 | 6 | 12 | 5 | 16 | 72 | 770 | 304 | 466 |
| %reg | 85 | 79 | 33 | 92 | 60 | 88 | 81 | 84 | 83 | 84 |

Table A6.15 Relative marker choice in *Edward III* – whole text

| | | restrictive | | non-restrictive | | | |
|---|---|---|---|---|---|---|---|
| | | *sub* | *obj* | *sub* | *obj* | *totals* | *%* |
| who(m) | personal | 0 | 1 | 7 | 6 | 14 | |
| | | | | | | 17 | 8 |
| | non-personal | 0 | 0 | 3 | 0 | 3 | |
| which | personal | 0 | 0 | 1 | 0 | 1 | |
| | | | | | | 21 | 10 |
| | non-personal | 6 | 2 | 3 | 9 | 20 | |
| that | personal | 44 | 4 | 12 | 0 | 60 | |
| | | | | | | 132 | 65 |
| | non-personal | 27 | 31 | 13 | 1 | 72 | |
| zero | personal | 3 | 0 | 3 | 0 | 6 | |
| | | | | | | 33 | 16 |
| | non-personal | 8 | 19 | 0 | 0 | 27 | |
| | | | | | | N=203 | |

Table A6.16 Relative marker choice in *Edward III* acts 1-2

| | | restrictive | | non-restrictive | | | |
|---|---|---|---|---|---|---|---|
| | | *sub* | *obj* | *sub* | *obj* | *totals* | *%* |
| who(m) | personal | 0 | 0 | 2 | 2 | 4 | |
| | | | | | | 7 | 8 |
| | non-personal | 0 | 0 | 3 | 0 | 3 | |
| which | personal | 0 | 0 | 1 | 0 | 1 | |
| | | | | | | 13 | 14 |
| | non-personal | 3 | 1 | 3 | 5 | 12 | |
| that | personal | 14 | 2 | 4 | 0 | 20 | |
| | | | | | | 57 | 63 |
| | non-personal | 14 | 17 | 6 | 0 | 37 | |
| zero | personal | 2 | 0 | 0 | 0 | 2 | |
| | | | | | | 14 | 15 |
| | non-personal | 5 | 7 | 0 | 0 | 12 | |
| | | | | | | N=91 | |

Table A6.17 Relative marker choice in *Edward III* acts 3-5

| | | *restrictive* | | *non-restrictive* | | | | |
|---|---|---|---|---|---|---|---|---|
| | | *sub* | *obj* | *sub* | *obj* | *totals* | | *%* |
| who(m) | personal | 0 | 1 | 5 | 4 | 10 | 10 | 9 |
| | non-personal | 0 | 0 | 0 | 0 | 0 | | |
| which | personal | 0 | 0 | 0 | 0 | 0 | 8 | 7 |
| | non-personal | 3 | 1 | 0 | 4 | 8 | | |
| that | personal | 30 | 2 | 8 | 0 | 40 | 75 | 67 |
| | non-personal | 13 | 14 | 7 | 1 | 35 | | |
| zero | personal | 1 | 0 | 3 | 0 | 4 | 19 | 17 |
| | non-personal | 3 | 12 | 0 | 0 | 15 | | |
| | | | | | | N=112 | | |

Table A6.18 Auxiliary 'do' use in *Edmond Ironside*

| | *1.01* | *1.02* | *1.03* | *2.01* | *2.02* | *2.03* | *3.01* | *3.02* | *3.03* | *3.04* | *3.05* | *3.06* |
|---|---|---|---|---|---|---|---|---|---|---|---|---|
| reg | 69 | 19 | 13 | 13 | 27 | 56 | 20 | 17 | 21 | 7 | 51 | 6 |
| unreg | 13 | 5 | 4 | 5 | 6 | 23 | 6 | 10 | 0 | 0 | 11 | 0 |
| N= | 82 | 24 | 17 | 18 | 33 | 79 | 26 | 27 | 21 | 7 | 62 | 6 |
| %reg | 84 | 79 | 72 | 72 | 82 | 71 | 77 | 63 | 100 | 100 | 82 | 100 |

| | *4.01* | *4.02* | *4.03* | *4.04* | *5.01* | *5.02* | *totals* |
|---|---|---|---|---|---|---|---|
| reg | 48 | 19 | 11 | 13 | 33 | 75 | 518 |
| unreg | 13 | 3 | 4 | 4 | 10 | 16 | 133 |
| N= | 61 | 22 | 15 | 17 | 43 | 91 | 651 |
| %reg | 79 | 86 | 73 | 77 | 77 | 82 | 80 |

Table A6.19 Auxiliary 'do' use in *Sir Thomas More*

(a) Original text (hand S)

| *scene* | *1* | *2* | *3* | *4* | *5* | *6* | *7* | *8a* | *8b* | *9* | *10* | *11* |
|---|---|---|---|---|---|---|---|---|---|---|---|---|
| reg | 41 | 50 | 29 | 12 | 10 | 21 | 40 | 23 | 24 | 84 | 25 | 33 |
| unreg | 4 | 8 | 5 | 2 | 0 | 2 | 8 | 3 | 6 | 17 | 4 | 5 |
| N= | 45 | 58 | 34 | 14 | 10 | 23 | 48 | 26 | 30 | 101 | 29 | 38 |
| %reg | 91 | 86 | 85 | 86 | 100 | 91 | 83 | 89 | 80 | 83 | 86 | 87 |

| | *12* | *13* | *14* | *15* | *16* | *17* |
|---|---|---|---|---|---|---|
| reg | 12 | 57 | 17 | 14 | 26 | 33 |
| unreg | 1 | 6 | 3 | 2 | 2 | 2 |
| N= | 13 | 63 | 20 | 16 | 28 | 35 |
| %reg | 92 | 91 | 85 | 88 | 93 | 94 |

(b) Additions (hands A-E)

| | addition 1 | addition 2 | | | addition 3 | addition 4 | | addition 5 | addition 6 |
|---|---|---|---|---|---|---|---|---|---|
| scene | 8 | 4 | 5 | 6 | 8 | 8 | 8 | 10 | 9 |
| hand | A | B | C | D | C | C | E | C | B |
| reg | 25 | 14 | 16 | 27 | 2 | 55 | 10 | 10 | 13 |
| unreg | 4 | 3 | 6 | 6 | 0 | 11 | 2 | 0 | 4 |
| N= | 29 | 17 | 22 | 33 | 2 | 66 | 12 | 10 | 17 |
| %reg | 86 | 82 | 73 | 82 | 100 | 83 | 83 | 100 | 77 |

(c) Totals:

| | *S* | *A* | *B* | *C* | *D* | *E* | *Whole play* | *Original text a* | *Original text b* |
|---|---|---|---|---|---|---|---|---|---|
| reg | 552 | 25 | 27 | 83 | 27 | 10 | 724 | 202 | 350 |
| unreg | 80 | 4 | 7 | 17 | 6 | 2 | 116 | 40 | 40 |
| N= | 632 | 29 | 34 | 100 | 33 | 12 | 840 | 242 | 390 |
| %reg | 87 | 86 | 79 | 83 | 82 | 83 | 86 | 84 | 90 |

# Bibliography

(Place of publication is London unless otherwise stated.)

Abbott, E., 1869, *A Shakespearean Grammar* (reprinted 1966)

Adams, G., 1974, '*The Woman's Prize*', unpublished PhD thesis, University of New Brunswick

Adams, J. (ed.), 1917, *Dramatic Records of Sir Henry Herbert*, New Haven (reprinted New York, 1963)

Adams, R., 1988, 'The Defoe file', *The New York Review of Books*, 22 December, pp. 58–60

Aitchison, Jean, 1991, *Language Change: Progress or Decay?* (2nd edition), Cambridge

Alexander, Peter, 1930, 'Conjectural history, or Shakespeare's *Henry VIII*', *Essays and Studies of the English Association*, 16, ed. H. Grierson, pp. 85–120

1939, *Shakespeare's Life and Art*

Appleton, W., 1956, *Beaumont and Fletcher; A Critical Study*

Ard, J., 1982, 'Auxiliary "do": support or emphasis?', *Linguistics*, 20, pp. 445–66

Baghdikian, S., 1979, 'The structure of negative sentences in 16th century English', *Linguistics in Belgium* (papers from the third December meeting of the Belgian Linguistic Circle, Dec. 1978), eds. S. de Vriendt, M. Dominicy, C. Peeters, Brussels, pp. 11–19

1982, 'A functional perspective of the system of negation in early Modern English', *Folia Linguistica Historica*, III/2, pp. 153–61

1985, '"He did not seek" or "He seeketh not": are you a queen or a country woman?', *Communicating and Translating: Essays in Honour of Jean Dierickx*, eds. J. van Noppen and G. Debusscher, Brussels, pp. 241–8

Bailey, R., 1978, *Early Modern English*, Hildesheim

Baker, J., 1988, 'Pace: a test of authorship based on the rate at which new words enter an author's text', *Literary and Linguistic Computing*, 3.1, pp. 1–11

Baker, W., 1967, *Syntax in English Poetry, 1870–1930*, Berkeley, CA

Barber, C., 1976, *Early Modern English*

1981, '"You" and "Thou" in Shakespeare's *Richard III*', *Leeds Studies in English*, 12, pp. 273–89

Bawcutt, N. (ed.), 1977, *The Two Noble Kinsmen*, Harmondsworth

Beebe, L. M., and H. Giles, 1984, 'Speech-accommodation theories: a discussion in terms of second-language acquisition', *International Journal of the Sociology of Language*, 46, pp. 5–32

Bentley, G., 1948, 'Shakespeare and the Blackfriars theatre', *Shakespeare Survey*, 1, pp. 38–50

1971, *The Profession of Dramatist in Shakespeare's Time, 1590–1642*, Princeton, NJ

Berry, F., 1958, *Poets' Grammar: Person, Time and Mood in Poetry*

Berry, L., 1960, 'Biographical notes on Richard Fletcher', *Notes and Queries*, October, pp. 377–8

1964, 'The Life of Giles Fletcher, the Elder', *The English Works of Giles Fletcher, the Elder*, University of Wisconsin Press, Madison, WI, pp. 3–49

Bertram, P., 1961, 'The date of *The Two Noble Kinsmen*', *Shakespeare Quarterly*, 12, pp. 21–32

1965, *Shakespeare and The Two Noble Kinsmen*, New Jersey

Biber, D., 1988, *Variation Across Speech and Writing*, Cambridge

1989, 'A typology of English texts', *Linguistics*, 27.1, pp. 3–43

Blake, N., 1983, *Shakespeare's Language*

1987, 'Levels of language in *Henry IV* part one', *Stylistica*, eds. M. Gomez Lara and J. Prieto Pablos, Alfar, Seville, pp. 189–207

Bowers, F. (gen. ed.), 1966–, *The Dramatic Works in the Beaumont and Fletcher Canon*, seven volumes to date: 1 (1966), 2 (1970), 3 (1976), 4 (1979), 5 (1982), 6 (1985), 7 (1989), Cambridge

Boyle, R., 1880–5, '*Henry VIII*. An investigation into the origin and authorship of the play', *Transactions of the New Shakespeare Society 1880–5*, pp. 443–87

Bradford, Gamaliel, 1910, '*The History of Cardenio* by Mr. Fletcher and Shakespeare', *Modern Language Notes*, 25, pp. 51–6

Bradley, A.C., 1929, *A Miscellany*

Brainerd, B., 1979, 'Pronouns and genre in Shakespeare's drama', *Computers and the Humanities*, 13, pp. 3–16

Brook, G., 1976, *The Language of Shakespeare*

Brown, R., and A. Gilman, 1960, 'The pronouns of power and solidarity', *Style in Language*, ed. Thomas Sebeok, New York and London, reprinted in *Communication in Face to Face Interaction*, eds. J. Laver and S. Hutcheson, 1972, Harmondsworth, pp. 128–45

1989, 'Politeness theory and Shakespeare's four major tragedies', *Language in Society*, 18, pp. 159–212

Brown, P., and S. Levinson, 1987, *Politeness: Some Universals in Language Usage*, Cambridge (first published 1978 in E. Goody (ed.), *Questions and Politeness*, Cambridge, 1987 reissued with new introduction and corrections)

Burton, D.M., 1968, *Shakespeare's Grammatical Style*

Byrne, G., 1936, *Shakespeare's Use of the Pronoun of Address, its Significance in Characterisation and Motivation*, New York

Calvo, Clara, 1992, 'Pronouns of address and social negotiation in *As You Like It*', *Language and Literature*, 1, pp. 5–27

Cawley, A., and B. Gaines (eds.), 1986, *A Yorkshire Tragedy*, Manchester

Chambers, E., 1944, *Shakespeare Gleanings*, Oxford

Clinch, N. (ed.), 1987, *Monsieur Thomas*, New York

Collinson, Patrick, 1983, 'Cranbrook and the Fletchers: popular and unpopular religion in the Kentish Weald', *Godly People: Essays on English Protestantism and Puritanism*, pp. 399–428

Craig, D. H., 1991, 'Plural pronouns in Roman Plays by Shakespeare and Jonson', *Literary and Linguistic Computing*, 6, pp. 180–6

Dekeyser, X., 1987, 'Relative clause formation in the *Anglo-Saxon Chronicle*', *Folia Linguistica Historica*, VII/2, pp. 351–61

Denison, David, 1985, 'The origins of periphrastic do: Ellegard and Visser reconsidered', *Papers from the Fourth International Conference on English Historical Linguistics*, eds. R. Eaton, O. Fischer, W. Koopman, W. van der Leek, Amsterdam, pp. 45–60

Devitt, Amy, 1989, *Standardizing Written English: Diffusion in the Case of Scotland 1520–1659*, Cambridge

Dominik, M., 1985, *William Shakespeare and The Birth of Merlin*

Donawerth, J., 1984, *Shakespeare and the Sixteenth-century Study of Language*, Urbana

Doran, M., 1960, Review of Foakes 1957, *Journal of English and Germanic Philology*, 59, pp. 287–91

Edwards, P., and C. Gibson, 1976, *The Plays and Poems of Philip Massinger*, 5 volumes, Oxford

Ellegard, A., 1953, *The Auxiliary Do. The Establishment and Regulation of its Use in English*, Stockholm

Elliot, Ward, and Robert Valenza, 1991a, 'Was the Earl of Oxford the true Shakespeare? A computer-aided analysis', *Notes and Queries*, 38/4, pp. 501–6

1991b, 'A touchstone for the bard', *Computers and the Humanities*, 25, pp. 199–209

Ellis-Fermor, U., 1961, *Shakespeare the Dramatist, and Other Papers*, ed. K. Muir

Engblom, V., 1938, *On the Origin and Development of the Auxiliary Do*, Lund

Everitt, E., 1954, *The Young Shakespeare: Studies in Documentary Evidence*, Anglistica II

Farmer, J. (ed.), 1910, *The Two Noble Kinsmen*, Tudor Facsimile Texts (reprinted New York, 1970)

Farnham, W., 1916, 'Colloquial contractions in Beaumont, Fletcher, Massinger and Shakespeare as a test of authorship', *Publications of the Modern Language Association of America*, 31, pp. 326–58

Fleay, F.G., 1874, *Transactions of the New Shakespeare Society*, pp. 1–84, 130–51, 195–209, 285–317, 339–66, Appendix, pp. 23, 61–4

Foakes, R. (ed.), 1957, *Henry VIII* (Arden, revised 1964)

Fox, B., and S. Thompson, 1990, 'A discourse explanation of the grammar of relative clauses in English conversation', *Language*, 66, pp. 297–316

Frazier, Harriet C., 1968, 'The rifling of beauty's stores: Theobald and Shakespeare', *Neuphilologische Mitteilungen*, 79, pp. 232–56

1974, *A Babble of Ancestral Voices: Shakespeare, Cervantes, and Theobald*, The Hague

Freehafer, John, 1969, '*Cardenio*, by Shakespeare and Fletcher', *PMLA*, 84, pp. 501–13

Friedrich, P., 1972, 'Social context and semantic feature: the Russian pronominal usage', eds. J. Gumperz and D. Hymes, *Directions in Sociolinguistics*, New York, pp. 270–300

Frye, Northrop, 1965, *A Natural Perspective: the Development of Shakespearean Comedy and Romance*

Furbank, P., and W. Owens, 1988, *The Canonisation of Daniel Defoe*

Gillet, P., 1974, 'Me, U, and Non-U: class connotations of two idioms', *Shakespeare Quarterly*, 25, pp. 297–309

Glover, A., and A. Waller (eds.), 1905–12, *The Works of Francis Beaumont and John Fletcher*, 12 volumes, Cambridge

Greg, W.W., 1955, *The Shakespeare First Folio, its Bibliographical and Textual History*, Oxford

1957, *A Bibliography of the English Printed Drama to the Restoration*

Gurr, A., 1982, 'You and thou in Shakespeare's sonnets', *Essays in Criticism*, 32, 9–25

Hammond, Brean S., 1984, 'Theobald's *Double Falshood*: an "Agreeable cheat"?', *Notes and Queries*, 229, pp. 2–3

Hart, A., 1934, 'Shakespeare and the vocabulary of *The Two Noble Kinsmen*', *Review of English Studies*, 10, pp. 274–87, (reprinted in *Shakespeare and the Homilies, and Other Pieces of Research into Elizabethan Drama*, Melbourne, 1934)

Hausmann, R., 1974, 'The origin and development of modern English periphrastic "do"', *Historical Linguistics*, 1, Proceedings of the First International Conference on Historical Linguistics, North Holland linguistic series 12a, eds. J. Anderson and C. Jones, Amsterdam, pp. 159–89

Hensman, B., 1974, *The Shares of Fletcher, Field and Massinger in Twelve Plays of the Beaumont and Fletcher Canon*, 2 volumes, Salzburg

Hickson, S., 1847, 'The shares of Shakespeare and Fletcher in *The Two Noble Kinsmen*', *The Westminster and Foreign Quarterly Review*, 47, pp. 59–88 (reprinted in *Transactions of the New Shakespeare Society 1874*, Appendix, pp. 25–61)

1850, Letter on Spedding 1850, *Notes and Queries*, 2, August, p. 198

Hoeniger, F. (ed.), 1963, *Pericles* (Arden)

Holdsworth, Richard, 1982, 'Middleton and Shakespeare: the case for Middleton's hand in *Timon of Athens*',unpublished PhD thesis, University of Manchester

Honigmann, E., 1967, 'On the indifferent and one way variants in Shakespeare', *The Library*, pp. 189–204

Hope, Jonathan, 1990a, 'Socio-historical linguistic evidence for the authorship of renaissance plays: test cases in the Shakespeare, Fletcher, and Massinger canons', unpublished PhD thesis, University of Cambridge

1990b, 'Applied historical linguistics: socio-historical linguistic evidence for the authorship of renaissance plays', *Transactions of the Philological Society*, 88/2, pp. 201–26

1993, 'Second person singular pronouns in records of early Modern "spoken" English', *Neuphilologische Mitteilungen*, 94/1, pp. 83–100

forthcoming, 'The status of auxiliary do', paper read at the Seventh International Conference on English Historical Linguistics, Valencia, September 1992

Horton, Thomas Bolton, 1987, *The Effectiveness of the Stylometry of Function Words in Discriminating between Shakespeare and Fletcher*, thesis number CST–48–87, published by the Department of Computer Science, University of Edinburgh

Hoy, Cyrus, 1956–62, 'The shares of Fletcher and his collaborators in the Beaumont and Fletcher canon', *Studies in Bibliography*, 7 (1956), pp. 129–46; 9 (1957), pp. 143–62; 11 (1958), pp. 85–106; 12 (1959), pp. 91–116; 13 (1960), pp. 77–108; 14 (1961), pp. 45–67; 15 (1962), pp. 71–90

1976, 'Critical and aesthetic problems of collaboration in renaissance drama', *Research Opportunities in Renaissance Drama*, 19, pp. 3–6

1984, 'Fletcherian Romantic Comedy', *Research Opportunities in Renaissance Drama*, 27, pp. 3–11

1985, 'Massinger as a collaborator: the plays with Fletcher and others', *Philip Massinger: a Critical Reassessment*, ed. D. Howard, Cambridge, pp. 51–82

Hudson, Richard, 1980, *Sociolinguistics*, Cambridge

Humphreys, A. (ed.), 1971, *Henry VIII*, Harmondsworth

Ingram, J., 1874, 'On the 'weak endings' of Shakespeare, with some account of the history of the verse-texts in general', *Transactions of the New Shakespeare Society*, pp. 442–51

Jackson, MacD., P., 1962, 'Affirmative particles in *Henry VIII*', *Notes and Queries*, 207, pp. 372–4

1965, '*Edward III*, Shakespeare, and Pembroke's Men', *Notes and Queries*, 210, pp. 329–31

1979, *Studies in Attribution: Middleton and Shakespeare*, Salzburg

1990, '*Pericles* acts I and II: new evidence for George Wilkins', *Notes and Queries*, 235, June, pp. 192–6

1993a, 'Rhyming in *Pericles*: more evidence of dual authorship', *Studies in Bibliography*, 96, pp. 239–49

1993b, 'The authorship of *Pericles*: the evidence of infinitives', *Notes and Queries*, 238, pp. 197–200

Johnson, A., 1966, 'The pronouns of direct address in 17th century English', *American Speech*, 41, pp. 261–9

Jones, G., 1981, 'You, thou, he or she? The master-mistress in Shakespearean and Elizabethan sonnet sequences', *Cahiers Elisabethains*, 19, pp. 73–84

Kenny, A., 1982, *The Computation of Style*

Kermode, F., 1948, 'What is Shakespeare's *Henry VIII* about?', *Durham University Journal*, new series 9, pp. 48–55

1963, *William Shakespeare; The Final Plays*

Kermode, F. (ed.), 1954, *The Tempest*, Arden

Kerrigan, John, 1983, 'Revision, adaptation, and the fool in *King Lear*', *The Division of the Kingdoms: Shakespeare's Two Versions of King Lear*, eds. G. Taylor and M. Warren, Oxford, pp. 196–245

1986, 'Diary', *The London Review of Books*, 6 February, p. 21

1990, '*Henry IV* and the Death of Old Double', *Essays in Criticism*, pp. 24–53

Kerrigan, John (ed.), 1986, *The Sonnets and A Lover's Complaint*, Harmondsworth

Knight, G., 1947, '*Henry VIII* and the poetry of conversion', *The Crown of Life; Essays in Interpretation of Shakespeare's Final Plays*, pp. 256–336 (2nd ed. 1948)

Knutson, R., 1985, '*Henslowe's Diary* and the economics of play revision for revival, 1592–1603', *Theatre Research International*, 10, pp. 1–18

Kroch, A., 1989, 'Function and grammar in the history of English: periphrastic "do"', *Language Change and Variation*, eds. R. Fasold and D. Schiffrin, Amsterdam, pp. 133–172

Kroeber, A., 1958, 'Parts of speech in poetry', *Publications of the Modern Language Association of America*, 73, pp. 309–14

Kukowski, Stephan, 1990, 'The hand of John Fletcher in *Double Falshood*', *Shakespeare Survey*, 43, pp. 81–9

Labov, William, 1972, *Sociolinguistic Patterns*, Philadelphia

Lake, David, 1975, *The Canon of Thomas Middleton's Plays: Internal Evidence for the Major Problems of Authorship*, Cambridge

Lancashire, A., and J. Levenson, 1973, 'Anonymous Plays', *The Predecessors of Shakespeare: A Survey and Bibliography of Recent Studies in English Renaissance Drama*, eds. T. Logan and D. Smith, Nebraska

1975, 'Anonymous Plays', *The Popular School: A Survey and Bibliography of Recent Studies in English Renaissance Drama*, eds. T. Logan and D. Smith, Nebraska

Lass, Roger (ed.), forthcoming, *The Cambridge History of the English Language*, volume three, Cambridge

Law, R., 1957, 'Holinshed and *Henry VIII*', *Texas Studies in English*, 36, pp. 3–11

1959, 'The double authorship of *Henry VIII*', *Studies in Philology*, 56, pp. 471–88

Leech, C., 1962a, *Shakespeare; the Chronicles*

1962b, *The John Fletcher Plays*

Lehmann, C., 1986, 'On the typology of relative clauses', *Linguistics*, 24.4, pp. 663–80

Leith, Dick, 1983, *A Social History of English*

1984, 'Tudor London: sociolinguistic stratification and linguistic change', *Anglo-American Studies*, 4.1, Salamanca, Spain, pp. 59–72

Lightfoot, David, 1979, *Principles of Diachronic Syntax*, Cambridge

Littledale, H. (ed.), 1876, *The Two Noble Kinsmen*, 3 volumes: I (type facsimile), II (edition with commentary), III (1885, introduction and word index)

Logan, T., and D. Smith, 1978, *The Later Jacobean and Caroline Dramatists: A Survey and Bibliography of Recent Studies in English Renaissance Drama*, Nebraska

Maxwell, B., 1923, 'Fletcher and Shakespeare', *Manly Anniversary Studies*; revised in *Studies in Beaumont, Fletcher, and Massinger*, New York, 1939

1935, '*The Woman's Prize, or the Tamer Tamed*', *Modern Philology*, 32, pp. 353–63

1939, *Studies in Beaumont, Fletcher and Massinger* (reprinted London, 1962)

1956, *Studies in the Shakespeare Apocrypha*

Maxwell, J.C., 1950, 'Peele and Shakespeare: a stylometric test', *Journal of English and Germanic Philology*, 49, pp. 557–61

Maxwell, J.C. (ed.), 1962, *Henry VIII*, Cambridge

McIntosh, A., 1963a, '*King Lear* act 1, scene 1. A stylistic note', *Review of English Studies*, New Series 14, pp. 54–6

1963b, '*As You Like It*: a grammatical clue to character', *Review of English Literature*, 4, pp. 68–81

Merriam, Thomas, 1982, 'The authorship of *Sir Thomas More*', *Association for Literary and Linguistic Computing Bulletin*, 10, pp. 1–8

1985, 'The consonance of literary elements with mathematical models: a study of authorship in the Huntingdon plays', unpublished M. Phil. thesis, King's College, University of London

1989, 'Taylor's statistics in *A Textual Companion*', *Notes and Queries*, September, pp. 341–2

1992a, 'Chettle, Munday, Shakespeare, and *Sir Thomas More*', *Notes and Queries*, September, pp. 336–41

1992b, '*Pericles* I–II revisited and considerations concerning literary medium as a systematic factor in stylometry', *Notes and Queries*, September, pp. 341–5

Merriam, T., and M. Smith, 1986, 'The authorship controversy of *Sir Thomas More*', [comment by Merriam on previous work and debate, reply by Smith], *Literary and Linguistic Computing*, 1.2, pp. 104–8

Metz, G., 1982, *Four Plays Ascribed to Shakespeare*, New York

1985, 'Disputed Shakespearean texts and stylometric analysis', *TEXT*, 2, pp. 149–72

1989, '"Voyce and Credyt": the scholars and *Sir Thomas More*', *Shakespeare and Sir Thomas More: Essays on the Play and its Shakespearean Interest*, ed. T. Howard-Hill, Cambridge

Milroy, Lesley, 1987, *Observing and Analysing Natural Language: A Critical Account of Sociolinguistic Method*, Oxford

Mincoff, Marco, 1952, 'The authorship of *The Two Noble Kinsmen*', *English Studies*, 33, pp. 97–115

1960, '*Henry VIII* and Fletcher', *Shakespeare Quarterly*, 12, pp. 239–60

1964, 'Fletcher's early tragedies', *Renaissance Drama*, 7, pp. 70–94

1966, '*The Faithful Shepherdess*: a Fletcherian experiment', *Renaissance Drama*, 9, pp. 163–77

Morton, A.Q., 1978, *Literary Detection*

1986, 'Once. A test of authorship based on words which are not repeated in the sample', *Literary and Linguistic Computing*, 1.1, pp. 1–8

Muir, Kenneth, 1954, 'The kite-cluster in *The Two Noble Kinsmen*', *Notes and Queries*, 189, pp. 52–3

1960, *Shakespeare as Collaborator*

Muir, Kenneth (ed.), 1970, *Double Falshood*, Cornmarket Press Facsimile (general editor H. Neville Davies)

Mulholland, J., 1967, '"Thou" and "You"' in Shakespeare: a study in the second person pronoun', *English Studies*, Amsterdam, 48, pp. 34–43

Nagucka, R., 1980, 'Grammatical peculiarities of the contact-clause in early Modern English', *Folia Linguistica*, I/1, pp. 171–84

Nevalainen, Terttu, 1991, 'Motivated archaism: the use of affirmative periphrastic do in Early Modern English liturgical prose', *Historical English Syntax* (Topics in English Linguistics 2), ed. Dieter Kastovsky, Berlin, pp. 303–20

Nevalainen, Terttu, and Matti Rissanen, 1985, 'Do you support the *Do*-support? Emphatic and non-emphatic Do in auxiliary statements in present-day spoken English', *Papers from the Third Scandinavian Symposium on Syntactic Variation*, ed. S. Jacobson, Stockholm, pp. 35–50

Nicholson, M., 1922, 'The authorship of *Henry VIII*', *Publications of the Modern Language Association of America*, 37, pp. 484–502

Nosworthy, J. (ed.), 1955, *Cymbeline* (Arden)

Oliphant, E., 1927, *The Plays of Beaumont and Fletcher; An Attempt to Determine Their Respective Shares and the Shares of Others*, New Haven

Ogura, Mieko, 1993, 'The development of periphrastic *do* in English: a case of lexical diffusion in syntax', *Diachronica*, 10, pp. 51–85

Oras, A., 1953, 'Extra monosyllables' in *Henry VIII* and the problem of authorship', *Journal of English and Germanic Philology*, 52, pp. 198–213

Pafford, J. (ed.), 1963, *The Winter's Tale* (Arden)

Partridge, A.C., 1949, *The Problem of Henry VIII Reopened*, Cambridge

1964, *Orthography in Shakespearean and Elizabethan drama*

Pennel, C., and W. Williams, 1968, *Francis Beaumont-John Fletcher-Philip Massinger, 1937–65; John Ford, 1940–65; James Shirley, 1945–65*, Elizabethan Bibliographies Supplements, 8

Philippides, D., 1988, 'Literary detection in the *Erotokritos* and *The Sacrifice of Abraham*', *Literary and Linguistic Computing*, 3.1, pp. 1–11

Poel, W., 1913, 'The authors of *King Henry VIII*', *Shakespeare in the Theatre*, pp. 85–98

Poussa, Pat, 1990, 'A contact-universals origin for periphrastic *do* with special consideration of Old English-Celtic contact', *Papers from the Fifth International Conference on English Historical Linguistics*, eds. Sylvia Adamson, Vivien Law, Nigel Vincent and Susan

Wright, Amsterdam, pp. 407–34

Proudfoot, G.R., 1966, 'Shakespeare and the new dramatists of the King's Men', *Later Shakespeare*, Stratford-upon-Avon Studies 8, general eds. J.R. Brown and B. Harris, Stratford on Avon, pp. 235–61

1985, '*The Reign of King Edward The Third* (1596) and Shakespeare', *Proceedings of the British Academy*, 71 (published 1986), pp. 159–186

Proudfoot, G.R. (ed.), 1970, *The Two Noble Kinsmen*, Regents Renaissance Drama Series

Quirk, Randolf, 1957, 'Relative clauses in educated spoken English', *English Studies*, 38, pp. 97–109

Quirk, Randolf, Sidney Greenbaum, Geoffrey Leech, Jan Svartvik, 1972, *A Grammar of Contemporary English*

1985, *A Comprehensive Grammar of the English Language*

Rissanen, Matti, 1985, 'Periphrastic 'Do' in affirmative statements in early American English', *Journal of English Linguistics*, 18.2, pp. 163–83

1991, 'Spoken language and the history of *do*-periphrasis', *Historical English Syntax* (Topics in English Linguistics 2), ed. Dieter Kastovsky, Berlin, pp. 321–42

Rogers, P., 1989, 'Defoe or the devil', *The London Review of Books*, 2 March, pp. 16–7

Romaine, Suzanne, 1981, 'Syntactic complexity, relativization and stylistic levels in Middle Scots', *Folia Linguistica Historica*, II/1, pp. 71–97

1982, *Socio-Historical Linguistics*, Cambridge

1984, 'On the problem of syntactic variation and pragmatic meaning in sociolinguistic theory', *Folia Linguistica*, XVIII/3–4, pp. 409–38

Rydén, M., 1966, *Relative Constructions in Early Sixteenth Century English*, Uppsala

1970, *Coordination of Relative Clauses in Sixteenth Century English*, Uppsala

1979, *An Introduction to the Historical Study of English Syntax*, Stockholm Studies in English, 51, Stockholm

1983, 'The emergence of *who* as a relativizer', *Studia Linguistica*, 37.2, pp. 126–34

Salmon, V., 1967, 'Elizabethan colloquial English in the Falstaff plays', *Leeds Studies in English*, 1, pp. 37–70

1970, 'Some functions of Shakespearean word-formation', *Shakespeare Survey*, 23, pp. 13–26

Salmon, V., and E. Burness (eds.), 1987, *Reader in the Language of Shakespearean Drama*, Amsterdam

Sams, E., 1985, *Shakespeare's Lost Play: 'Edmund Ironside'*

1991, 'The painful misadventures of Pericles acts I–II', *Notes and Queries*, 236, March, pp. 67–70

Samuels, M., 1972, *Linguistic Evolution*, Cambridge

Sankoff, G., 1980, *The Social Life of Language*, Philadelphia, PA

Sarrazin, G., 1897, 'Wortechos bei Shakespeare', *Shakespeare Jahrbuch*, 33, pp. 121–65

1898, 'Wortechos bei Shakespeare', *Shakespeare Jahrbuch*, 34, pp. 119–69

Schoenbaum, Samuel, 1961, 'Internal evidence and the attribution of Elizabethan plays', *Bulletin of the New York Public Library*, 65, pp. 102–24

1966, *Internal Evidence and Elizabethan Dramatic Authorship*, Evanston

Schwartzstein, Leonard, 1954, 'The text of *The Double Falsehood*', *Notes and Queries*, 199, pp. 471–2

Seary, P., 1990, *Lewis Theobald and the Editing of Shakespeare*, Oxford

Sherbo, A., 1959, 'The uses and abuses of internal evidence', *Bulletin of the New York Public Library*, 63, pp. 5–20

Slater, E., 1988, *The Problem of 'The Reign of King Edward III': A Statistical Approach*, Cambridge

Smith, M.W.A., 1986, 'A critical review of word-links as a method for investigating Shakespearean chronology and authorship', *Literary and Linguistic Computing*, 1.4, pp. 202–6

1987a, 'Hapax legomena in prescribed positions: an investigation of recent proposals to resolve problems of authorship', *Literary and Linguistic Computing*, 2.3, pp. 145–52

1987b, 'The authorship of *Pericles*: new evidence for Wilkins', *Literary and Linguistic*

*Computing*, 2.4, pp. 221–30

1988, 'The authorship of acts I and II of *Pericles*: a new approach using first words of speeches', *Computers and the Humanities*, 22, pp. 23–41

1989a, 'A procedure to determine authorship using pairs of consecutive words: more evidence for Wilkins's participation in *Pericles*', *Computers and the Humanities*, 23, pp. 113–29

1989b, 'Forensic stylometry: a theoretical basis for further developments of practical methods', *Journal of the Forensic Science Society*, 29, pp. 15–33

1991a, 'The authorship of *The Raigne of King Edward the Third*', *Literary and Linguistic Computing*, 6, pp. 166–174

1991b, 'The authorship of *Timon of Athens*', *TEXT, The Transactions of the Association for Textual Scholarship*, 5, pp. 195–240

1991c, 'Statistical inference in *A Textual Companion* to the Oxford Shakespeare', *Notes and Queries*, 236, March, pp. 73–8

1991d, 'The authorship of *The Revenger's Tragedy*', *Notes and Queries*, 236, December, pp. 508–13

1992, 'The problem of acts I–II of *Pericles*', *Notes and Queries*, 237, September, pp. 346–55

1993, '*Edmund Ironside*', *Notes and Queries*, 238, June, pp. 202–5

Smith, M.W.A., and H. Calvert, 1989, 'Word-links as a general indicator of chronology of composition', *Notes and Queries*, 234, September, pp. 338–41

Spalding, W., 1833, 'A letter on Shakespeare's authorship of *The Two Noble Kinsmen*', Edinburgh; reprinted by the New Shakespeare Society, 1876

Spedding, J., 1850, 'Who wrote Shakespeare's *Henry VIII*?', *Gentleman's Magazine*, 178, August and October, pp. 115–23 (main essay) and 381–2 (letter in reply to Hickson 1850); reprinted as: 'On the several shares of Shakespeare and Fletcher in the play of *Henry VIII*', *Transactions of the New Shakespeare Society, 1874*

Spencer, T., 1939, '*The Two Noble Kinsmen*', *Modern Philology*, 36, pp. 255–76

Sprague, A., 1964, *Shakespeare's Histories: Plays for the Stage*

Stein, Dieter, 1985, 'Discourse markers in early Modern English', *Papers from the Fourth International Conference on English Historical Linguistics*, eds. R. Eaton, O. Fischer, W. Koopman, F. van der Leek, Amsterdam

1986, 'Syntactic variation and change: the case of do in questions in early Modern English', *Folia Linguistica Historica*, VII/1, pp. 121–49

1987, 'At the crossroads of philology, linguistics and semiotics: notes on the replacement of TH by S in the third person singular in English', *English Studies*, 5, pp. 406–31

1990, *The Semantics of Syntactic Change*, Amsterdam

Stillinger, Jack, 1991, *Multiple Authorship and the Myth of Solitary Genius*, Oxford

Strang, Barbara, 1970, *A History of English*

Stratil, M., and R. Oakley, 1987, 'A disputed authorship study of two plays attributed to Tirso de Molina', *Literary and Linguistic Computing*, 2.3, pp. 153–60

Street, R. J., and H. Giles, 1982, 'Speech accommodation theory: a social and cognitive approach to language and speech behaviour', *Social Cognition and Communication*, eds. M. Roloff and C. Berger, Beverly Hills, CA

Sykes, H., 1919, *Sidelights on Shakespeare*, Stratford on Avon

Taunton, Nina, 1990, 'Did John Fletcher the playwright go to university?', *Notes and Queries*, 235, June, pp. 170–2

Thomson, N., 1989, 'How to read articles which depend on statistics', *Literary and Linguistic Computing*, 4.1, pp. 6–11

Tieken, Ingrid, 1987, *The Auxiliary Do in Eighteenth-century English*, Dordrecht

Tucker Brooke, C. (ed.), 1908, *The Shakespeare Apocrypha*, Oxford

Visser, F., 1963–73, *A Historical Syntax of the English Language*, 3 volumes in 4, Leiden

Waith, E., 1952, *The Pattern of Tragicomedy in Beaumont and Fletcher*, New Haven

Waith, E. (ed.), 1989, *The Two Noble Kinsmen*, Oxford

Wales, Katie, 1983, 'Thou and you in early modern English: Brown and Gilman reappraised, *Studia Linguistica*, 37.2, pp. 107–25

Walker, A., 1953, *Textual Problems of the First Folio*

Waller, F., 1958, 'Printer's copy for *The Two Noble Kinsmen*', *Studies in Bibliography*, 11, pp. 61–84

1966, 'The use of linguistic criteria in determining the copy and dates for Shakespeare's plays', *Pacific Coast Studies in Shakespeare*, eds. W. McNeir and T. Grennfield, Oregon, pp. 1–19

Weber, H., 1812, 'Observations on the participation of Shakespeare in *The Two Noble Kinsmen*', *The Works of Beaumont and Fletcher*, ed. H. Weber, volume 13, Edinburgh

Wells, Stanley, and G. Taylor, (general eds.), 1986, *William Shakespeare: The Complete Works*, Oxford

Wells, Stanley, G. Taylor, with J. Jowett and W. Montgomery, 1987, *William Shakespeare: A Textual Companion*, Oxford

Wentersdorf, K., 1951, 'Shakespearean chronology and the metrical tests', *Shakespeare-Studien*, festschrift für H. Mutschmann, eds. W. Fischer and K. Wentersdorf, Marburg

Wilson, B., 1987, 'Deception in the comedies and tragicomedies of John Fletcher', unpublished PhD thesis, University of Tennessee

Woods, Anthony, Paul Fletcher, Arthur Hughes, 1986, *Statistics in Language Studies*, Cambridge

Wright, Susan, 1992, 'In search of history: the English language in the eighteenth century', Paper read at ICAME 1992, Nijmagen

Zandvoort, R., 1942, 'On the relative frequency of the forms and functions of "to do"', *English Studies*, 24, pp. 1–16

# Index